Handbook of Social Services
for
Asian and Pacific Islanders

HANDBOOK OF SOCIAL SERVICES
———————FOR———————
ASIAN AND PACIFIC ISLANDERS

Edited by
Noreen Mokuau

GREENWOOD PRESS
New York • Westport, Connecticut • London

Library of Congress Cataloging-in-Publication Data

Handbook of social services for Asian and Pacific Islanders / edited
  by Noreen Mokuau.
       p.   cm.
    Includes bibliographical references and index.
    ISBN 0–313–26116–4 (alk. paper)
       1. Social work with minorities—United States.   2. Asian
  Americans—Services for.   3. Oceanian Americans—Services for.
  I. Mokuau, Noreen.
  HV3198.A2H36   1991
  362.84′00973—dc20   91–11339

British Library Cataloguing in Publication Data is available.

Library of Congress Catalog Card Number: 91–11339
ISBN: 0–313–26116–4

First published in 1991

Greenwood Press, 88 Post Road West, Westport, CT 06881
An imprint of Greenwood Publishing Group, Inc.

Printed in the United States of America

The paper used in this book complies with the
Permanent Paper Standard issued by the National
Information Standards Organization (Z39.48–1984).

10 9 8 7 6 5 4 3 2 1

To my parents
Norman and Angeline Mokuau
who have given me a gift of Hawaiian heritage,

and to my husband
Frank Carlos, Jr.
who has encouraged my expression of Hawaiianness.

Contents

III. Contemporary Problems and Issues

Preface

Asian and Pacific Islander Americans (APIAs) are a diverse and quickly growing population. According to the Asian American Health Forum, Inc. (1990), Asian Americans have geographical origins in over twenty countries, with more than sixty different ethnicities represented and a multitude of languages and dialects. The heterogeneous nature of Pacific Islander groups is easily reflected in the distinctive languages, traditions, and values of the Polynesian, Micronesian, and Melanesian island cultures scattered throughout the 64 million square miles of the Pacific Ocean. The U.S. Bureau of the Census in the last few decades has indicated a rapid growth of the APIA population, from 1.5 million in 1970, to 3.7 million in 1980, and to approximately 7.3 million in 1990. Estimates on population demographics suggest that APIA groups will continue to increase in the 1990s and could reach 9.85 million by the year 2000 (Asian American Health Forum, Inc., 1990).

The diversity and quickly changing demographics of APIAs in the United States invite a focused and thorough examination of this population. As a population of color, APIAs experience political and economic oppression, which results in a an array of problems and issues associated with discrimination. The resolution of such problems and issues can only be expected when there is a comprehensive understanding of the historical traditions, cultural values, and behavioral lifestyles of these groups.

Social services is one professional arena in which efforts toward resolving human problems can be made. Defined as a variety of programs or activities employing helping professionals such as social workers, psychologists, physicians, nurses, public health workers, sociologists, anthropologists, and so on, social services are directed toward the overall goal of enhancing the quality of life. While the literature related to social services and people of color has increased in recent years, the literature focusing on social services and APIAs is still embryonic and incomplete. This handbook represents an effort to contribute to the establishment and growth of a knowledge base relevant to the provision of sensitive and appropriate social services of APIA populations.

The chapters of this handbook are divided into three areas. Part I provides an introduction to social services for APIA populations. Laura Uba and Stanley Sue document the scope and nature of social services for APIAs by identifying major population groups and postulating a range of social service models relevant for these groups. Noreen Mokuau and Debbie Shimizu explicate a conceptual model for examining social services for APIAs by identifying key elements of a basic framework. Paul Pedersen explores philosophical and historical underpinnings of APIA concepts of helping and draws broad implications for the applicability of such traditional concepts to the American social services system.

Part II is a focused examination of selected APIA groups in terms of historical background, sociodemographic information, cultural values and behavioral norms, problems and issues, and social service intervention. The largest Asian groups in the United States are included. Stephen Fugita, Jennifer Abe, Karen L. Ito, and David T. Takeuchi write on Japanese Americans; Karen Huang covers Chinese Americans; and Jonathan Y. Okamura and Amefil Agbayani author the chapter on Filipino Americans. Jon K. Matsuoka contributes the chapter on the largest new Asian immigrant group, the Vietnamese. Chapters on the three largest Pacific Islander groups are also incorporated: Kekuni Blaisdell and Mokuau compose the chapter on native Hawaiians; Mokuau and Nathan Chang write on Samoans; and Faye F. Untalan documents the background and social service needs of Chamorros. The uniqueness of this part of the book is its "how to" or applied social service information for dealing with the problems and issues of the various APIA groups and the uniformity of the information presented, as all chapter contributors follow the same general outline of major topics.

Part III highlights specific problems and issues within certain fields of practice of the social services, including children and family, gerontology, and education. Specifically, Jeannette C. Takamura details information for working with elderly APIAs; Sharlene Maeda Furuto addresses family violence among Pacific Islander populations; and Michael J. Manos examines social skills learning among APIA populations. The concluding chapter of the book by Daniel S. Sanders predicts futuristic trends of social services for APIAs.

There are many persons who deserve acknowledgment and credit for this handbook. I would like to recognize the expertise and diligent work of all the chapter contributors. Each contributor demonstrated a deep and passionate knowledge of their respective topics and a willingness to share their knowledge with others in the hopes of improving social services for APIAs. Special recognition needs to be given to chapter contributor, Dean, and Professor Daniel Sanders who devoted his life to the development of international and multicultural social welfare. Dean Sanders completed his chapter before his death in 1989.

In addition to the chapter contributors, many other persons are noteworthy in the evolution and development of this handbook. I would like to acknowledge the support of Professor Haunani Kay Trask, Director of Hawaiian Studies at the University of Hawaii, who has a vision of empowering native Hawaiian educators. I am deeply appreciative of the day-to-day support of many colleagues, but most importantly Debbie Shimizu and Professor Colette Browne, and the conscientious and dedicated work of my secretary Louise Young. Finally, there has been support from my entire family, and clearly the persons to whom I owe the most and to whom this book is dedicated are my parents, Norman and Angeline Mokuau, and my husband Frank Carlos, Jr.

REFERENCE

Asian American Health Forum, Inc. (1990). *Dispelling the myth of a healthy minority.* San Francisco: Asian American Health Forum, Inc.

I

Social Services for Asian and Pacific Islander Populations

CHAPTER 1

Nature and Scope of Services for Asian and Pacific Islander Americans

LAURA UBA AND STANLEY SUE

ASIAN AND PACIFIC ISLANDER AMERICANS

In 1980, the Asian and Pacific Islander American (APIA) population numbered about 3.7 million, with approximately 812,000 Chinese, 782,000 Filipino, 716,000 Japanese, 387,000 Asian Indians, 357,000 Koreans, 245,000 Vietnamese, 172,000 native Hawaiians, 40,000 Samoans, 31,000 Chamorros, and other groups of Asian and Pacific Islander ancestry (U.S. Bureau of the Census, 1988). Projections are that in the 20-year span from 1980 to 2000, the APIA population will more than double, making it the fastest growing ethnic minority group in the nation (Sue and Padilla, 1986). A 1987 Center for Migration Studies publication projected that the Asian populations in the United States will number 6.5 million in 1990 and 9.85 million by the year 2000 (Ponce, 1990).

The groups comprising the APIA populations are culturally and experientially diverse. The diversity is evident in such ways as their differing degrees of acculturation, migration experiences, occupational skills (Shu and Satele, 1977), worldviews and values (Mokuau, 1988), patterns of help-seeking from public services (JWK International Corporation, 1976), personality syndromes (Sue and Frank, 1973), and basic sociodemographic data including geographic residence, age, place of birth, and poverty levels (U.S. Bureau of the Census, 1988).

According to the 1980 Census, APIAs are not geographically distributed evenly across the United States. About 58 percent of the APIAs lived in the west (versus 29 percent of the total American population), particularly in California and Hawaii. Over two-thirds lived in California, Hawaii, New York, Illinois, or Texas.

This chapter was supported by NIMH Research Grant No. 1 R01MH 44331.

The gender distribution of APIAs ranged from 48 percent female (among Vietnamese) to 58 percent female (among Koreans). This compares to 51 percent of the total U.S. population being female.

The median age of APIA groups ranged from 19.2 years for Samoans to 33.5 years for Japanese Americans. The median age for all APIA groups together was 28.4 years compared to 30 years for the total U.S. population.

The percentage of foreign-born across APIA groups varies widely. For example, 93.9 percent of the Cambodians, 90.5 percent of the Vietnamese and Hmong (from Laos), 93.7 percent of the Laotians, 82 percent of the Thai, 81.9 percent of the Koreans, 70.4 percent of the Asian Indians, 64 percent of the Filipinos and Chinese, 35.6 percent of the Samoans, 28.4 percent of the Japanese, 9.5 percent of the Chamorro, and 1.6 percent of the Hawaiians were foreign-born according to the 1980 Census. Taken together, 59 percent of the APIAs were foreign-born compared with 6 percent of the total U.S. population. A second language was spoken by over 90 percent of the Vietnamese, Laotian, Hmong, and Cambodian families, while fewer than half of the Chamorro or Japanese American families spoke a second language.

There was also a wide range of poverty rates across APIA groups. In the United States as a whole, 9.6 percent of American families lived in poverty according to the 1980 Census. Over two-thirds of the Hmong and Laotians, almost half of the Cambodians, over one-third of the Vietnamese, and between 10.5 percent and 13 percent of the Chinese, Thai, and Korean families lived in poverty. Despite the reputed "success" of APIAs, only the Japanese, Filipinos, and Asian Indians had lower poverty rates than the U.S. population as a whole. The average income for APIAs ranged from $27,400 for Japanese families to $5,000 for Hmongs in America.

Such diversity suggests that different groups have varying needs for social services and that services would be most effectively provided in ways that are tailored for each group. This chapter serves as a general overview of all APIA populations by exploring options for social service models that have relevance for this group of people. The specific focus is on mental health service models. Prior to an examination of these models, consideration is given to APIA needs for mental health services, the underutilization of mental health services by APIA, and the reasons for this underutilization.

SOCIAL AND PSYCHOLOGICAL PROBLEMS AND ISSUES AMONG ASIAN AND PACIFIC ISLANDER AMERICAN POPULATIONS

Considerable evidence suggests that mental health problems have been underestimated or go unnoticed in the APIA population. For example, S. Sue and J. K. Morishima (1982) noted that many Asian American students exhibit higher levels of anxiety than non-Asian students. Yet, few such students ever use mental health services or come to the attention of mental health professionals. Furthermore, in comparisons between Asians and non-Asians who utilize mental health services, Asians are more severely disturbed. Asian American clients have been diagnosed as psychotic more often than white, black, Native American, or Hispanic clients (Sue, 1977). T. R. Brown, K. M. Stein, K. Huang, and D. E. Harris (1973) also found that Chinese inpatients tended to be more disturbed than a Caucasian control group. This pattern of low utilization but high levels of disturbance among users suggests that only the more severely disturbed APIAs seek treatment from mental health professionals. Those APIAs who have milder problems or who have adequate resources may avoid treatment in the mental health care systems. Furthermore, it should be noted that one particular Asian group, the Southeast Asian refugees, has been found to exhibit extremely high levels of mental disturbance, especially posttraumatic stress disorders and adjustment problems (Owan, 1985).

Although the popular belief is that APIAs experience few mental health problems, an analysis of the situation of this population would suggest that emotional disturbance may be quite prevalent. In addition to organic factors, mental health is determined by the presence of stressors and by a lack of resources or social supports.

APIAs face a number of stressors. Common stressors include conflicts between traditional Asian and Pacific Islander values and lifestyle practices with that of American norms. Cultural and intergenerational conflicts often arise from differences in acculturation between children and parents. For recent immigrants, factors common to the etiology of mental disturbance include traumas experienced before immigrating, communication difficulties, underemployment, difficulties adjusting to a new cultural milieu, separation from family, and loss of social supports.

APIAs also face identity conflicts. Even those who are Americans and whose families have been Americans for generations often are not fully accepted as Americans and are presumed to be foreign by other Americans. The American myth that the United States embraces all people and provides equal opportunity compounds the negative feelings accompanying the lack of acceptance. In addition, the APIAs have to deal with cultural stereotypes. Stereotypes of APIAs may keep people from appreciating APIAs as individuals, may confine APIAs' expression of their individuality, or may affect the APIAs' self-concepts. For example, if Asian American students study hard and receive good grades, they may feel they are reinforcing the stereotypes of Asian Americans as exceptional achievers. If they do not work hard, they may be considered a waste to society, an embarrassment to family, and an outcast to others. Many struggle over who they are as APIAs.

Finally, the issue of racism and minority status always exists. Many of the immigrant APIAs experience minority status and encounter racism for the first time when they come to the United States. Often APIAs, no matter how long they have been in the United States, whether citizens or not, have to deal with rampant cultural and institutional racism as well as individual racism.

PROBLEMS IN SERVICE DELIVERY

Underutilization of Services

The mental health needs of APIAs are largely unmet. As mentioned previously, widespread evidence indicates that APIAs do not use mental health services as much as would be expected based on the size of the APIA population (Hatanaka, Watanabe, and Ono, 1975). This underutilization does not appear to be a simple function of acculturation; there is no relationship between degree of acculturation and the tendency to use mental health services. For example, while Japanese Americans tend to be more acculturated than Chinese Americans (Sue and Kirk, 1973), the former use mental health facilities less often than the latter (Kitano, 1969a).

Furthermore, there is evidence that when Asian Americans use mental health services, they often terminate treatment prematurely. For example, in a large-scale study, S. Sue (1977) found that 30 percent of Caucasian patients failed to return for treatment after an initial contact with a mental health facility, while over 50 percent of the APIAs did so. He suggested that a mismatch between services needed and services provided may act as a deterrent to service utilization and result in premature termination.

Explanations for Underutilization of Services

The underutilization of services can be due to a number of factors. Underutilization is due partly to the characteristics of many APIAs and partly to the lack of responsiveness of the mental health service delivery system to those characteristics.

Worker-Client Mismatches in Interpersonal Styles and Values. Mental health services in the United States generally represent a particular (white, middle-class, European) worldview (Singer, 1976). The characteristics of American services may conflict with values, styles, and expectations commonly found among APIAs (Singer, 1976; Sue, 1978). This conflict may lead to underutilization of services.

Worldview biases may blur the distinction between pathology and sociocultural variance (Kranz, 1973; Singer, 1976). They may also account in part for the fact that APIAs are labeled with more severe diagnoses than Caucasian Americans. D. Li-Repac (1980) found that Chinese and Caucasian workers differed in their diagnostic ratings of Chinese and Caucasian clients, suggesting that ethnicity and background of workers affect the assessment process. It may be that when workers hold world-views that are different from those held by their clients, are unaware of the bases for these differences, and encounter cultural practices and behaviors that are difficult to understand, the workers are apt to mis-interpret behaviors as indicating psychopathology (Kitano, 1970). For example, self-deprecating statements do not necessarily reflect low self-esteem in an APIA; rather, such statements could reflect the adoption of cultural mores emphasizing modesty. That an APIA does not offer details about his or her life does not necessarily mean that he or she is resisting or denying but rather could simply reflect a cultural emphasis on not being conspicuous. Standing out is culturally frowned on by APIAs (Tung, 1985). The APIA client is often aware that the worker does not appreciate the APIA's perspective and is misinterpreting his or her behaviors.

Difficulties occur when the values, assumptions, and conceptions of mental health held by the worker and the client are conflicting. It has been noted that Asian clients often do not share in certain values that are implicitly relevant to traditional forms of intervention (e.g., valuing independence over interdependence, individualism over the family or group, verbal and emotional expressiveness over inhibition) (Sue and Morishima, 1982; Yamamoto, 1978). The worker's emphasis on Western values and Western approaches to problems frequently confuses or con-flicts with the orientation of the APIA client (Tsui and Schultz, 1988). Furthermore, there may be different assumptions held concerning the need to confront conflicts (Tsui and Schultz, 1988), the strategy to achieve change (e.g., through insight or willpower), and the client's ability to initiate change (Singer, 1976). Differences may exist in expectations con-cerning the client's openness, psychological sophistication, willingness to verbalize difficulties, and verbal skills (Brown et al., 1973; Yamamoto, 1978). Some APIA clients may be reticent to ask what is expected of them and what they can gain from treatment because to ask may appear to be criticism of the authority figure, the worker (Tsui and Schultz, 1988). For example, APIA clients, thinking that being quiet shows respect to the workers, may expect not to talk much in treatment since they anticipate that the workers will take an active role in providing infor-mation. Simultaneously, workers may expect their clients to talk and may interpret client silence as resistance to therapy.

Western values are manifested in the expectation of adherence to strict appointment schedules and orientation toward long-range solutions. Such expectations may conflict with those of some APIAs (Sue and Sue,

1977). For example, native Hawaiian clients rated mental health services that were not restrained by schedules (e.g., rigid appointment schedules, long waits) higher than services that were (Prizzia and Mokuau, forthcoming). This ignorance of the cultural conflicts experienced by the APIA client in treatment may render the worker insensitive and ineffective. In turn, this may deter APIAs from seeking mental health services.

As a result of the incongruence between services conducted in a Western style and the needs of some APIAs, workers may become anxious and lose confidence with APIA clients and thus want to end the intervention as soon as possible (Tung, 1985). Meanwhile, APIA clients may also feel uncomfortable and not want to "impose" too long on workers. In fact, APIAs receive shorter-term treatment and are less likely to encounter professionals than nonprofessionals at intake (Sue, 1977).

Shortages of Culturally Sensitive Personnel. Among the cultural factors that need to be understood and accepted by mental health service providers are the history, traditions, cultural symbols, parental roles, language styles, sex role differences, functions and responsibilities of the family, belief and value systems, and religious practices and beliefs of APIAs (Sanders, 1975). There is often a shortage of personnel who are sensitive to cultural characteristics found in APIAs.

Research indicates that APIAs are more likely to use services when bilingual, bicultural personnel are employed in the service setting (Wong, 1982). When the client and the worker share ethnic language and culture, there is a decrease in the client dropout rate and care is more effective (Lee, 1985; Wong, 1982). The lack of trained, bilingual, bicultural, or culturally sensitive paraprofessional and professional mental health workers may result in culturally inappropriate services for APIAs and may thereby indirectly deter APIAs from using available mental health services. Thus, a barrier to service utilization may be the failure to recruit, train, and distribute adequate numbers of such personnel. Available evidence indicates that there is a shortage of Asian bilingual and bicultural health personnel (Sue and Morishima, 1982).

Client Fears. APIA clients may fear that workers have different conceptions of mental health and have different goals for treatment. On the one hand, clients may be concerned that workers will try to turn them into adjusted Caucasians—namely, people adapted to white, middle-class standards of mental health. The APIAs may prefer to adjust to APIA standards of behavior. For example, APIA clients may not want to become independent, open, assertive, and direct in communication style when their subculture places more value on dependence than autonomy and stresses politeness more than directness. On the other hand, APIA clients may also fear that workers presume that they want to be adapted to particular, stereotypical APIA values when that is not what the clients want. Such fears and suspicions may deter APIAs from seeking services and undermine the worker-client relationship.

Clients may also be suspicious that services from APIA workers may lead to a lack of confidentiality. Inasmuch as APIA communities are often small, with much intragroup knowledge of other members of their ethnic group (see, for example, Kitano, 1969b), some clients may be concerned that their difficulties will be known to others within the ethnic community. Thus, the problems of trying to provide effective mental health services to the APIA population are quite complex.

Cultural Inhibitions Against Seeking Mental Health Services. A number of Asian cultural values inhibit the utilization of mental health services. Some common cultural inhibitions include the following.

1. Stigma of Mental Health Problems. Many APIAs believe that having psychological problems is shameful and disgraceful (Kitano, 1970) and that the ability to control the expression of personal problems is a sign of maturity (President's Commission on Mental Health, 1978). Some interpret the need for extrafamilial intervention to resolve personal problems as especially shameful. There is a fear of stigma and a desire not to disgrace the individual or the family by going to mental health professionals. P-W. Chen (1977), for example, found that 77 percent of his respondents said that they were embarrassed to ask for needed social services. Thus, the reticence of the individual to admit to the family and the community that mental health problems exist may account in part for the lack of service utilization.

2. Expression of Mental Health Problems. Crosscultural differences have been found in symptom expressions (Marsella, Kinzie, and Gordon, 1973). Ethnic response styles may account for differences in symptoms manifested (Marsella, Sanborn, Kameoka, Shizuru, and Brennan, 1975). APIAs may not seek mental health services because there is a tendency for psychological problems to be expressed as psychosomatic symptoms (Owan, 1985). Among many Asian cultures, having a physical problem is more socially acceptable than having a psychological one. Thus, they may seek the services of acupuncturists, herbalists, or physicians rather than mental health professionals.

3. Conceptions of Mental Health. Cultural differences exist in conceptions of mental health. Supernatural or spiritual events are often viewed as culturally acceptable rather than mentally dysfunctional by Southeast Asians (Owan, 1985) and native Hawaiians (Mokuau, 1990), and thus the services of priests, shamans, and other spiritual healers may be sought more than those of mental health workers. In addition, coming from a tradition in which people do not seek help for unhappiness, Southeast Asians rarely consider feelings and emotional problems to be legitimate reasons for seeking professional help (Tung, 1985).

Their belief is that everyone has hardships in life, so it is indiscreet to talk about one's problems. Feelings are considered essentially private matters, and lamenting one's problems is a sign of weakness and a lack of character. Southeast Asians often define mental disorders as only those disorders that upset the group (Tung, 1985). S. Sue, N. Wagner, D. Ja, C. Margullis, and L. Lew (1976) also found ethnic differences in conceptualizations of mental health and disturbance. Compared to whites, Asian Americans were more likely to believe that mental disturbances were caused by organic or bodily factors. A belief in the organic nature of mental disorders implies that medical or physical interventions, and not necessarily psychological ones, are appropriate.

4. Coping with Problems. There are interethnic and intraethnic differences in attitudes toward mental health services (Chen, 1977). Grounded in the cultural value placed on self-control, many APIAs believe that mental health is enhanced by not thinking about one's problems. Indeed, Asians are more likely than whites to believe that one should avoid morbid thinking to maintain mental health. This view may influence the low utilization of mental health services. Since treatment often requires self-disclosure of personal and intimate problems (i.e., focusing on morbid thoughts), many APIA clients do not believe that treatment is helpful. They may feel uncomfortable discussing intimate problems that they have culturally learned to avoid presenting to others. Among various Asian groups and particularly among Southeast Asians, it is thought that willpower can prevent people from having "inappropriate" emotions and can help them overcome pains in life (Tung, 1985). Southeast Asian cultures emphasize patience, resignation, and stoicism. One seeks help only as a last resort. Enduring through personal suffering is promoted and admired in some Asian religions (Wong, 1985). Therefore, seeking professional mental health services may be seen as inappropriate.

A large portion of the APIA population may not think that professional mental health services per se are helpful (Kitano, 1973). Rather than seeking these services like other Americans, APIAs tend to seek help from friends, family, physicians, and clergy before turning to mental health professionals (JWK International Corporation, 1976; Kitano, 1969a; Wong, 1985). Thus, in addition to inappropriate services being offered to APIAs, a salient problem in the delivery of mental health services may be the reluctance of APIAs to seek professional mental health services from anyone.

5. Acceptance of Public Services. Many APIAs believe that, for the sake of pride and self-respect, they must not accept public health services. Services geared toward those who cannot afford private care may carry welfare (and thus shame-inducing) connotations to some pro-

spective recipients. APIAs often have cultural values dictating the need to repay obligations, and these values may conflict with receiving mental health services at less than full cost (Wong, 1985).

Since many only halfheartedly believe that mental health services can help, they also eschew expensive private mental health care. Moreover, recent immigrants frequently do not have health insurance to help cover the cost of mental health services (Wong, 1985).

6. Language Difficulties. There are also language barriers in the delivery of services for many APIAs. Difficulties with English may impede some APIAs from learning about available services, filling out forms, and interacting with personnel. Many are fearful of seeking services from people who do not speak their language (Shu and Satele, 1977). Several studies of foreign-speaking patients have suggested that the language barrier is important in the treatment process in relation to diagnosis, conversational styles, frequency of misinterpretations, client attitudes, accessibility to a range of client services, and treatment effectiveness (see, for example, Marcos and Alpert, 1976; Marcos, Alpert, Urcuyo, and Kesselman, 1973).

Furthermore, when non-English-speaking clients seek services, they are often told to come back at another time with a neighbor or a child who can translate (Office for Civil Rights, 1973). This acts as a deterrent to the delivery of services since the clients are often reluctant to disclose private information in front of their neighbors or children. The non-English-speaking client is, in effect, denied confidentiality and is embarrassed.

In addition, an interpreter may not have the linguistic or mental health background to translate adequately for the client (Citizen's Advisory Council, 1979), may make changes in translating and try to explain what the patient means, may cause subtle nuances in connotation to be lost in translation (Wong, 1985), may cause therapy sessions to take twice as long (Larsen, 1975), and may cause the worker to feel uncertain of the communication and unsure of his or her own adequacy in the therapeutic situation. This in turn could lead the worker to drive the client away because of the worker's frustration, annoyance, and loss of interest (Larsen, 1979). These problems with interpreters are significant insofar as language plays a role in manifestations and diagnoses of disorders, effectiveness of treatment, and willingness to receive services. It appears that the problem of the shortage of bilingual personnel cannot be satisfactorily assuaged by the use of interpreters.

7. Knowledge of Available Services and Geographic Inaccessibility. Ignorance of the availability of services has been a prevalent reason social services have not been sought by APIAs (Division of Asian American Affairs, 1977; Chen, 1977). It is largely due to a lack of coordination

between mental health services and other religious and health services within the ethnic communities that could act as referral resources for mental health services.

The location of mental health services and the inadequacy of public transportation that feeds into the site of the local mental health facility may also be barriers to service utilization (Lum, 1985). Little consensus exists regarding where facilities would be most effectively located. Some suggest that the delivery site should be within the ethnic community, immediately visible, accessible, and integrated into the community. Others suggest that the mental health centers should be located near but not in the ethnic community since potential clients are ashamed and embarrassed by their need for services and do not want others in the ethnic group to see them receiving services.

MODELS FOR SERVICE DELIVERY

Underutilization of services does not necessarily imply an incompatibility between intervention and APIA clients. Rather, it highlights the need for modification in services and service delivery such that cultural compatibility of service and client is assured. The question is, what types of resources in the way of facilities and personnel can most effectively make these modifications?

A range of mental health service delivery system options exists (Uba, 1980). Three prototypes of culturally sensitive mental health service delivery systems for APIAs include: (a) mainstream facilities in which there are no specific personnel assigned to working with APIAs, (b) mainstream facilities in which specific personnel are trained to provide culturally sensitive services to APIAs, and (c) facilities that are physically separate from mainstream facilities and in which all of the personnel specialize in providing culturally sensitive services to APIA clients.

Mainstream Facilities and General Personnel

Services for APIAs may be integrated into mainstream facilities in which all of the personnel would be trained to provide culturally sensitive services. For example, staff at a community mental health center could receive inservice training on how to work with APIA clients.

There are limitations to this approach. For all personnel to be able to provide culturally sensitive services, a major revamping of traditional mental health service training (to include instruction on numerous APIA cultures and values) would be required. Such change may be resisted by professional organizations, universities, and students. The structural changes needed for training would elevate costs and require new training materials on cultural factors and would be considered major obstacles. In addition, this policy of embedding culturally appropriate services within mainstream facilities may compound consumer ignorance of mental health services for APIAs by minimizing the visibility of such services and serve to limit service accessibility (Gilbert, 1972).

Nevertheless, advantages to this approach are apparent. Since APIAs exhibit a great deal of heterogeneity, staff can provide services that are appropriate for unacculturated as well as acculturated APIAs. The services would not be segregated, in that a mental health facility could serve a wide range of culturally diverse clients, and staff would increase their ability to work with different kinds of clients.

Mainstream Facilities and Special Personnel

Within mainstream facilities, there may be culturally sensitive teams of service providers to provide services for APIAs. In this model, bilingual and bicultural workers would be employed to work specifically with certain populations.

A disadvantage to this approach is that the establishment of culturally sensitive teams within centralized, mainstream services may create internal contentiousness, administrative confusion, and unnecessary duplication of services between the mainstream and the semiautonomous, pluralistic services (Anders, Parlade, Chatel, and Peele, 1977). Moreover, difficulties may exist in finding personnel who can work with specific Asian and Pacific Islander groups.

There are many advantages to this approach as well. The lack of culturally sensitive personnel could be alleviated by judicious use of extant culturally sensitive personnel. Furthermore, rather than automatically and indiscriminantly being sent to separate APIA facilities without considering the appropriateness of such services for the individual client, having both mainstream and culturally specialized services available within the same setting gives consumers a clear choice of services. Offering a choice of services may increase the chance of an effective matching of needs and services and increase the use of services by APIAs. In addition, fewer changes in mental health training would be called for because only those who worked with APIAs would need to receive special training. Thus, this option would also be more economical for the delivery system than either of the other options. Finally, the cultural sensitivity of all personnel in mainstream facilities may be heightened by having the special unit housed within the mainstream facilities.

Segregated Facilities

Services for APIAs may be provided in culturally sensitive facilities that are in a different location than the mainstream services (perhaps under an umbrella of social services for APIAs). Separate facilities would probably focus their limited resources on those APIAs who most need culturally sensitive and bilingual services (e.g., immigrants).

Several drawbacks exist in this approach. Concentrating a large portion of the mental health service providers trained to work with APIAs in segregated facilities would limit opportunities to promote understanding of APIAs among service providers in mainstream facilities. The APIA clients who appear at mainstream facilities may be referred to a segregated facility or may receive culturally unresponsive treatment. On the other hand, more acculturated APIA clients who are referred to separate facilities for APIAs may not benefit from these specialized services. Thus, the more acculturated APIAs may fall through the service delivery cracks in that mainstream facilities are unprepared to deal with cultural issues, while segregated services are not geared for those who are highly acculturated. In addition, the number of these specialized, segregated centers would be small. Clients who need the services may find them located far from where they reside. Moreover, adopting this option could, in the long run, leave APIAs without culturally sensitive services inasmuch as when there are budgetary cutbacks, these programs may lose their funding if separate services for APIAs are perceived as secondary or superfluous.

There are advantages to this approach. Some APIAs feel welcome or understood only in facilities that are specifically for APIAs. Another advantage to this approach is that it may afford institutional flexibility to meet the needs of APIAs: receptionists who can speak more than one language, scheduling that accommodates the patterns and needs of APIAs, locations near or in APIA communities, service delivery centers that provide training, and so on. The high visibility of separate facilities may increase public awareness of services and may attract potential APIAs into mental health service delivery. Concentrating culturally sensitive personnel in a few facilities may circumvent shortages of culturally sensitive service providers (President's Commission on Mental Health, 1978). The opportunity for community involvement in the planning and implementation of services for APIAs may be increased when there are separate facilities, presumably run by APIAs (Lum, 1985). Services that are effective and frequently used tend to be community based with providers being either members of or known in the ethnic community (Wong, 1985).

Appropriateness of Models

Not all APIAs are equally subject to barriers to service delivery. There are large interethnic differences in terms of acculturation, mental health service needs (Kim, 1973), and patterns of help-seeking (JWK International Corporation, 1976), as well as intraethnic differences in attitudes toward the treatment of mental disorders (Chen, 1977). Furthermore, the relevance of ethnicity in the development, manifestation, or treatment of mental disorders may vary widely across individual members of the heterogeneous APIA population.

Experience and research have shown that one form of service delivery is not clearly and always preferable to another, although it is clear that culturally sensitive services are needed. Work in Los Angeles (Hatanaka et al., 1975), San Francisco (Kitano, 1969b), and Seattle (Sue and McKinney, 1975) has demonstrated that culturally relevant services dramatically increase APIA use of mental health services.

The first mainstream option would be most apt when there are few APIAs in the service area, when there are few who need bilingual services, and when many of the existing mental health providers are culturally sensitive. The mainstream facilities could also have special teams to serve APIAs. The special teams options, a variation of which has been adopted by the Asian American Task Force of the County of Los Angeles/ University of Southern California Hospital Mental Health Services, would be particularly appropriate when financial and spatial resources are limited and when there are only a limited number of people who could provide services in a culturally sensitive way. The teams have an advantage over simply having one ethnic specialist, in that efforts would not be limited to one person, and the team could represent different ethnic groups. In the past, services that have provided one specialist in minority mental health care have not had much impact (Wu and Windle, 1980).

The segregated services option, which has been adopted at a number of places including the Asian/Pacific Counseling and Treatment Center in Los Angeles and the Richmond Maxi-Center in San Francisco, would be particularly apt when APIAs are concentrated in a small area, when mainstream facilities are situated far from APIA populations, or when there are many immigrant APIAs needing services.

The existence of separate mental health facilities for APIAs has increased utilization rates. For example, when San Francisco's Richmond Maxi-Center was established, more patients were seen in the first three months than were seen in the previous five to six years in that catchment area (Murase, n.d.; Wong, 1977). In Seattle, an APIA counseling and referral service was used as much in one year as eighteen other community mental health centers were used by APIAs over a three-year period (Sue and McKinney, 1975). During the two years that H. L. Kitano (1969b) worked at a child guidance clinic serving San Francisco public schools, there were no cases of children of Japanese ancestry being referred. In contrast, a family service agency developed by the Japanese community served an average of thirty active counseling cases per month. Similar findings for Asian American mental health facilities in Los Angeles have been reported (Hatanaka et al., 1975).

CONCLUSION

The policy options presented here are not mutually exclusive. A combination of these delivery systems is probably needed to meet the heterogeneous range of APIA needs. Since APIAs are generally reticent to seek mental health services, it may be premature to stress outpatient treatment and overlook the importance of outreach. Whether mainstream or segregated services are established, there is a need for adjunctive measures including educating the APIA public about mental health services.

The 1990s will be a period of increased growth for APIA populations, and social service professionals must make a concerted and responsive effort to enhance and increase the accountability of services to this diverse population.

REFERENCES

Anders, A., R. Parlade, J. Chatel, and R. Peele (1977). Why we did not establish a separate complete program for Spanish speaking patients. In E. R. Padilla and A. M. Padilla (eds.), *Transcultural Psychiatry: A Hispanic Perspective.* Los Angeles: Spanish Speaking Mental Health Research Center.

Brown, T. R., K. M. Stein, K. Huang, and D. E. Harris (1973). Mental illness and the role of mental health facilities in Chinatown. In S. Sue and N. Wagner (eds.), *Asian-Americans: Psychological Perspectives.* Palo Alto, Calif.: Science and Behavior Books.

Chen, P-W. (1977). *Chinese-Americans View Their Mental Health.* San Francisco: R and E Research Associates.

Citizen's Advisory Council, State of California, Health and Welfare Agency, Department of Mental Health Services (1979). Multi-cultural issues in mental health services: Strategies toward equity. Sacramento, CA.

Division of Asian American Affairs, Office of Special Concerns, Assistant Secretary for Planning and Evaluation, Office of the Secretary, Department of Health, Education, and Welfare (1977). Asian American Field Survey: Summary of the Data. Washington, D.C.: U.S. Government Printing Office.

Gilbert, N. (1972). Assessing service delivery methods: Some unsettled questions. *Welfare in Review* 10: 25–33.

Hatanaka, H. K., W. Y. Watanabe, and S. Ono (1975). The utilization of mental health services by Asian Americans in Los Angeles. In W. H. Ishikawa and N. A. Hayashi (eds.), *Delivery of Services in Pan Asian Communities.* San Diego: San Diego Pacific Asian Coalition Mental Health Training Center, San Diego State University.

JWK International Corporation (1976). Identification of problems in access to health care services and health careers for Asian Americans. Department of Health, Education, and Welfare (DHEW), Public Health, Health Resources Opportunity, contract #HRA–230–75–0193.

Kim, B-L. (1973). Asian Americans: No model minority. *Social Work* 18 (3): 44–53.

Kitano, H. L. (1969a). Japanese-American mental illness. In S. Plog and R. Edgerton (eds.), *Changing Perspectives on Mental Illness*. New York: Holt, Rinehart and Winston.

———(1969b). *Japanese Americans: The Evolution of a Subculture*. Englewood Cliffs, N.J.: Prentice-Hall.

———(1973). Japanese crime and delinquency. In S. Sue and N. Wagner (eds.), *Asian Americans: Psychological Perspectives*. Palo Alto, CA: Science and Behavior Books.

———(1970). Mental illness in four cultures. *Journal of Social Psychology* 80: 121–134.

Kranz, P. (1973). Towards achieving more meaningful encounters with minority clients. *Hospital and Community Psychiatry* 24: 343–444.

Larsen, J. K. (1979). Reflections of a tender-minded radical. In W. P. Lebra (ed.), *Transcultural Research in Mental Health, Volume 2: Mental Health Research in Asia and the Pacific*. Honolulu: University Press of Hawaii.

Lee, E. (1985). Inpatient psychiatric services for Southeast Asian refugees. In T. Owan (ed.), *Southeast Asian Mental Health: Treatment, Prevention, Services, Training, and Research*. Washington, D.C.: U.S. Department of Health and Human Services.

Li-Repac, D. (1980). Cultural influences on clinical perception: A comparison between Caucasian and Chinese-American therapists. *Journal of Cross-Cultural Psychology* 11: 327–342.

Lum, R. G. (1985). A community-based mental health service to Southeast Asian refugees. In T. Owan (ed.), *Southeast Asian Mental Health: Treatment, Prevention, Services, Training, and Research*. Washington, D.C.: U.S. Department of Health and Human Services.

Marcos, L. R., and M. Alpert (1976). Strategies and risks in psychotherapy with bilingual patients: The phenomenon of language independence. *American Journal of Psychiatry* 133 (11): 1275–1278.

Marcos, L. R., M. Alpert, L. Urcuyo, and M. Kesselman (1973). The effect of interview language on the evaluation of psychopathology in Spanish-American schizophrenic patients. *American Journal of Psychiatry* 130 (5): 549–553.

Marsella, A. J., D. Kinzie, and P. Gordon (1973). Ethnic variations in the phenomenology of emotions: I. Shame. *Journal of Cross-Cultural Psychology* 4 (4): 435–458.

Marsella, A. J., K. O. Sanborn, V. Kameoka, L. Shizuru, and J. Brennan (1975). Cross-validation of self-report measures of depression among normal populations of Japanese, Chinese, and Caucasian ancestry. *Journal of Clinical Psychology* 31 (2): 281–287.

Mokuau, N. (1990). The impoverishment of native Hawaiians and the social work challenge. *Health and Social Work* 15 (3): 235–242.

Mokuau, N. (1988). Social work practice with individuals and families in a crosscultural perspective. In D. Sanders and J. Fischer (eds.), *Visions for the Future: Social Work and Pacific-Asian Perspectives.* Honolulu: University of Hawaii, School of Social Work.

Murase, K. (n.d.). Summary of report of subpanel on mental health of Asian/ Pacific Americans, President's Commission on Mental Health. Unpublished manuscript.

Office for Civil Rights (1979). Untitled. Department of Health, Education, and Welfare report.

Owan, T. (1985). Southeast Asian mental health: Transition from treatment to prevention—a new direction. In T. Owan (ed.), *Southeast Asian Mental Health: Treatment, Prevention, Services, Training, and Research.* Washington, D.C.: U.S. Department of Health and Human Services.

Ponce, N. (1990). Asian and Pacific Islander health data: Quality issues and policy recommendation. Paper presented at the Asian American Health Forum Conference, Washington, D.C.

President's Commission on Mental Health (1978). Report of the President's Commission on Mental Health. Washington, D.C.: U.S. Government Printing Office.

Prizzia, R., and N. Mokuau (forthcoming). Mental health services for native Hawaiians: The need for culturally relevant services. *Journal of Health and Human Resources Administration.*

Sanders, D. S. (1975). Dynamics of ethnic and cultural pluralism: Implications for social work education and curriculum innovations. *Journal of Education for Social Work* 11 (3): 95–100.

Shu, R., and A. S. Satele (1977). *The Samoan Community in Southern California: Conditions and Needs.* Occasional Paper #2. Los Angeles: Asian American Mental Health Research Center.

Singer, K. (1976). Cross-cultural dynamics in psychotherapy. In J. R. Masserman (ed.), *Social Psychiatry, Volume 2: The Range of Normal in Human Behavior.* New York: Grune and Stratton.

Sue, D. W. (1978). World views and counseling. *Personnel and Guidance Journal* 56: 458–462.

Sue, D. W., and A. C. Frank (1973). A typological approach to the psychological study of Chinese and Japanese American college males. *Journal of Social Issues* 29 (2): 129–148.

Sue, D. W., and B. Kirk (1973). Differential characteristics of Chinese-American students. *Journal of Counseling Psychology* 19 (6): 471–478.

Sue, D. W., and S. Sue (1977). Barriers to effective cross-cultural counseling. *Journal of Counseling Psychology* 24 (5): 420–429.

Sue, S. (1977). Community mental health services to minority groups: Some optimism, some pessimism. *American Psychologist* 32 (8): 616–624.

Sue, S., and H. McKinney (1975). Asian Americans in the community mental health care system. *American Journal of Orthopsychiatry* 45 (1): 111–118.

Sue, S., and J. K. Morishima (1982). *The Mental Health of Asian Americans.* San Francisco: Jossey-Bass.

Sue, S., and A. M. Padilla (1986). Ethnic minority issues in the United States: Challenges for the educational system. In California State Department of Education (ed.), *Beyond Language: Social and Cultural Factors in Schooling*

Language Minority Students. Los Angeles: Evaluation, Dissemination and Assessment Center, California State University.

Sue, S., N. Wagner, D. Ja, C. Margullis, and L. Lew (1976). Conceptions of mental illness among Asian and Caucasian American students. *Psychological Reports* 38 (3): 703–708.

Tsui, P., and G. L. Schultz (1988). Ethnic factors in group process: Cultural dynamics in multi-ethnic therapy groups. *American Journal of Orthopsychiatry* 58 (1): 136–142.

Tung, T. M. (1985). Psychiatric care for Southeast Asians: How different is different? In T. Owan (ed.), *Southeast Asian Mental Health: Treatment, Prevention, Services, Training, and Research*. Washington, D.C.: U.S. Department of Health and Human Services.

Uba, L. (1980). *Approaches to Mental Health Service Delivery for Asian Americans in Los Angeles County*. Nashville, Tenn.: Vanderbilt Institute for Public Policy Studies.

U.S. Bureau of the Census (1988). *We, the Asian and Pacific Islander Americans*. Washington, D.C.: U.S. Government Printing Office.

Wong, H. Z. (1982). Asian and Pacific Americans. In L. R. Snowden (ed.), *Reaching the Underserved: Mental Health Needs of Neglected Populations*. Beverly Hills, Calif.: Sage Publications.

Wong, H. Z. (1985). Training for mental health service providers to Southeast Asian refugees: Models, strategies, and curricula. In T. Owan (ed.), *Southeast Asian Mental Health: Treatment, Prevention, Services, Training, and Research*. Washington, D.C.: U.S. Department of Health and Human Services.

Wong, N. (1977). Psychiatric education and training of Asian American psychiatrists. Paper presented at annual meeting of the American Psychiatric Association, Toronto, Ontario, Canada.

Wu, I., and C. Windle (1980). Ethnic specificity in the relationship of minority use and staffing of community mental health centers. *Community Mental Health Journal* 16: 156–168.

Yamamoto, J. (1978). Therapy for Asian Americans. *Journal of the National Medical Association* 70: 267–270.

CHAPTER 2

Conceptual Framework for Social Services for Asian and Pacific Islander Americans

NOREEN MOKUAU AND DEBBIE SHIMIZU

INTRODUCTION

Ethnic-Competent Practice

Social services that reflect a mastery of knowledge and skills and a compassionate responsiveness to the values, traditions, and lifestyle experiences of Asian and Pacific Islander groups can be referred to as ethnic-competent practice. Specifically, ethnic competence is an informed capacity to understand and utilize a body of knowledge and skills that are compatible with different ethnic groups. Inherent in this definition is the assumption that in addition to the utilization of an existing body of knowledge, a new body of knowledge appropriate for the unique concerns of the diverse groups of Asian and Pacific Islanders must be simultaneously created.

Ethnic competence also refers to an awareness of one's own ethnic worldview, an awareness of the worldviews of other ethnic groups, and a responsiveness to facilitate an improved quality of life for all ethnic minority peoples. This idea of ethnic competence highlights the importance of the personal attributes of the social worker. L. Wilson (1982) identifies the personal attributes that contribute to ethnic competence: (1) personal qualities of warmth, empathy, and genuineness; (2) acceptance of and openness to differences among people; (3) a willingness to learn to work with clients of different ethnic minority groups; (4) a commitment to alleviate racism and poverty; and (5) a definition of one's personal values, stereotypes, and biases about ethnicity and the effects of accommodation or conflict (in Gallegos, 1984, p. 7).

The Ethnic-Competent Worker

The worker who subscribes to ethnic-competent practice is a mediator who moves across group boundaries in a manner appreciative of the transactions of people (Green, 1982) and is able to function effectively in more than one culture (Gallegos, 1984). J. W. Green's transactional perspective focuses on the relations of the larger society and persons who identify themselves with an ethnic group. This perspective stipulates that "values, signs, and behavioral styles" define the boundaries of groups and suggests that workers adopt the role of "mediators" in facilitating the interactions across group boundaries. J. S. Gallegos (1984) validates the importance of transactions of people and states that the "ethnically competent" worker must be able to practice in any cross-cultural situation (p. 3).

This chapter proposes a framework for acquiring ethnic-competent practice with Asian and Pacific Islanders. The framework identifies dimensions of practice by synthesizing major themes from existing models of minority practice into an organizational structure that is relevant for Asian and Pacific Islanders. The foundation for this framework is a discussion affirming the importance of social services for ethnic minorities and an overview of the historical evolution of such work.

JUSTIFICATION OF SOCIAL SERVICES FOR ETHNIC MINORITIES

It would appear that a rationale for designing and delivering ethnic-competent social services for ethnic minorities is self-evident. However, the relative invisibility of ethnicity in the social work literature (Green, 1982) and the underemphasis in social service professions on ethnic minority groups (Lum, 1986) would suggest that a discussion affirming the importance of ethnic-competent social services is warranted. The following discussion focuses on a justification of services as it relates to ethnic minorities of color and, in particular, Asian and Pacific Islanders.

"People of color deserve adequate, effective, and sensitively attuned treatment" (Jacobs and Bowles, 1988, p. x). Justification is based on the acknowledgment of ethnic minorities of color as a people and as an oppressed population. This justification is reinforced by the ethical mandates of several professional groups including psychologists, psychiatrists, marriage and family therapists, school counselors, rehabilitation counselors, and social workers (Corey, Corey, and Callanan, 1988).

J. G. Hopps (1982) indicates that while "many forms of exclusion and discrimination exist in this country, none is so deeply rooted, persistent and intractable as that based on color" (in Devore and Schlesinger, 1987, p. 13). Literature attests to the historical oppression experienced by people of color such as blacks, Native Americans, Hispanics, and Asians; however, there is a myth that Asians in the 1990s are less affected by oppression, and there is minimal information on the neglected minority group, Pacific Islanders. Many Asians, such as the Japanese and Chinese, are no longer viewed as an oppressed population because they have made gains in education, occupation, and income that are comparable to mainstream society, but W. Devore and E. G. Schlesinger (1987) note that these Asians still confront persistent and subtle racism related to their color (pp. 12–13). Furthermore, immigrant and refugee Asian groups of the 1970s and 1980s, such as the Vietnamese, Cambodians, and Hmong, are strongly affected by racism and poverty. Finally, Pacific Islander groups such as native Hawaiians, previously unrecognized in the social services literature, are gaining attention because of their severe health and mental health profiles (Mokuau, 1990). Asian and Pacific Islanders are entitled to competent and sensitive social services, as are all other persons, but their needs become more pronounced when viewed in context of the risks involved in being a population of color.

The provision of social services by professionals from interdisciplinary fields is guided by professional codes of conduct and policy mandates. Such policies support the development of a social service perspective unique to ethnic minorities of color. For example, the National Association of Social Workers and the Council on Social Work Education, the two largest social work organizations, have articulated and promoted reports and policies that mandate attention to ethnic minority concerns (Dieppa, 1984; Gallegos, 1984). D. D. Bowles (1988) states that social work education policies require that students acquire a body of knowledge that will allow them to adequately meet the needs of people of color who are victimized by racism and oppression (p. 1). While most ethnic specialists concur that strides in progress have been made in knowledge development and service delivery, there is also a consensus that the current state of social services is still inadequate in meeting the needs of ethnic minority populations (Devore and Schlesinger, 1987; Lum, 1986; Green, 1982). A review of the historical evolution of social services for ethnic minorities may be helpful in providing further insight into this area.

HISTORICAL EVOLUTION OF SOCIAL SERVICES FOR ETHNIC MINORITIES OF COLOR

The origin and evolution of social services in the United States is associated with advocacy for oppressed peoples. However, for one group of oppressed people, ethnic minorities of color, this has been more rhetoric than reality (Mokuau, forthcoming). Several reports document that oppressed people of color have historically been excluded and denied access to social services (Solomon, 1976; Morales, 1976; Lum, 1986). "Social welfare agencies served mainstream society and White immigrants, while people of color struggled to exist in isolated geographic ghetto areas. They were targets of exploitation and oppression in the United States" (Lum, 1986, p. 6).

L. E. Davis (1984) notes that W.E.B. Du Bois predicted, over eighty years ago, that the problem of the twentieth century would be the problem of color. A historical overview of social services would appear to confirm that there was limited improvement to services to ethnic minorities of color in the first half of the century and then increasing, albeit inadequate, attention paid to the needs of this population in the second half of the century. The evolution of services, with some focus on counseling, can be depicted in three different periods in the twentieth century.

Period 1: 1900–1960. In general, in the period from 1900 through 1960, the attention paid to people of color was negligent. The early empirical research on crosscultural counseling is limited, and what is available focuses on the counseling difficulties arising from the effects of a worker-client relationship in which the worker is white and the client is black. According to this literature, the disparity between the worker and the client generated problems such as: (1) varying interpretations of symptoms and problems (Ellenberger, 1960), (2) difficulties in establishing rapport (Bernard, 1953; Seward, 1956), and (3) difficulties in being genuine (Records, 1966). While this research raised the level of consciousness about crosscultural relations, it was not instrumental in effecting relevant societal changes.

Period 2: 1960–1980. Prompted by social unrest and dissatisfaction and the passage of civil rights legislation in the 1960s, there was a concerted increase in research and services directed toward ethnic minorities of color in the period 1960–1980. The research in the 1960s corroborated earlier research findings about the importance of ethnic and cultural variables in counseling, while the research in the 1970s became more specialized and focused on blacks and other minorities of color such as Hispanics, Native Americans, and Asians. Examples of the specialized nature of research include investigations of the interactive effects of: (1) ethnicity and social class (Wolkon, Moriwaki, and Williams, 1973), (2) ethnicity and counselor experience (Acosta and Sheehan, 1976), (3) ethnicity and counseling style (Atkinson, Maruyama, and Matsui, 1978), and (4) ethnicity and intragroup attitudinal differences (Furlong, Atkinson, and Casas, 1979). In addition to research, social service organizations reflected a stronger commitment to people of color (Lum, 1986) in terms of the hiring and retention of bilingual workers and the placement of agencies such as multipurpose centers in ethnic communities.

Period 3: 1980–1990. The momentum of the previous two decades diminished in the 1980s because of the conservative political atmosphere. But the efforts of that period bore fruit in the publication of a significant number of social service textbooks focusing on ethnic minorities (Jacobs and Bowles, 1988; Devore and Schlesinger, 1987; Ho, 1987; Lum, 1986; White, 1984; Green, 1982). Predominant topics in these texts included: (1) theoretical and conceptual perspectives appropriate for ethnic minorities of color, (2) information related to the social and political realities for oppressed peoples, (3) information on cultural norms and values for specific groups, and (4) information on specific problems and concerns of the various groups. The expansion of knowledge has contributed to improved ways of dealing with those who are ethnically different. It is anticipated that the 1990s will continue to show a commitment to ethnic minorities of color in terms of innovative research and service delivery.

In these three periods, the emphasis in knowledge development and subsequently service delivery has been on worker-client relationships in which the workers are of Anglo-Saxon and European descent and the clients are persons of color. However, new information will need to be generated in the future because of the changing demography of the nation. According to Davis (1984), "demographers predict that the number of non-white minorities will increase from their 1980 proportion of approximately 17 percent to approximately 30 percent of the American populace by the year 2000" (p. 3). This would mean that approximately one of every three Americans will be a person of color by the year 2000. The implications are that more white social workers will be working with clients of color and that more practitioners of color will be working with white clients as well as other clients of color.

A FRAMEWORK FOR SOCIAL SERVICES WITH ASIAN AND PACIFIC ISLANDERS

As noted in the previous section, the publication of various textbooks on ethnic minorities of color in the period 1980–1990 was testimony to the development of new knowledge. A major thrust of this new literature has been on the formulation of conceptual models and approaches in which to organize information relevant to ethnic minorities of color. Several noteworthy models and approaches include D. Norton's (1978) dual perspective, J. Green's (1982) cultural awareness approach, Gallegos's (1984) ethnic-competent practice, D. Lum's (1986) process-stage approach, Devore and Schlesinger's (1987) ethnic-sensitive practice approach, and Lee's (1990) cultural-competent model. There are varying emphases within these models on the role of the worker, the client, and the process of helping. These models and approaches reflect cumulative knowledge building in that these authorities review and critique existing frameworks on minority social work practice and then propose new perspectives. Devore and Schlesinger (1987) go one step further; in addition to reviewing existing frameworks for minority social work practice, they also assess prevailing approaches to social work practice, such as the problem-solving approach or the systems approach, for relevance for people of color.

The framework for Asian and Pacific Islanders is based on a synthesis of some of the major themes drawn from these models on minority social work practice. In particular, the works of Green (1982) and Devore and Schlesinger (1987) are briefly described and major themes extrapolated for the framework for Asian and Pacific Islanders.

Cultural Awareness Approach: Help-Seeking Model

Green's (1982) conceptualization of the help-seeking model is grounded in the idea that it is important to understand and work through the nature and the degree of the cultural distinctiveness of the worker and the client. The model emphasizes the significance of ethnographic understanding in the planning and delivery of culturally responsive services. In this model, the worker needs to be aware of his or her own cultural values and biases and of the cultural perspective of the client. The help-seeking model has four major components that pertain to the client's culture: (1) the client's definition of the problem, (2) the client's use of language, (3) the availability of indigenous helping resources, and (4) client-oriented criteria for determining problem resolution (p. 31).

Defining an experience as a problem is largely attributed to cultural interpretations. Different cultures have distinctive ways of explaining the etiology of problems, recognizing the symptoms, identifying treatment options, and so on. Because there is the likelihood of the client and the worker "defining" the problem differently, Green (1982) indicates that it is critical to recognize the manner in which the client views the problem. Related to this is the importance of language as a primary vehicle in which the meaning of the problem is communicated. It becomes necessary for the worker to comprehend the linguistic symbols of a culture in order to understand best how that culture views the world and the problems experienced. Defining and communicating the problem within the client's frame of reference facilitates the matching of an intervention style that is based on cultural criteria and assures that a satisfactory resolution is achieved based on the client's values. Finally, the incorporation of indigenous strategies of problem intervention, including folk healing, may be useful to clients who place greater legitimacy on such strategies over those of professional social services.

Ethnic-Sensitive Practice Approach

Devore and Schlesinger (1987) present an ethnic-sensitive practice approach identifying major assumptions and principles related to working with ethnic minorities. Social services must pay attention to "ethnicity and social class and how these contribute to individual and group identity, dispositions toward basic life tasks, coping styles, and problems likely to be encountered. These, together with individual history, and genetic and physiological disposition, contribute to the development of personality and group life" (p. 149).

The four assumptions of ethnic-sensitive practice are: (1) individual history and collective history influence the formulation and resolution of problems; (2) the present is most important; (3) ethnicity significantly influences individual identity development; and (4) ethnicity is a source of strength as well as a source of strain and discord (p. 150). Historical experiences of oppression and discrimination affect the status and adjustment of cultural groups and have relevance for the scope of problems evident and the means in which the group resolves those problems in contemporary times. The development of an individual's identity significantly derives from ethnic experiences that are habitual and routine and provide a sense of belonging and historical continuity. Elements of this ethnic reality, including the family, rituals and celebrations, ethnic schools, and language, present themselves as both strengths and stressors of a culture.

These four assumptions lead to two major principles prominent in ethnic-sensitive practice. The first principle is that problem definition and intervention are affected by the path that is taken by the client to get to the worker; these paths may range on a continuum from one that is totally coercive to one that is totally voluntary. Devore and Schlesinger (1987) suggest that the initial problem definition is influenced by the path to the social worker; however, regardless of that path, efforts must be made to place the problem in context of the client's cultural frame of reference. The second principle is that attention must be given to the integration of individual and systemic change efforts as a basic component of ethnic-sensitive practice. In recognizing the institutional basis for racism, workers must simultaneously effect change in the environment as well as change in the individual.

There are two dominant themes in the help-seeking model and the ethnic-sensitive practice approach that are useful in conceptualizing a framework for Asian and Pacific Islanders: (1) importance of self-understanding as it relates to the identification of one's own values and traditions and an understanding of how these values and traditions influence our relationships with others; and (2) awareness of the client's cultural frame of reference as it pertains to the ways in which problems are defined and communicated and the strategies for problem resolution. Awareness also involves knowing the impact of history on the group's evolution to present times.

DIMENSIONS OF SUCH A FRAMEWORK

There are several dimensions of a framework of social services for Asian and Pacific Islanders. These dimensions focus on the capabilities of the worker to be self-aware, knowledgeable about the culture, and skilled in social services intervention. Dimensions help guide the worker in achieving ethnic-competent practice in terms of knowledge building and may partially support the development of those personal attributes that are critical for such work. The hypothesis is that being informed may contribute to the increased sensitivity and commitment of the worker. The dimensions are broad in scope so that applicability to the diverse groups of the Asian and Pacific Islander population, in any social service setting, is possible.

Self-Awareness

A worker's awareness of his or her worldviews is tantamount to an understanding of his or her role with the client and can positively influence the worker-client relationship. D. W. Sue (1981) points out that the worker should feel comfortable with the racial and philosophical differences between himself or herself and the client. There should be a respect for each individual being equally human. The worker should also be sensitive to his or her own limitations when working with others and should keep open the possibilities of referring the client to other workers or even consulting with indigenous healers.

J. G. Draguns (1976) suggests that an ideal perspective of worldviews would reflect a flexible balance and appreciation of two opposing frames of reference: *etic* (culture-general), which views cultural information in light of categories and concepts external to the culture but universal in their applicability; and *emic* (culture-specific), which views cultural data as indigenous or unique to a culture. N. Mokuau (1986) indicates that an overemphasis toward the culture-general occurs when the worker defines the dynamics of the relationship and prescribes intervention according to a monocultural set of assumptions. A popular example is the Asian American client who is believed to be "resistive" to treatment because of his or her lack of verbal self-disclosure. In this example, the worker, operating from a school of treatment that prescribes open verbal communication, is imposing values that are contrary to the client's value base, which promotes verbal reticence. On the other hand, Mokuau (1986) continues that an overemphasis on the culture-specific results in a focus on the culture, not the individual. An illustrative example is giving an Asian client a medical or health pamphlet in a language other than English because the assumption is that "all Asians do not speak English." The ideal, therefore, is an integration of both perspectives so that there is a respect for the universal qualities of human functioning with an understanding, if not sharing, of worldviews drawn from different cultures. It is imperative that this blending is done by giving primacy to the individual in the context of culture.

Knowledge

The appropriateness and sensitivity of assessment, intervention, and evaluation are largely dependent on the worker's knowledge of key variables relevant to Asian and Pacific Islanders. A theoretical or conceptual framework is valuable in the organization of information. In addition, specific cultural information on history, sociodemography, values, lifestyle practices, and presenting problems is necessary in a knowledge base.

History. With the exception of native Hawaiians, all other Asian and Pacific Islander groups immigrated to the United States and experienced differing forms of oppression and racism in their adjustment to the United States. Native Hawaiians, indigenous to the Hawaiian islands, also experienced oppression and racism, not as immigrants, but as a people colonized in their own homeland. The severity of historical oppression is manifested in such events as the internment of Japanese Americans during World War II, exclusion acts preventing Chinese from becoming citizens in the early 1900s, and the abrogation of native Hawaiian government and religion since the arrival of Westerners in 1778. Refugee populations in the 1970s and 1980s, such as the Vietnamese, Laotian, and Hmong, displaced from their own countries because of war, also faced critical situations of poverty and maladjustment in the United States. The collective and individual experiences of racism and oppression influence the development of personality, interpersonal relationships, and position and status in society. It is vital that workers have a knowledge of the historical background of the clients in order to best understand their present circumstances.

Sociodemography. The sociodemographic nature of a population in terms of population census, geographical residence, levels of income, poverty, and education is important in assessment and intervention. Such data inform the worker of the social class of the client, possible stressors in his or her life, and the degree of ethnic community resources and support available. For example, the majority of Asian and Pacific Islanders reside in five states: California, New York, Texas, Hawaii, and

Illinois. Implications for these states with high-density Asian and Pacific Islander populations include the existence of ethnic enclaves as well as the demonstration of high levels of racism due to the increased visibility of such minorities. This type of information is invaluable for the worker involved with the Asian and Pacific Islander client. Another example illustrating the importance of sociodemographic data relates to poverty levels. The 1980 Census indicates a national poverty level averaging 12.4 percent, with Asian and Pacific Islanders ranging from a low of 6.6 percent for Japanese Americans to a high of 65.9 percent for Laotians (U.S. Bureau of the Census, 1988). These data inform the worker of the varying levels of survival stressors relating to employment, housing, and subsistence and may help to pinpoint the area for intervention.

Values and Behavioral Norms. The values and lifestyle practices of the Asian and Pacific Islander client provide significant information for the worker. The development of a client's values, worldviews, and behavioral patterns is a complicated interplay of many variables involving collective ethnic and individual experiences. Recognizing that the worker examines his or her worldviews according to etic and emic perspectives, it is also useful to acknowledge that the client enters social services with a unique pattern of values that may also be similarly categorized. Mokuau (1986) suggests that three perspectives—culture-general, bicultural, and culture-specific—may be visualized as markers on a continuum. An individual who maintains a culture-general perspective views the world in ways compatible with the dominant or mainstream culture and can be referred to as acculturated. An individual who is bicultural holds simultaneous membership in two different cultures, and thus there is a commitment to the values of both the dominant and ethnic cultures. An individual who maintains a culture-specific perspective views the world in ways compatible with the parameters of his or her specific cultural group and can be referred to as traditional (p. 154).

The nature of an individual's worldviews and values interfaces with the behavioral norms that are adopted. For example, language as the symbolic expression of a culture can be perceived as a behavioral norm deriving from and interfacing with the values and worldviews of a group. In Asian and Pacific Islander cultures, there is great diversity in the retention of indigenous languages, ranging from a low of 0.5 percent native Hawaiians who speak a language other than English at home to a high of 81.9 percent for Cambodians who speak their native tongue (Asian American Health Forum, Inc., 1990). The implications are that native Hawaiians hold a values position of acculturated and that Cambodians hold a values position perceived as traditional. While this may serve as a useful point of departure in the assessment of a client's background, in this particular example a comprehensive examination of the history of native Hawaiians will reveal that they may not be acculturated individuals but rather victims of colonization who were forced to give up their language.

An Asian and Pacific Islander client may hold dear values and traditions that fall into an infinite number of places on the culture-general/bicultural/culture-specific continuum. A worker's understanding of what the values are, where they fall on the continuum, and how the values interface with behavioral norms can facilitate the assessment of problems and the selection of appropriate intervention.

Social and Psychological Problems and Issues. Being informed about the nature and severity of social and psychological problems confronting the various Asian and Pacific Islander groups facilitates assessment and the appropriate utilization of intervention strategies. The problems may vary between fourth-generation Japanese and a recent refugee population such as the Vietnamese, but the underlying factor of institutional racism permeates the development of all problems. An array of problems evident in Asian and Pacific Islander cultures includes poverty, unemployment, poor health profiles, and mental health problems such as depression, anxiety, and low self-esteem.

It is also important for the worker to understand the client's perception of the problem and cultural ways of problem resolution. For example, in Samoan culture, the use of physical discipline in child-rearing is acceptable, and Samoan parents who are found to be perpetuators of child abuse in the American system are sometimes confused, angry, and resistive to treatment. While condoning of child abuse is abhorrent, the worker who operates within the parameters of Samoan culture will probably have the best results in altering child-rearing behaviors. These cultural parameters may include working with the entire family as well as respected Samoan community members such as the chiefs or pastors.

Social Services Intervention

The conceptualization of social services intervention is driven by a knowledge of the client's background. The information on history, sociodemography, values, behavioral norms, and problems contributes to accurate and appropriate social service intervention. Such information guides workers in their selection of appropriate models or theories of practice and pinpoints the specific skills that may be the most useful.

Theoretical and Conceptual Models. There are many theories and models on personality development, human behavior, and social service intervention that may apply to Asian and Pacific Islanders. While these theories and models may have been originally developed for culture-general or white, middle-class populations, their usefulness resides in their match to the client's background. Devore and Schlesinger (1987) review several prevailing approaches to social work practice, including the psy-

chosocial, problem-solving, task-centered, structural, systems, and ecological approaches, and assess the extent to which they pay attention
to the ethnic reality. Mokuau and J. Matsuoka (1986) examine personality
theories categorized as psychodynamic, existential-humanistic, and cog-
nitive-behavioral for their relevance for Asian American populations.
These "mainstream" theories and models seem to be the most useful
for Asian and Pacific Islanders who have adopted some of the values
and worldviews of the mainstream culture. They may also be useful, if
modified, to fit the needs of the ethnic client.

Various cultures have developed their own models on human behavior
and intervention. Indigenous models may be used in conjunction with
culture-general theories or may have merit in being used by themselves.
These indigenous models may have greatest use with those Asian and
Pacific Islanders who adhere to the worldviews and traditions of their
ethnic groups. For example, Japanese culture has *Morita* and *Naikan*
therapy, and in native Hawaiian culture, there is *Ho'oponopono*, a family-
centered approach.

The ethnic-competent worker must have a knowledge of the array of
theories available, both culture-general and culture-specific, and be able
to modify or translate these theories to match the client's background.

Skills. The worker's ability to translate theories and conceptual models
to be consistent with the background of the client reflects skills of accurate assessment, informed selection, utilization of intervention strategies, and systematic evaluation. Lum (1986) identifies the role of the
worker and the skills necessary in each of the stages of the helping
process: contact, problem identification, assessment, intervention, and
termination. He further differentiates the skills in working at three levels
of practice: with individuals, groups, and communities. While there are
a multitude of skills and tasks proposed, the basis of all suggested derives
from the worker's capacity to develop plans that help the ethnic client
to fulfill his or her needs in context of existing social and environmental
parameters.

Gallegos (1984) delineates several skills required for ethnic-competent
practice. The skills listed are not intended to be a comprehensive package
of skills but serve as a stimulus for thinking about ethnic-competent
practice. The worker should be able to:

1. establish techniques for learning the cultures of ethnic minority clients and
   their communities;
2. assess the meaning of ethnicity for individual clients;
3. master interviewing techniques that reflect an understanding of the role of
   language in the client's culture;
4. utilize the concept of empowerment on behalf of ethnic minority clients and
   their communities;

5. evaluate the validity and applicability of new techniques, research, and knowledge for work with ethnic minorities;

6. understand the impact of social policies and services on minority clients; and

7. recognize and combat individual and institutional racism and racial stereo-types. (p. 8)

CONCLUSION

We have reviewed how the social service profession has struggled historically to develop a body of knowledge to meet the needs of ethnic minorities. While the evolution has been slow, there has been a major thrust since the 1980s to formulate several conceptual models. In this chapter we have focused on two approaches, the cultural awareness approach (Green, 1982) and the ethnic-sensitive practice approach (Devore and Schlesinger, 1987). The underlying themes in these models contribute to the conceptualization of a framework for Asian and Pacific Islanders, which we have identified in this chapter. Two themes highlighted in these models are: (1) the importance for the worker to understand his or her own values and traditions and their influence on relationships with others; and (2) the importance to have knowledge of the client's cultural history and frame of reference as it pertains to the definition, communication, and resolution of problems. The worker who understands and utilizes these concepts is an ethnically competent worker.

Specifically, the framework includes several dimensions that help to develop ethnic-competent practice. These dimensions focus on the worker's:

1. self-awareness. Ideally this is balanced between etic (culture-general) and emic (culture-specific) views.

2. knowledge about culture. This includes cultural history, sociodemography, values, behavioral norms, and social and psychological problems and issues.

3. knowledge and skills in social service intervention. This includes the selection of models and theories and the worker's ability to translate them into practice.

The following chapters utilize this framework to present the historical background, sociodemographic overview, values and behavioral norms, profile of social and psychological problems and issues, and social service intervention with selected Asian and Pacific Islander groups (Japanese Americans, Chinese Americans, Filipino Americans, Vietnamese Americans, native Hawaiians, Samoan Americans, and Chamorro Americans). Three chapters also deal with contemporary problems and issues facing Asian and Pacific Islanders (the elderly, family violence, and social literacy among the youth), and another chapter underscores the importance of the concept of balance in these cultures. The final chapter discusses future directions in social services for Asian and Pacific Islanders.

With the projected increase of nonwhite minorities in the United States, the need for social service professionals to become ethnically competent is crucial. Gallegos (1984) contends that ethnic competence must be an educational goal for all helping professionals. Bowles (1988) urges educators and service delivery providers to "be responsible for considering issues of ethnicity and race when developing curricula; when making diagnostic formulations and treatment plans; when formulating research questions, methodology, and design; when assessing the service needs of the community; and when critiquing social policies" (p. 2). For example, the Council on Social Work Education and schools of social work should assure that ethnic minority content and skills for crosscultural practice are part of the curriculum. Social service agencies should hire ethnic minority staff and supervisors and support schools in educating students and other professionals about working with ethnic minority clients. Ethnic minority professionals should be encouraged and supported to develop research, present lectures and workshops, and serve as consultants. Social workers should work to empower their clients, the consumers of services, to take an active role in changing policies that impact their lives.

We are hopeful that the information gained through this book will equip social service professionals with the knowledge to become ethnically competent, culturally sensitive, and stronger advocates for ethnic minorities.

REFERENCES

Acosta, F. X., and J. G. Sheehan (1976). Psychotherapist ethnicity and expertise as determinants of self-disclosure. In M. Miranda (ed.), *Psychotherapy with the Spanish-Speaking: Issues in Research and Service Delivery*, monograph no. 3. Los Angeles: Spanish Speaking Mental Health Research Center, UCLA.

Asian American Health Forum, Inc. (1990). *Asian and Pacific Islander American Population Statistics*. San Francisco.

Atkinson, D. R., M. Maruyama, and S. Matsui (1978). Effects of counselor race and counseling approach on Asian Americans' perceptions of counselor credibility and utility. *Journal of Counseling Psychology* 25 (1): 76–83.

Bernard, V. W. (1953). Psychoanalysis and members of minority groups. *Journal of the American Psychoanalytical Association* 1: 256–268.

Bowles, D. D. (1988). Introduction to Part 1: Practice issues. In C. Jacobs and D. D. Bowles (eds.), *Ethnicity and Race: Critical Concepts in Social Work*. Silver Spring, Md.: National Association of Social Workers, Inc.

Corey, G., M. S. Corey, and P. Callanan (1988). Appendix. *Issues and Ethics in the Helping Professions*. Monterey, Calif.: Brooks/Cole Publishing Company.

Davis, L. E. (1984). The significance of color. *Ethnicity in Social Group Work Practice*. New York: Haworth Press.

Devore, W., and E. G. Schlesinger (1987). *Ethnic-Sensitive Social Work Practice*. Columbus, Ohio: Merrill Publishing Company.

Dieppa, I. (1984). Trends in social work education for minorities. In B. White (ed.), *Color in a White Society*. Silver Spring, Md.: National Association of Social Workers, Inc.

Draguns, J. G. (1976). Counseling across cultures: Common themes and distinct approaches. In P. Pedersen, J. Draguns, W. Lonner, and J. Trimble (eds.), *Counseling Across Cultures*. Honolulu: University of Hawaii Press.

Ellenberger, H. J. (1960). Cultural aspects of mental illness. *American Journal of Psychotherapy* 14: 158–173.

Furlong, M. J., D. R. Atkinson, and J. M. Casas (1979). Effects of counselor ethnicity and attitudinal similarity on Chicano students' perceptions of counselor credibility and attractiveness. *Hispanic Journal of Behavioral Sciences* 1 (1): 41–53.

Gallegos, J. S. (1984). The ethnic competence model for social work education. In B. White (ed.), *Color in a White Society*. Silver Spring, Md.: National Association of Social Workers, Inc.

Green, J. W. (ed.) (1982). *Cultural Awareness in the Human Services*. Englewood Cliffs, N.J.: Prentice-Hall.

Ho, M. K. (1987). *Family Therapy with Ethnic Minorities*. Newbury Park, Calif.: Sage Publications.

Hopps, J. G. (1982). Oppression based on color. *Social Work* 27 (1): 3–5.

Jacobs, C., and D. D. Bowles (1988). *Ethnicity and Race: Critical Concepts in Social Work*. Silver Spring, Md.: National Association of Social Workers, Inc.

Lee, E. (1990). Culturally competent practice. Paper presented at the Asian American Health Forum Conference, Washington, D.C.

Lum, D. (1986). *Social Work Practice and People of Color: A Process-Stage Approach*. Monterey, Calif.: Brooks/Cole Publishing Company.

Mokuau, N. (1986). Ethnic minorities. In H. Gochros, J. Gochros, and J. Fischer (eds.), *Helping the Sexually Oppressed*. Englewood Cliffs, N.J.: Prentice-Hall.

Mokuau, N. (forthcoming). Ethnic minority curriculum in baccalaureat social work program. *Journal of Multicultural Social Work*.

Mokuau, N. (1990). The impoverishment of native Hawaiians and the social work challenge. *Health and Social Work* 15 (3): 235–242.

Mokuau, N., and J. Matsuoka (1986). Appropriateness of practice theories for working with Asian and Pacific Islanders. Paper presented at the Council on Social Work Education Annual Conference, Miami, Fla.

Morales, A. (1976). The Mexican American and mental health issues. In M. Sotomayor (ed.), *Cross Cultural Perspectives in Social Work Practice and Education*. Houston: University of Houston Graduate School of Social Work.

Norton, D. (1978). *The Dual Perspective: Inclusion of Ethnic Minority Concept in the Social Work Curriculum*. New York: Council on Social Work Education.

Records, W. (1966). Counseling and color: Crisis and conscience. *Integrated Education* 4: 34–41.

Seward, G. (1956). *Psychotherapy and Culture Conflict.* New York: Ronald Press.

Solomon, B. B. (1976). *Black Empowerment: Social Work in Oppressed Communities.* New York: Columbia University Press.

Sue, D. W. (1981). The culturally skilled counselor. *Counseling the Culturally Different: Theory and Practice.* New York: John Wiley and Sons.

U.S. Bureau of the Census (1988). *We, the Asian and Pacific Islander Americans.* Washington, D.C.: U.S. Government Printing Office.

White. B. (ed.) (1984). *Color in a White Society.* Silver Spring, Md.: National Association of Social Workers, Inc.

Wilson, L. (1982). Ethnic competence: Skills, attitudes, knowledge. Unpublished paper. Seattle: Multi-Ethnic Mental Health Training Project, School of Social Work, University of Washington.

Wolkon, G. H., S. Moriwaki, and K. J. Williams (1973). Race and social class as factors in the orientation toward psychotherapy. *Journal of Counseling Psychology* 20 (4): 312–316.

CHAPTER 3

Balance as a Criterion for Social Services for Asian and Pacific Islander Americans

PAUL PEDERSEN

If you asked most Western-trained social service providers to describe what they do, many if not most would say they make people feel more pleasure and less pain, more happiness and less sadness, and experience more success and less failure. This is a one-directional approach to social services. An alternative criterion that this chapter attempts to describe is a two-directional balance where both pain and pleasure, both happiness and sadness, both success and failure are equally important accommodations. The most widely understood example of balance in relationships would be the *Yin* and *Yang* symbol where light and darkness become part of the same sphere and are inseparable from one another.

By helping to define or restore balance in a person's life, social services can help that person integrate both pain and pleasure in a meaningful way. The models for defining and restoring balance as a criterion for social service are best found in Asian and Pacific models of health (Tseng and Wu, 1985; Sheikh and Sheikh, 1989; Blowers and Turtle, 1987; Roland, 1988; Bond, 1986).

ASIAN AND PACIFIC PSYCHOLOGIES

The separation of Asian and Western cultures sometimes obscures more than it illuminates. H. Nakamura (1964) discounts various attempts to identify cultural traits that contrast East and West. He claims the common features of one hemisphere are either partly or imperfectly understood in the other hemisphere or were conspicuous in a particular country at a particular time and then generalized to include the whole hemisphere. Thus, he says, "We must acknowledge the fact that there exists no single Eastern feature but rather that there exists diverse ways of thinking in East Asia characteristic of certain people but not of the whole of East Asia" (p. 19). The whole idea of national character is in some disrepute among social scientists, as are research findings suggesting innate racial differences in personality. There is indeed a special uniqueness in each culture that has evolved for whatever reason. For example, India emphasizes the spiritual, China emphasizes the social, and Western culture emphasizes the rational aspects of human behavior. At the same time, we must realize that Asia includes a wide range of distinctive cultures, and this precludes accurate generalizations about the thinking of Asians. After surveying each separate tradition, the cultural systems of India, China, and Japan will be contrasted with one another and with Western notions of psychology, emphasizing similarities and differences.

The assumptions underlying Asian psychological thinking relate to basic collective or corporate philosophical assumptions of the self in a context of human existence. There is much less emphasis on individualism and more on a corporate identity that balances aspects of the self. Likewise, there is a more positive interpretation of dependence and interdependencies within the unit, the family, and society. The family plays a particularly significant role as a model for defining the balance of roles for institutional social relationships of society. Many Asian cultures define the personality in relational terms, focusing on the space between individuals rather than on the individuals themselves. The emphasis in these Asian systems is mainly on the structure of family, clan, class, and state thought in which individuals relate to one another. Asian thinking is by no means unimodal, however, as Nakamura (1964) asserts.

Indian Psychologies

Psychological explanation is not a Western invention. Ancient Indians developed a variety of personality theories originally based on the *gunas*, or attributes of the mind, dating back to Vedic literature of about 800–500 B.C. Each succeeding religiophilosophical system in India modified views of personality in its own way, generally emphasizing practical aspects of organizing, classifying, and understanding persons in relation to the family, society, and abstract values.

These Indian systems were developed into specific ways of thinking through the classical Hindu literature of the Rg-Veda, the Upanishads, yoga, and the Bhagavad-Gita. The revolutionary teachings of Gotama Buddha, born in 563 B.C., spread throughout Asia to China and Japan, carrying, modifying, and adapting original ideas of the Aryans, who invaded India between 2000 and 1000 B.C.

From Aryan philosophy there is the notion of mind, soul, or spirit rooted in the changeless reality of an inner self or *atman*, considered to be the core of reality both for individuals and for a cosmic unity. G. Murphy and L. Murphy (1968) observe: "From this philosophy of the *atman* develops a conception of purity, changeless nobility, freedom from deception, freedom from passion, deceit, and delusion which reappears in almost all the forms of Indian philosophy" (p. 6). The emphasis in Asian thought, however, is not on the *atman* as an individual entity or basic unit, but rather on the principle of an "Absolute," which approximates the Western notion of God.

The development of psychological concepts in India went through a period emphasizing magic, in which people tried to understand nature, and a period emphasizing human concerns, as in Buddhism, in which inner harmony and psychic consciousness became the key to freedom (Govinda, 1961). Awareness of suffering is a constant theme of Indian psychology whereby the wise person escapes enslavement to selfishness by realizing the true nature of the universe.

Four basic concepts are needed to understand Indian psychology:

1. *Dharma*: Codes and rules that define goodness, maturity, and appropriateness of behavior.
2. *Karma*: The propulsion from previous incarnations, present deeds, and future destiny (which has been wrongly characterized as "fatalism").
3. *Maya*: The illusion of real knowledge and causes (which Westerners might describe as "reality").
4. *Atman*: The person, not as an individual and separate "self," but as part of an ultimate cosmic unity or Absolute.

These concepts were taught in the legends of the Ramayana, the Mahabharata, in the religious literature of the Upanishads and Bhagavad-Gita. All are concerned with the struggle between good and evil.

The Upanishads ask the question "Who am I?" in a variety of contexts. The person is variously described as the one who sees, who speaks, who discriminates—the ear of the ear; mind of the mind; agency for memory and volition, austerity, and self-control. The Upanishads emphasize the connection between an individual and the cosmic Absolute rather than taking any aspect separately.

Yoga likewise discriminates between self and the time-defined context in which the self exists. The person is considered to exist outside the sphere represented by pure self. Undifferentiated consciousness separates self as "knower" from the object "known," which contaminates the pure self. The separation of individual self-serene and changeless-form thought process is evident in disciplined self-training through the system of Raja-yoga (royal Yogo) and the physiological discipline of

Hatha-yoga (yoga of force), concerned with cultivating extraordinary bodily control (Murphy and Murphy, 1968).

The Bhagavad-Gita presents three classifications of goal orientation and modes of existence (*gunas*) for persons: the Tamas, Rajas, and Sattwa systems. The Tamas and Rajas emphasize self-diminuation, while the Sattwa emphasizes self-enhancement and self-realization. "Individuals abiding in Tamas prefer to lead an easy-going life. They are generally sluggish and lethargic and totally indifferent to any constructive action which calls for a rigorous discipline in life" (Beg, 1970, p. 13). The state of Rajas more clearly defines goals of power and the accumulation of wealth, perceiving others as objects for exploitation. Both Tamas and Rajas emphasize a closed system, depriving human relationships of harmony, happiness, and dignity. Sattwa stresses the goal of cosmic awareness, ecstasy, bliss, altruism, unitive consciousness, and spiritual enlightenment, emphasizing the value of nonattachment. Sattwa emancipates human mind and body from bondage of passions, pride, anxiety, and the wasteful action of biological needs. There is an emphasis on human and transcendental values, ethical behavior, and "self-actualization" beyond the physical or psychological realities of life in a "transpersonal" psychology of personality.

Buddhism emphasizes the four noble truths and the eightfold path. The four noble truths are: (1) All life is subject to suffering; (2) desire to live is the cause of repeated existences; (3) the annihilation of desire gives release from suffering; and (4) the way of escape is through the eightfold path. The eightfold path is right belief, right thought, right speech, right action, right livelihood, right effort, right mindfulness, and right concentration to escape from desire. These ideas spread throughout Asia to influence the understanding of personality in a variety of settings.

R. A. Schweder (1982) provides a summary of how concepts of personality contrast between American and East Indian cultures. Since many of the Asian psychological perspectives we discuss in this chapter began in India, it is particularly important to understand the complexity of Indian psychology.

Chinese Psychologies

When Buddhism was imported to China around the first century B.C., it was modified to emphasize the social responsibility of Buddha's ethical teaching. The Chinese have been fairly characterized as valuing common sense and utilitarian ways of thinking. Even their philosophical teachings are based on practical subjects and include everyday examples of morality, politics, and a lifestyle that results in successful living.

Many of the teachings of Taoism dwell on the art of self-protection, on the method of attaining success, or on the right way of governing. Confucianism, which occupied the highest position in Chinese thought, is also largely a system of ethics for the governing class and a set of precepts for governing the people. (Nakamura, 1964, p. 234)

The indigenous Chinese view of personality developed from the teaching of Confucius (551–479 B.C.), emphasizing aspects of "characterological theory" (Hiniker, 1969). The basic aspects of this view emphasize the notions of face, filial piety, and proper conduct. The notion of face brings out an individual's felt moral worth, assessed according to his or her loyalty to his or her group rather than according to universal principles, with social deviance controlled more by public shaming than private guilt. Filial piety describes a compliant and submissive posture toward authority. Proper conduct (*Li*) defines the duty of persons and the necessity of observing proper forms of conduct for each social situation. These truths are described in four books: *Confucian Analects, The Book of Mencius, The Great Learning,* and *The Doctrine of the Mean.* The task of Chinese philosophy is to describe the "way" (*Tao*) to perfection of the personality along practical lines, synthesizing Confucian this-worldliness and Taoist other-worldliness to achieve sageness within and kingliness without. Chinese philosophy can be described according to five basic social relationships between: (1) sovereign and subject; (2) father and son; (3) elder and younger brother; (4) husband and wife; and (5) friend and friend. Each contrasting layer of Chinese philosophy, from early Confucianism to contemporary Maoism, emphasizes variants of these basic themes.

F.L.K. Hsu (1985) describes the very concept of being a person (*jen*) in Chinese culture as involving a dynamic balance, which he calls "psychosocial homeostasis." For every living human being, *jen* is not a fixed entity. Like the human body it is in a state of dynamic equilibrium. It is a matrix or a framework within which every human individual seeks to maintain a satisfactory level of psychic and interpersonal equilibrium, in the same sense that every physical organism tends to maintain a uniform and beneficial psychological stability within and between its parts (pp. 33–34).

K. S. Yang (1986) cites research indicating that Chinese adults tend to display a cognitive style of seeing things in wholes rather than in parts—a proclivity for global or holistic perception—while Westerners do the reverse.

F.M.C. Cheung (1986) describes traditional medical beliefs in the classical and folk traditions through a series of relationships.

In the classical tradition, illnesses are discussed in terms of the balance of the *Yin* and *Yang* forces, the five fundamental elements (metal, wood, water, fire and earth), the *ching-lo* (meridian) system, and the circulation of *chi* (vital energy).

The aetiology of illnesses is attributed to three groups of factors: six seasonal influences (wind, heat, fire, cold, moisture and dryness), several internal emotions (joy, grief, fear, anger, love, hatred and desire) and situational conditions such as trauma, fatigue, deregulation of diet and insects. (p. 171)

Cheung (1986) goes on to describe empirical studies of both normal and abnormal Chinese subjects that demonstrate multiple causal attributions and coping strategies for problem solving, suggesting, and interactional paradigm. Psychological variables, somatic factors, and situational contexts all contribute to the Chinese understanding of the psychological. A systems model is more adequate to examine the multiple factors and to prescribe treatment. This interactional approach is similar to the bio-psychological model of medicine gaining popularity in Western medicine.

Chinese psychological thinking as described in the *Confucian Analects, The Book of Mencius, The Great Learning,* and *The Doctrine of the Mean* describes a "way" or *Tao* that synthesizes this-worldliness with other-worldliness. The five basic social relationships between sovereign and subject, father and son, elder and younger brother, husband and wife, and friend and friend provide models of harmony and balance for achieving psychological health.

Japanese Psychologies

The Japanese, influenced by both India and China, adapted and expanded these models of balance and harmony through the uniquely Japanese perspective of Zen. Zen Buddhism believes that persons who are emancipated from the dualistic bondage of subjectivity and objectivity of mind and body are awakened to their own true nature, or the condition of *Satori* or enlightenment. In that state the person is finely tuned to both inner and outer reality. D. K. Reynolds (1980) in his Zen center emphasizes "phenomenological operationalism" where the uneasy mind is refocused and regulated.

The Japanese way of thought was strongly influenced by both India and China, particularly in the period before the Meiji Restoration in 1868. Evidence of these influences is apparent both in the language and philosophies of the Japanese culture. Chinese writings and thought were introduced in Japan in the sixth century A.D., with particular emphasis on Confucianism and Buddhism. The Japanese selectively adapted these viewpoints to develop their own unique way of thinking, emphasizing what Nakamura (1964) calls the limited social nexus of the Japanese people themselves.

Relationships in Japanese culture stress the group rather than the individual. While the basic social unit in the West is the individual, and groups of individuals compose the state, the Japanese society is more accurately understood as an aggregation of family units. Considerable importance is attached to esteem of the hierarchical order, with each person well defined in his or her role. Special attention is given to the family, clan, and nation as instrumental in defining loyalty through mutual exchange of obligation.

In abstract terms, human relations are divided into "vertical" categories, such as the parent-child and superior-inferior relationship, or "horizontal" ones, such as that between siblings or collegial associates. While the horizontal relationship has contributed to the formation of concepts of caste, as in India, or of class, as in America, the vertical relationship in Japan has taken the form of *oyabun-kobun,* as for example patron and protégé, landlord and tenant farmer, or master and disciple, in the Japanese bureaucracy. Hierarchy in the group is usually determined by a seniority system, and this frustrates modern Japanese management systems, which emphasize individual competency. The sense of Japanese honor is closely tied to high esteem for a hierarchical order. Nakamura (1964) claims this hierarchy motivates the moral faculty of Japanese self-reflection and identity: "It posits before man the ideal of the infinite good that he should strive for, it induces him to reflect, by contrast, upon the sorry fact that he himself is too weak and helpless to refrain from doing evil; and thus it awakens within him the consciousness of [man]" (p. 513).

C. Nakane (1972) contrasts the notion of attribute, or any specific quality of an individual, with the notion of frame of reference, or groups of individuals who share the same situation by living in the same neighborhood, working in the same company, or belonging to the same organization. The practical significance of a Japanese individual identifying himself or herself according to his or her frame of reference rather than his or her individualized attributes is readily seen.

Role behavior, therefore, becomes the means of self-realization for even the modern Japanese. The individual is dedicated to and inseparable from his or her role, which probably dates back to basic Confucian values embodied in the samurai elite of the nineteenth century. Carefully prescribed role relationships, beginning with the family, have significantly contributed to the stability of Japanese society in spite of rapid social change, at the cost of deemphasizing a sense of personal self. Achievement is not considered an individual phenomenon but rather the result of cooperation, both collaterally and hierarchically, in the combined and collective efforts of individuals. G. DeVoss (1973) says: "Internalized sanctions make it difficult to conceive of letting down one's family or one's social groups and occupational superiors. In turn, those in authority positions must take paternal care of those for whom they have responsibility" (p. 185).

The importance of human relations is further evidenced in elaborate rules of propriety. The exchange of greetings, for example, is elaborate rather than simple. There is an abundance of honorific words and phrases in the Japanese language. "It is said that if all such honorific words were taken out of Lady Murasaki's *Tale of Genji*, the book would be reduced to one half its length" (Nakamura, 1964, p. 407). At the same time, there is an acknowledgment and acceptance of natural desires or sentiments as they are. It is in the social realm that conduct is carefully regulated; within one's inner self one can think whatever one pleases. The strong collectivity orientation in Japanese culture stresses stability and security but can result in stagnation, while the American adjustment, through self-orientation and individual freedom, can result in anomie.

Horizontal relationships of equals are not emphasized in traditional Japanese culture. Outside the family there is more instrumentally directed cooperative behavior than is generally recognized. "A great deal of social cohesion and social control is exercised through constrained participation in a wide variety of organizations directed to community betterment. How the individual feels about participating is beside the point—one is impelled to meet the social expectations of others as one subordinates self to social role" (DeVoss, 1985).

M. Nakakaki (1973) discusses the psychodynamic mechanisms in Japanese culture that are reconciled in a balance of contrasting tendencies. In the title of her book on Japan, R. Benedict (1946) juxtaposes the symbolism of a "chrysanthemum" for the soft, tranquil delicacy of aesthetic character in tension with the militaristic, authoritative attitude of a "sword." There is a similar dynamic balance throughout Japanese culture, which reconciles self-expression against conformity throughout society. These contrasts are related to a basic tension between narcissism and masochism (Nakakaki, 1973). The narcissistic element is indicated by achievement orientation, competitiveness, and ambitiousness in a self-centered, omnipotent, and grandiose manner. The Japanese self-consciously strive for higher goals to realize their ego-ideal and are further motivated in this direction by a family-related, shame-oriented drive to be successful. The masochistic lifestyle is demonstrated in attitudes toward work, illness, and death whereby the person is duty-bound to repay obligations. The ideals of self-denial are prominent in Japanese culture. The traditional Japanese family provides models in a narcissistic father through his omnipotence in the household and a masochistic mother whose task it is to maintain harmony in the family. The narcissistic pattern is related to shame and the masochistic pattern to guilt, as these two tendencies coexist in Japanese culture. The individual reconciles this tension by living in accord with prescribed roles within family and society. The source of conflict most likely to occur is between individual ambition and role responsibility.

Mental health, therefore, depends on keeping these two opposing tendencies in balance so that the individual can move freely from masochistic hard work in the daytime to narcissistic relaxation at home, without either tendency taking control of him or her. It is necessary for the individual to transcend these categories by balancing them without weakening either tendency.

Pacific Island Psychologies

While the literature on Pacific Islanders is less developed (Mokuau, 1985), the studies that have been done suggest that (1) mental health facilities are being underutilized largely due to a conflict of philosophies, (2) culture-specific approaches such as "talking therapy" are being developed on indigenous values, and (3) prescriptive treatment studies matching the method with the context of each Pacific Island culture are being developed. The family unit is clearly the force and model that unifies Pacific Islanders and is the resource for healing and treatment. In Hawaiian culture, for example, *ho'oponopono*, which means setting to right or the restoration and maintenance of good relationships among family and supernatural powers, demonstrates the importance of balance or harmony in social services (Pukui, Haertig, Lee, and McDermott, 1979; Paglinawan, 1983).

More recently, Ayurvedic medicine, based on Indian and Asian traditions such as yoga, has grown out of holistic health movements, combining the influence of mind and body in the definition of interactive health. Biofeedback techniques, meditation, the study of alpha and beta rhythms, and the importance of feeling states have perpetuated this Asian-based search for balance in the search for psychological health. Transpersonal psychology (Tart, 1975) contrasts the Asian emphasis on balance with the Western emphasis on solutions in an attempt to combine both positions.

THE DEFINITION OF BALANCE

The fourth alternative, which M. Maruyama (1978) favors, is a homeostatic reciprocal and "morphogenetic," or organic, analogy to living forms, which looks at a balance of variables beyond the explanation of casual relationships. The morphogenetic analogy is more familiar to non-Western culture, as in the dynamic balance of *Yin* and *Yang*, hot and cold, male and female throughout nature (Berry, 1980). In many non-Westernized systems there is less emphasis on separating the person or persons from the presenting problem or source of difficulty than in Western cultures.

Balance suggests a broad frame of reference to the system or field surrounding each unit or identity. While Western approaches acknowledge the importance of "solutions," there is less understanding of how "problems" are also important in social services. Counseling is typically described as a one-directional process emphasizing the value of pleasure, happiness, and utopian resolution of conflict rather than a two-directional process with a dynamic balance of positive and negative forces requiring reconciliation. In many non-Westernized systems there is less emphasis on separating the person or persons from a presenting problem or source of difficulty than there is in Westernized systems. There is also less of a tendency to locate the problem inside an isolated individual and more of an attempt to relate the individual's problem to other persons or even the cosmology. Balance in the context of social services is a condition of order and dynamic process within a context where all elements, pain as well as pleasure, serve a useful and necessary function. This non-Western emphasis is typically more holistic in acknowledging the interaction of persons and environments in both their positive and negative aspects. Happiness is achieved indirectly as a by-product of harmonious, two-directional balance.

This definition of balance is different from consistency theory defined by F. Heider (1958), T. M. Newcomb (1953), or W. J. McGuire (1966), where inconsistency among elements is an unpleasant state that individuals avoid in preference to a more pleasant harmony. Because of this preference, balanced structures, according to consistency theory, are easier to learn, more stable, and less volatile. Cognitive balance in this perspective is achieved by changing, ignoring, differentiating, or transcending inconsistencies. Inconsistency leads to dissonance and a change of cognition or feelings about a situation (Triandis, 1977). Consistency theory seeks to *create* a balance in order to increase pleasure or positive outcomes.

The restoration of balance provides an alternative goal to the more individualized goal of solving social problems. In the context of balance as a criterion, social change is perceived as an unresolved ambiguity, tension, and reciprocity of contrasting alternatives rather than resolving differences in favor of either alternative. Balance is a process rather than a conclusive event. In a similar mode, the pain and otherwise negative aspects of social problems also provide necessary resources for creating a dynamic balance with pleasure and positive aspects of the same situation.

The Conceptual Framework of Balance

P. Pedersen (1986) suggests that one look at the problem in four different ways illustrative of its role in the balanced approach to multicultural counseling. On the basis of working with Asian clients, particularly

Indonesian and Chinese clients, Pedersen (1986) discovered that the problem was more frequently anthropomorphized as a source of influence. As a result of working with Asian clients, the problem was now seen as an externalized force in the interview. Where the problem was first perceived as just bad, it was now perceived as both good and bad, judging from the client's perspective. If the problem was unambiguously negative in its effect, the client would have a much easier time disengaging. It is the bittersweet ambiguity that makes problems difficult. Second, a problem is complex much like a personality. A problem is not simply bad grades, sleeplessness, or overdrinking. A problem is a very complex configuration that draws from the total environment of the client, persons significant to the client, and perhaps even the counselor to develop its identity. Third, the problem is active rather than passive, with an ability to change and constantly adapt to the dynamic context. What appears to be the problem at one point in the interview may quickly change to another form within the interview. Unlike a lump of clay, a stick, or other inert object that can be moved from one place to another, the problem can maneuver elusively to escape whatever defenses the counselor and client may set up. The problem draws aspects of its identity from many different independent sources, even though none of these sources has control over the problem. For all practical purposes, the problem is perceived as an independent force with an independent identity. Fourth, the problem is not an abstraction but, from the client's viewpoint, very concrete. It is here and now, sitting beside the client to coach the client through the interview. Most research on the problem emphasizes its abstract qualities from the therapist's viewpoint rather than as a client-perceived reality. It is important to constantly adjust the therapist intervention to facilitate a balanced perspective between the client, counselor, and problem.

Counseling occurs in a force field of push and pull factors in which the counselor seeks to be helpful, the client seeks to reconcile internalized ambiguity, and the problem seeks to continue controlling the client—all aspects of which are culturally mediated. In the mode of social power theory, counseling occurs in the context of an equilibrium between the counselor seeking coalition with the client against the resistance of a problem. Negotiating a coalition between the client and the counselor describes the task functions of counseling in operational terms.

Figure 3.1 describes this triadic interaction between the counselor, client, and problem in which the client is initially being dominated by the problem and the counselor is intervening to restore a balance of power for the client. Counseling, then, becomes a process whereby a client's contribution of power or influence is increased and, as an inverse function of this process, the problem's capacity for power or influence is decreased. The client is encouraged to accept a greater share of the

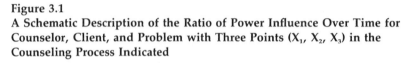

Figure 3.1
A Schematic Description of the Ratio of Power Influence Over Time for Counselor, Client, and Problem with Three Points (X₁, X₂, X₃) in the Counseling Process Indicated

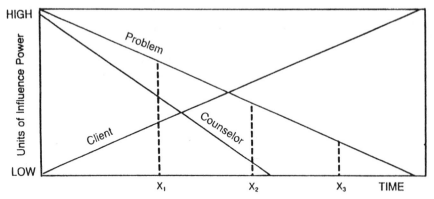

power and, as an inverse function of this process, the problem will control a lesser share of the power. The counselor intervenes to encourage client progress up the slope through a client-counselor coalition that balances the power influence of the problem.

As Figure 3.1 illustrates, at any point along the scale, the power of the counselor plus the power of the client should be approximately equal to the power of the problem ($C_0 + C_1 = P$). Since the power is distributed unequally in a constantly changing dynamic situation, the effective counselor needs to vary the power of intervention accordingly. If a counselor assumes too much power the client will withdraw from counseling in preference to the problem as less threatening. If the counselor assumes too little power the client will also withdraw from the problem because of the ineffective counselor.

The three situations (X_1, X_2, and X_3) are indicated in Figure 3.1. In X_1, the client has little power and is dominated by the problem, requiring the counselor to exert greater power than the client. In X_2, the client is able to exert enough power so that the counselor's power is reduced. Situation X_3 shows the client able to manage the problem almost independently and maintain a balance. The measures of high and low power influence are relative and not absolute to accommodate a relatively effective client facing a difficult problem and a relatively ineffective client facing a mild problem.

The counselor needs to coordinate the power of intervention according to the variable rate and direction of a client's movement to maintain a client-counselor coalition and maintain balance in the interview. Counselors might exert more power through confrontation and interpretation and less power through reflection and nondirective accommodation. When a counselor and client come from different cultures, it is particularly difficult to maintain the appropriate balance of power inside the counseling interview. However, the research indicating that the counseling "relationship" is the most important predictor of success in therapy suggests that this balance of power must be maintained. This model provides a conceptual framework for operationalizing the counseling interaction and for defining the goal of training as increasing a counselor's skill in maintaining an effective balance in counseling.

APPLICATIONS OF BALANCE TO THERAPY

There is evidence that successful therapy systems have a tendency to compensate for the social context by restoring a balance. Explorational, open-ended, insight-oriented therapy is less successful in cultures favoring authoritarian or totalitarian political regimes (Draguns, 1981). E. D. Wittkower and H. Warnes (1974) suggest that crosscultural preferences in therapy depend on etiological views and ideological differences, which is why they claim psychoanalysis gained ground in the United States through individualism, work therapy in the Soviet Union because of Marxist ideology, autogenic training in Germany and Morita therapy in Japan because of culturally imposed, rigid self-discipline. W. S. Tseng and J. Hsu (1980) further discuss how therapy compensates for culturally different features so that highly controlled and overregulated cultures might encourage therapies that provide a safety-valve release for feelings and emotions while underregulated or anomic cultures might encourage therapies with externalized social control at the expense of self-expression. T. Y. Lin and M. C. Lin (1978) attribute mental illness to five harmful emanations affecting the *Yin* and *Yang* when they are disturbed or "out of balance."

A. W. Watts (1961) describes counseling as a social game based on conventional rules that defines boundaries between the individual and the cultural context. It is then the duty of a therapist to involve participants in a "counter game" that restores a unifying perspective of ego and environment so that the person can be liberated and a balanced context restored. J. G. Draguns (1981) suggests several guidelines for adjusting balance through therapy. The more complex the social and cognitive structure, the more a society will prefer hierarchy and ritual characterized by elaborate techniques for countering psychological distress. The stronger a society believes in the changeability of human nature and plasticity of social roles, the more they will favor therapy techniques as vehicles of change. The more attitudes toward psychological disturbance reflect deep-seated prejudices about human nature, the less tolerant and accepting they will be of the mentally ill. The emphasis in adjusting the balance is a dynamic rather than static variable across cultures.

In some cases the balance has been restored through therapy by bringing in a third person or "mediator" in addition to the counselor and client. W. Bolman (1968) advocates the approach of using two professionals, one from each culture, collaborating in crosscultural counseling with traditional healers as cocounselors. H. Weidman (1975) introduces the notion of a "culture broker" as an intermediary for working with culturally different clients. C. W. Slack and E. N. Slack (1976), in working with chemically dependent clients, suggest bringing in a coclient who has already effectively solved similar problems. V. Satir (1964) has introduced mediators in family therapy for problems of pathogenic coalitions with the therapist mediating to change pathogenic-related styles. In some cultures, such as Native American cultures, a third person as mediator might work better than in others (Trimble, 1981). If the mediator is poorly chosen, bringing in a third person as mediator or interpreter may seriously distress Hispanic clients through embarrassment, misinterpretations, inaccuracies, invasions of privacy and for a variety of other reasons (LeVine and Padilla, 1980). If counselors are themselves trained to be bicultural and bilingual, the mediating function is internalized within the counselor's range of skills. This internalized mediation goes back to the earliest Greek role of the counselor as a mediator between the client and a superordinate world of powers and values (Meadows, 1968).

Internalization of balance requires full awareness of the relevant social system variables. Functional and interactional social system variables have been the focus of the most promising research on behavior and sociocultural context (Bandura, 1977) and the assessment of social variables from their cultural context (Endler and Magnusson, 1976; Mischel, 1979). Cultural variables can intervene in a counseling interview in at least three different ways: through the cultures of the client, through the cultures of the counselor, through the cultures of the problem, which define the context of a counseling interview and take on characteristics from contributing cultural aspects of the environment. Particularly in multicultural counseling it is important to account for the cultural influences of the problem in the interview. Effective counselor training must consider the problem as well as the solution.

BEHAVIORS TO FACILITATE A BALANCED PERSPECTIVE IN THERAPY

A balanced perspective requires attention to both positive and negative elements in the interview. A one-directional approach emphasizes either a consistently positive perspective or a consistently negative perspective.

A two-directional or balanced perspective includes both the positive and negative implications as a means toward understanding the meaningful role of both positive and negative elements in the situation. As the social service provider observes the consumer, the provider might attend to the frequency of the following ten sets of behaviors. These behaviors have been developed to suggest a balanced perspective in the interview (Pedersen, 1990).

1. *The ability to see positive implications from an otherwise negative experience.* As suggested earlier, each problem is a problem because it makes a positive as well as a negative contribution. It would be simplistic of a provider to assume that the negative experiences of a client are not also related to positive outcomes and consequences. Ambivalence is derived from this mixture of positive and negative elements and can best be illuminated by not focusing exclusively on negative aspects.

2. *The ability to anticipate potential negative implications from an otherwise positive experience.* Providers are most vulnerable to the illusion of a solution. We would like to solve each problem finally and absolutely with more or less "magical" perfection. Each solution we bring to a client will almost certainly also have potential negative effects that must also be considered from the client's viewpoint. By counterbalancing a client's enthusiasm for simplistic solutions, the provider may provide a useful long-range alternative.

3. *The ability to articulate statements of meaning that help to interpret or integrate positive and negative events in a constructive way.* The role of the social service provider is to help clients articulate the meaning of an otherwise difficult situation in their lives and in their future. The meaning of each event includes both positive and negative elements that must be understood in context. By making accurate and appropriate statements, the provider is able to provide that meaningful context.

4. *The ability to avoid simple solutions to complex problems.* Each problem, as was mentioned earlier, is almost like a separate living personality in its complexity. At times the problem seems almost to argue back in its own defense. Thinking of the problem as a third force in the interview, with its own complicated agenda, helps the provider avoid simple solutions. Many problems in many cultures do not require or even prefer solutions. Matching solutions to problems is itself a culturally biased perspective.

5. *Sensitivity to the human ecology of forces influencing the interviewee's behavior.* How often in the interview are external forces mentioned as influencing the client's situation? There is an ecological balance of forces in the interview just as there is in nature. Both the provider and the client need to be aware of this balance of outside forces taking a lively interest in the interview's outcome. Any solution derived independent of these external forces is not likely to be satisfactory or appropriate.

6. *Sensitivity to the changing power of the interviewee over time.* As indicated earlier, a provider will work with a low-power client quite differently than with a high-power client. The ever-changing power level of the client must be matched with a corresponding change by the provider to stay in tune and maintain the harmony of the interview. If the provider is not aware of changing power levels in the client, even a well-conceived interview will soon fail.

7. *Sensitivity to the changing power of the interviewee across different topical areas.* Just because a client is inadequate in one aspect of his or her life does not mean he or she is inadequate in all others. Similarly, clients may be strong and effective in some of their relationships but not in others. As the topic and venue of the interview changes, is the provider sensitive to the changed power level with regard to this new topic?

8. *Sensitivity to the changing power of the interviewee in different social roles.* Clients who function at a very adequate level in some roles may not function adequately in other roles. All of us vary in our ability to succeed or fail across the various roles of our lives. Is the provider sensitive to the different power levels of a client across roles?

9. *The ability to adjust the amount of influence by the interviewer to facilitate the independent growth of the interviewee.* In order to facilitate a balanced perspective, the provider needs to provide enough but not too much control, influence, or power in the interview. If the provider exerts too much control to a strong client, the client will rebel and reject the provider as more troublesome than the problem. If the provider exerts too little control toward a weak client, the client will abandon the provider as inadequate and unable to provide the necessary protection.

10. *The ability to maintain harmony within the interview.* It is difficult to define harmony but easy to recognize its presence or absence in the rapport between the client and provider. In the considerable research on counseling and therapy, the only variable to emerge as an absolutely necessary but not always sufficient aspect of good social service is relationship. To the extent that a balanced perspective contributes to a meaningful and helpful relationship between the provider and client, it provides evidence of harmony within the interview.

These ten skills to facilitate a balanced perspective in therapy are not the only skills available to providers. These examples are provided to illustrate the implications of balance as a criterion of social services for the practice of counseling and therapy.

CONCLUSION

There are several implications of considering balance as a criterion for social services for Asian and Pacific Islander Americans. Each implication contributes toward a capability for understanding and facilitating a balanced perspective in multicultural social services.

Concepts of knowledge must be enlarged to go beyond the boundaries of rational process. Knowledge in other cultures has many forms. There are other ways to gain knowledge, such as intuition and other forms of knowledge accumulated through experience. While reasoning is a valuable skill, it is presumed to get in the way of knowledge in many non-Western cultures and cut off sources of information. For that reason, logical inconsistency and paradox become valuable approximations of truth in many societies. Logic is only one form of validation, dependent on a scientific, rational, or abstract principle to describe human behavior. The criterion of balance suggests other sources of validation as well.

The importance of relationships must be recognized when working in societies that do not emphasize individualism. In many societies, individual development is a lower stage of growth toward "fulfillment." Appropriate spiritual alternatives describe the self as participating in a unity with all things and not limited by the changing illusions of self and nonself. In the non-Western perspective, an individual's unity with the universe goes beyond the self to cosmic unity. The individual exists in a context of relationships between people in a cosmos.

Westernized perspectives, which have dominated the field of mental health, must not become the criteria of "modernized" perspectives. While non-Western cultures have had a profound impact on the West in recent years, many non-Western cultures seem more determined than ever to emulate the West as a social model. There is also evidence that the more modernized a society is, the more its problems and solutions resemble those of Westernized society. While Western society is fearful of technological domination that might deteriorate social values and destroy the meaning of traditional culture, non-Western societies are frequently more concerned that the technology will not be available to them. The task is one of differentiating between modernized alternatives outside the Western model. Otherwise we end up teaching Westernization in the name of modernization. We need indigenous, non-Western models of modernity to escape from our own reductionistic assumptions.

Change is not inevitably a positive and good outcome of social services. A balanced perspective between changing and unchanging values requires that we recognize that many cultures do not accept change and development as desirable. Western cultures dictate "If you don't know what to do, at least do something!" In Western cultures there is a strong predisposition toward valuing change itself as intrinsically good, moving toward a solution, reconciling ambiguity, and promising better things for the future. A contrasting perspective suggests that change may be bad. In order to understand this change process, we need to identify those values that do not change but rather become the hinges on which the door of change swings. In a cosmic perspective it is possible to deny the reality of change entirely, along with cause-and-effect thinking, in favor of an external, unchanging picture of ultimate reality.

We do not control our environment, but neither does our environment control us. In the range of value orientations there is a clear division between those who believe it is our right and even responsibility to control the environment, those who teach just as firmly that we are controlled by our environment, and a third group who teaches that we interact with our environment so that the question of control is irrelevant. Whichever basic assumption is made will profoundly affect the criteria for intercultural training in any situation. An increased awareness of ecological balance helps us to understand the interaction with persons and environment as a complex and certainly not a simple phenomenon.

Ability to recover from mistakes is more important than perfection as a criterion for social service. I teach my students that if they are working in an intercultural environment and not making mistakes, then they are not taking enough chances. The skilled professional will make as many errors as the novice. The difference is the skilled professional will be able to recover and the novice will not. In learning about intercultural criteria it is important to break out of a "success/fail" dichotomy because ultimately the outcomes of social interaction are seldom defined clearly as a success or as a failure. The emphasis in identifying intercultural criteria needs to go beyond dichotomies to develop the potentially positive effects of each problem, as an analogue or a range of possibilities.

Very few institutions offer specializations in crosscultural mental health, although increasingly departments are offering isolated courses in crosscultural communication. There is a need for a network across disciplines and institutions to coordinate the efforts of multicultural social services. There is furthermore a need to involve the "real world" of the community and reduce the artificiality of classroom training through simplistic one-directional criteria.

The literature on intercultural mental health is diffused, varies a great deal in quality, and is published in journals of limited circulation. There is a need for a series of review publications that establish the threshold for quality control in previous as well as current publications. In the same regard there is a need for more attention to multicultural issues in national meetings of professional associations, which presently invest less than 2 percent of their time on crosscultural papers. There is a need for developing criteria from research on the range of non-Western alternatives to "talk therapy."

Finally, intercultural research has failed to develop grounded theory for multicultural social services. There are a number of reasons why this is true. First, the emphasis of multicultural research has been on abnormal rather than normal behavior across cultures. Second, only in the

1970s did research identify universal aspects across cultures and then only for the more serious categories of disturbance such as schizophrenia and affective psychoses. Third, the complexity of multicultural variables in research is difficult to quantify. Fourth, the multicultural research that is available lacks an applied emphasis and has remained largely theoretical or abstract. Fifth, there has not been sufficient interdisciplinary collaboration among mental-health-related disciplines on multicultural research. Sixth, the emphasis of multicultural research has been on the symptom rather than the interaction of person, profession, institution, and community.

We are at the starting point in developing multicultural balance as a criterion for social services. Only those who are able to escape being caught up in the web of their own assumptions and maintain a balanced perspective will be able to communicate effectively with other cultures. The dangers of cultural encapsulation and the dogma of increasingly technique-oriented definitions of social services have been frequently mentioned in the rhetoric of professional associations in the social services as criteria for accreditation. In order to escape from what G. Wrenn (1962; 1985) calls cultural encapsulation, social service providers need to challenge the cultural bias of their own untested criteria. To leave our assumptions untested or, worse yet, to be unaware of our culturally learned assumptions is not consistent with the standards of good and appropriate social service.

REFERENCES

Bandura, A. (1977). *A Social Learning Theory*. Englewood Cliffs, N.J.: Prentice-Hall.
Beg, A. (1970). The theory of personality in the Bhagavad Gita: A study in transpersonal psychology. *Psychologia* 15: 12–17.
Benedict, R. (1946). *The Chrysanthemum and the Sword*. Boston: Houghton Mifflin.
Berry, J. W. (1980). Ecological analysis for cross cultural psychology. In N. Warren (ed.), *Studies in Cross Cultural Psychology*. New York: Academic Press.
Blowers, G. H., and A. M. Turtle (1987). *Psychology Moving East: The Status of Western Psychology in Asia and Oceania*. Boulder, Colo.: Westview Press.
Bolman, W. (1968). Cross cultural psychotherapy. *American Journal of Psychiatry* 124: 1237–1244.
Bond, M. H. (ed.) (1986). *The Psychology of the Chinese People*. New York: Oxford University Press.
Cheung, F.M.C. (1986). Psychopathology among Chinese people. In M. H. Bond (ed.), *The Psychology of the Chinese People*. New York: Oxford University Press.
DeVoss, G. (1985). Dimensions of the self in Japanese culture. In A. J. Marsella, G. DeVoss, and F.L.K. Hsu (eds.), *Culture and Self: Asian and Western Perspectives*. New York: Tavistock.

——— (1973). *Socialization for Achievement: Essays on the Cultural Psychology of the Japanese*. Berkeley: University of California Press.

Draguns, J. G. (1981). Cross cultural counseling and psychotherapy: History, issues, current status. In A. J. Marsella and P. Pedersen (eds.), *Cross Cultural Counseling and Therapy*. Elmsford, N.Y.: Pergamon Press.

Endler, N. S., and D. Magnusson (eds.) (1976). *Interactional Psychology and Personality*. Washington, D.C.: Hemisphere Publishers.

Govinda, L. A. (1961). *The Psychological Attitude of Early Buddhist Philosophy*. London: Rider.

Heider, F. (1958). *The Psychology of Interpersonal Relations*. New York: John Wiley and Sons.

Hiniker, P. (1969). Chinese reactions to forced compliance: Dissonance reduction or national character. *Journal of Social Psychology* 77: 157–176.

Hsu, F.L.K. (1985). The self in cross cultural perspective. In A. J. Marsella, G. DeVoss, and F.L.K. Hsu (eds.), *Culture and Self: Asian and Western Perspectives*. New York: Tavistock.

LeVine, E. S., and A. M. Padilla (1980). *Crossing Cultures in Therapy: Pluralistic Counseling for the Hispanic*. Monterey, Calif.: Brooks/Cole Publishing Company.

Lewin, K. (1935). *A Dynamic Theory of Personality*. New York: McGraw-Hill.

Lin, T. Y., and M. C. Lin (1978). Service delivery issues in Asian–North American communities. *Asian Journal of Psychiatry* 135 (4): 454–456.

Maruyama, M. (1978). Psychotopology and its application to cross-disciplinary, cross-professional and cross-cultural communication. In R. Holloman and S. Arutiunov (eds.), *Perspectives on Ethnicity*. Paris: Mouton.

McGuire, W. J. (1966). The current status of cognitive consistency theories. In S. Feldman (ed.), *Cognitive Consistency*. New York: Academic Press.

Meadows, P. (1968). The cure of souls and the winds of change. *Psychoanalytic Review* 55 (3): 491–504.

Mischel, W. (1979). On the interface of cognition and personality. *American Psychologist* 34: 740–754.

Mokuau, N. (1985). Counseling Pacific Islander–Americans. In P. Pederson (ed.), *Handbook of Cross Cultural Counseling and Therapy*. Westport, Conn.: Greenwood Press.

Murphy, G., and L. Murphy (1968). *American Psychology*. New York: Basic Books.

Nakakaki, M. (1973, September). Japanese cultural and mental health: Psychodynamic investigation. Paper presented at the 9th International Congress of Anthropological and Ethnological Sciences, Chicago.

Nakamura, H. (1964). *Ways of Thinking of Eastern Peoples: India, China, Tibet, Japan* (Trans. Philip P. Wiener, ed.). Honolulu: East-West Center Press.

Nakane, C. (1972). *Human Relations in Japan*. Tokyo: Ministry of Foreign Affairs.

Newcomb, T. M. (1953). An approach to the study of communicative acts. *Psychological Review* 60: 393–404.

Paglinawan, L. (1983). Ho'oponopono. In E. V. Shook (ed.), *Ho'oponopono*. Honolulu: University of Hawaii, School of Social Work.

Pedersen, P. (1990). The constructs of complexity and balance in multicultural counseling theory and practice. *Journal of Counseling and Development* 68 (5): 550–554.

———— (1986). Developing interculturally skilled counselors: A prototype for training. In H. Lefley and P. Pedersen (eds.), *Cross Cultural Training for Mental Health Professionals*. Springfield, Ill.: Charles C. Thomas.

Pukui, M. K., E. W. Haertig, C. A. Lee, and J. F. McDermott (1979). *Nānā I Ke Kumu*, volume 2. Honolulu: Hui Hānai.

Reynolds, D. K. (1980). *The Quiet Therapies*. Honolulu: University Press of Hawaii.

Roland, A. (1988). *In Search of Self in India and Japan: Toward a Cross Cultural Psychology*. Princeton, N.J.: Princeton University Press.

Satir, V. (1964). *Conjoint Family Therapy*. Palo Alto, Calif.: Science and Behavior Books.

Schweder, R. A. (1982). Does the concept of the person vary cross culturally? In A. J. Marsella and G. M. White (eds.), *Cultural Conceptions of Mental Health and Therapy*. Boston: Reidel.

Sheikh, A. A., and K. S. Sheikh (1989). *Eastern and Western Approaches to Healing*. New York: John Wiley and Sons.

Slack, C. W., and E. N. Slack (1976). It takes three to break a habit. *Psychology Today* (February): 46–50.

Tart, C. (1975). *Transpersonal Psychologies*. New York: Harper and Row.

Triandis, H. C. (1977). *Interpersonal Behavior*. Monterey, Calif.: Brooks/Cole Publishing Company.

Trimble, J. (1981). Value differentials and their importance in counseling American Indians. In P. Pedersen, J. Draguns, W. Lonner, and J. Trimble (eds.), *Counseling Across Cultures*, rev. and expanded ed. Honolulu: University of Hawaii Press.

Tseng, W. S., and J. Hsu (1980). Minor psychological disturbances of everyday life. In H. Triandis and J. Draguns (eds.), *Handbook of Cross Cultural Psychology: Psychopathology*, volume 6. Boston: Allyn and Bacon.

Tseng, W. S., and D.Y.H. Wu (1985). *Chinese Culture and Mental Health*. Orlando, Fla.: Academic Press.

Watts, A. W. (1961). *Psychotherapy East and West*. New York: Mentor Press.

Weidman, H. (1975). Concepts as strategies for change. *Psychiatric Annals* 5: 312–313.

Wittkower, E. D., and H. Warnes (1974). Cultural aspects of psychotherapy. *American Journal of Psychotherapy* 28: 566–673.

Wrenn, G. (1985). Afterword: The culturally encapsulated counselor revisited. In P. Pedersen (ed.), *Handbook of Cross Cultural Counseling and Therapy*. Westport, Conn.: Greenwood Press.

———— (1962). The culturally encapsulated counselor. *Harvard Educational Review* 32: 444–449.

Yang, K. S. (1986). Chinese personality and its change. In M. H. Bond (ed.), *The Psychology of the Chinese People*. New York: Oxford University Press.

Zuk, G. (1971). *Family Therapy: A Triadic Based Approach*. New York: Behavioral Publications.

II

Asian and Pacific Islander Populations

CHAPTER 4

Japanese Americans

STEPHEN FUGITA, KAREN L. ITO, JENNIFER ABE, AND DAVID T. TAKEUCHI

INTRODUCTION

Social service and mental health planners in the United States are increasingly turning their attention to three areas: developing continuums of care, increasing linkages among service providers, and containing costs. A frequent by-product of these efforts is the implementation of standardized procedures for organizations and individuals providing services. Unfortunately, this strategy may cause organizations and providers to ignore cultural and social factors that affect both the presentation of problems and the acceptability of services.

This chapter describes some cultural and social factors that are important in planning for and providing services to Japanese Americans. We explore the legacy of the Japanese immigrants who came to the United States, their cultural values, and how these values may influence the presentation and resolution of social and psychological problems and issues. One caveat should be given: We intend to outline some central cultural and social issues that may be important in providing social services to Japanese Americans, and in doing so, we walk a thin line between describing general guidelines and stereotyping. The material in this chapter should be seen as a baseline from which to understand Japanese American behavior. Service providers can use this knowledge to solicit additional information to develop service plans that are sensitive to the unique needs of the Japanese American individual.

HISTORICAL BACKGROUND

Japanese immigration to the United States and the territory of Hawaii began in significant numbers around 1885, peaked in the decade between 1900 and 1910, and virtually stopped after 1924. The decline in Japanese immigration after 1924 was the result of the National Origins Act, which barred Asians from entering the country.

This sharply constrained immigration pattern produced a unique generational layering of the Japanese American community. The *Issei* or first-generation immigrants are largely in their 80s or older. The *Nisei*, or second generation, were the first generation born in the United States and are approximately 50 to 70 years old. A subset of *Nisei* who were educated in Japan are called *Kibei*. *Sansei* are the third generation and range in age from mid-30s to 50s. The fourth generation, *Yonsei*, are largely school-aged children to young adults.

Each generation has integrated Japanese and American cultural patterns differently and experienced distinct historical events in the United States. Not surprisingly, Japanese culture is the most salient for *Issei* and becomes less so in each succeeding generation as American cultural elements become more prominent. However, it is important to note that cultures are not static systems and are constantly being changed, integrated, destroyed, and recreated.

The Early Years

United States. The Japanese experience in the continental United States has been heavily agricultural and small-business oriented (Glenn, 1986). When the immigrant generation (*Issei*) first arrived, most with little money, they started out as farm laborers working in Japanese crews led by Japanese labor contractors. For example, in the first decade of the twentieth century, the majority of grape pickers in the Fresno, California, area were Japanese (U.S. Immigration Commission, 1911). It was not long, though, before the *Issei* 'moved into sharecropping and leasing because they believed that it was one of a few ways they could realize their sojourner dream of making enough money to return to Japan. The sojourner outlook of temporarily living in America to amass a small fortune and then returning to Japan was the dominant perspective of the immigrants who came to America (Moriyama, 1984; Bonacich and Modell, 1980).

Prior to World War II, the Japanese were the targets of a considerable amount of *de jure* and *de facto* discrimination. When Japanese Americans started to become established in small-scale farming, alien land laws were passed that attempted to push them out of independent farming. As mentioned earlier, in 1924 they were barred from entering the country. On a more personal level, they were frequently prevented from buying homes in desirable parts of town, using certain public facilities (e.g., swimming pools and theaters), and entering many professions. *Nisei* (second-generation) women could not teach in the very schools in which they had recently excelled (Kitano, 1976, pp. 97–98).

Hawaii. In the early nineteenth century, Hawaii's sugar cane growers sought contract workers from foreign countries to alleviate personnel shortages in the plantation economy. Chinese laborers were the first Asian group to immigrate to the territory of Hawaii during the period of 1823 to 1898. Immigrants from Japan followed the Chinese, coming in three different waves from 1868 to 1924.

Workers lived under deplorable conditions on the plantations. One factor in the Japanese American adjustment to and subsequent exit from the plantations was the establishment of the family unit. While many Japanese workers came to the plantations alone, they, like the Japanese in the continental United States, eventually sent for their families or negotiated for a "picture bride" from Japan. The establishment of the family unit made plantation life and conflicts more tolerable and provided the foundation for a Japanese American community in Hawaii.

Japanese workers frequently left the plantations as soon as it became feasible. Approximately 22 percent of the 180,000 Japanese immigrants returned to Japan, and a similar percentage went to the continental United States. The majority remained and formed communities in Hawaii called "camps." After leaving the plantations and finding entry into certain occupations closed, the Japanese established their own businesses, became artisans, or entered the helping professions such as social work, nursing, and teaching. They found service occupations acceptable partly because of the influence of Buddhism on their cultural values; these occupations were also seen as another avenue for entry into the middle class when other paths were blocked (Rogers and Izutsu, 1980).

The Internment

United States. Discrimination against Japanese Americans climaxed during World War II, resulting in the only mass incarceration of a civilian population in modern American history. Economic competition was a major factor in the removal and incarceration of Japanese Americans from the west coast. This is clearly illustrated in the following statement made in the Delano, California, Chamber of Commerce in reaction to the Attorney General who was sympathetic to the Japanese:

Is it any wonder that prices of vegetables have advanced when the average wage per hour has advanced from 25 cents to $1.00 and more? Do you think a white man can subsist on rice and fish and live in a miserable hovel like the Jap does? Do you want us to lower our standards of living to the level of the Jap? Did you personally ever thin lettuce, pick asparagus or perform other stoop labor tasks? . . . And yet you want our white laborers to do it for the same wages the Jap expected and received? We will admit the Jap vegetable growers were stiff competition. They were for two reasons. First, the Jap and his entire family worked from dawn to dusk in the field. Second, the Jap farmer was subsidized by the Japanese Imperial Government and did not worry if he lost money year after year. Of that we have no doubt. (Taylor, 1945, p. 391)

On February 19, 1942, President Franklin D. Roosevelt issued Executive Order 9066, which initiated the mass incarceration of the west coast Japanese, two-thirds of whom were American citizens. At that time, there were 127,000 Japanese Americans living in the United States; 113,000 lived in the Pacific coast states of Washington, Oregon, and California. California had nearly 80 percent of the Pacific coast total (93,000). In the spring of that year, the west coast Japanese were forced to move to temporary quarters until more permanent facilities could be hastily built in the interior part of the country. These temporary quarters were called assembly centers and were most often fair grounds or race tracks. By the fall of 1942, most of the evacuees had been moved to one of the ten crudely erected "relocation camps."

Hawaii. Even though Hawaii was much closer to the war zone, the Japanese American community was not incarcerated except for about 1,000 individuals. Most of the Hawaii internees were sent to the continental United States; a few were detained on Oahu (Kotani, 1985). President Roosevelt was in favor of incarcerating all of the Japanese in Hawaii; however, the military convincingly argued that there were not enough ships to handle the mass migration and that Japanese labor was critically needed to rebuild the damaged island economy. After all, the Japanese comprised about 30 percent of the population and a large proportion of the skilled laborers in Hawaii at that time (Culley, 1984).

Effects of the Incarceration

Although it will never be possible to measure fully the impact of the evacuation, incarceration, and resettlement on Japanese Americans, some facts are incontrovertible. The most obvious is that many persons suffered catastrophic economic losses. One *Issei* farmer reported shortly after the war:

Before war I had 20 acres in Berryessa. Good land, two good houses, one big. 1942 in camp everybody say sell, sell, sell. Maybe lose all. Lawyer write, he say sell. I sell $650 acre. Now the same land $1500 acre. I lose, I cannot help. All gone. Now I live in hostel. Work like when first come to this country. Pick cherries, pick pears, pick apricots, pick tomatoes. Just like when first come.

Pretty soon, maybe one year, maybe two years, find place. Pretty hard now. Now spend $15,000 just for (half as much) land. No good material for house. No get farm machinery. No use look back. Go crazy think about all lost. Have to start all over again like when come from Japan, but faster this time. (War Relocation Authority, 1947, p. 53)

The psychological sequelae of the camp experience are subtle and extremely difficult to verify empirically. Nevertheless, the stress from long periods of uncertainty, separation from family members, economic losses, and stigmatization have no doubt left their marks on those who were forced to endure internment. It is clear that the experience produced greater dependency in some *Issei*. Before World War II, very few *Issei* received public aid, but after the war significant numbers appeared on the rolls (War Relocation Authority, 1946).

Among the *Nisei*, the incarceration created a degree of cynicism and distrust of government that, not surprisingly, persists to this day. In telling euphemisms, *Nisei* refer to this bifurcation of their lives as "before camp" and "after camp" or "before the war" and "after the war." The psychological effect of these events is subtly portrayed in Monica Sone's book, *Nisei Daughter* (Sone, 1953). Before the war, relocation, and internment, the main character is an outgoing, slightly brash, highly Americanized teenager full of spunk and adventure. After the internment, she is a self-contained, reserved, and cautious young woman. The transformation of this character may serve as a metaphor for the social and psychological experiences of west coast and some Hawaii Japanese Americans.

Postwar Accommodation

Although there was initially some violence directed against the returning evacuees, the postwar period saw an opening up of the occupational opportunity structure for Japanese Americans, particularly for the *Nisei* who were just beginning to establish careers. The Japanese could not return to the west coast until 1945. Prior to 1945, they resettled primarily in the midwest or on the east coast. Before World War II, about 200 Japanese lived in Chicago. However, by the end of the war, it had become a major resettlement destination. At the peak of the exodus out of the concentration camps, over 1,000 Japanese per month moved into the city. For the most part, *Nisei* reported that they felt more welcome in areas outside the west coast. This is not to say that most escaped the sting of discrimination and prejudice. For example, attempts to buy a house in an all-white neighborhood frequently resulted in petitions from neighbors or pressure from real estate agents. Most *Nisei* did not resist these pressures and purchased homes in areas where the neighbors were more receptive.

Social changes also occurred rapidly in Hawaii after World War II. A large number of *Nisei* began pursuing higher education and majoring in fields such as law and medicine, which were previously inaccessible. Many of them used the GI Bill of Rights to help reach their educational goals. They formed political alliances with liberal Caucasians in the Democratic party and the labor unions.

Shortly after it achieved statehood in 1959, Hawaii's political structure changed from one dominated by the Caucasian-run Republican party to one dominated by the Democratic party, in which Japanese Americans were influential (Coffman, 1973). Since the early 1960s, Japanese Americans have been well represented in the professions and overrepresented in a number of fields such as teaching and government. Ironically, given their historical background, the Japanese in Hawaii presently are perceived by several ethnic groups as a source of discrimination in state and local government.

SOCIODEMOGRAPHIC OVERVIEW

In 1980, there were approximately 716,331 Japanese living in the United States. Immigration during the past decade has been quite low, less than 5,000 annually. California contained the largest number, 268,814 (37.5 percent); Hawaii was second with 239,734 (33.5 percent). Even though many Japanese resettled in the midwest and the east after the incarceration, most eventually returned to their former homes on the Pacific coast.

An important demographic difference between Japanese American communities in California and Hawaii is the proportion of the state population they represent. In California, Japanese Americans are the third largest Asian American group but make up only 1.1 percent of the state's population. Compare these figures to Hawaii where Japanese Americans are the second largest ethnic group in the state and the largest Asian American group, comprising 25 percent of the state's population. The differences in political fortunes, local histories, and sociodemographic characteristics between the Japanese on the continental United States and in the state of Hawaii cannot help but lead to different psychosocial profiles between the two groups.

With regard to current income, the 1980 Census documents that most Japanese Americans were solidly middle class, their average family income being $30,537, the highest of any Asian American group. Their family income was also higher than the mean white family income of $23,092. However, this difference is somewhat misleading. It is partly a function of more working family members and a disproportionate number residing in areas with a high cost of living. For example, the high cost of living in Hawaii forces many individuals to work at more than one job.

The Japanese American emphasis on education is also reflected in the Census figures. The percentage of Japanese Americans who had completed high school in 1980 was 87.5 percent for those aged 25 to 64, while the corresponding white figures were 75.3 percent (Barringer, Takeuchi, and Xenos, 1990).

The age distribution of the Japanese American population has important social service implications. Japanese Americans have the highest median age (33.5) of all the Asian American ethnic groups. They also have one of the highest percentages of adults who are 65 years old and over (7.3 percent). These data suggest the importance of social service programs for the elderly in Japanese American communities.

VALUES AND BEHAVIORAL NORMS

This section explores some general cultural values and behavioral norms that may be useful in understanding Japanese Americans and enhancing social services. Specific terms will be used to describe the cultural values that appear to influence Japanese American behavior. Japanese culture is distinct from other Asian cultures. Moreover, there are multiple ways of expressing a Japanese heritage. Over time, Japanese Americans have adapted traditional Japanese cultural values to fit the unique social, political, and economic structures of their community and the larger society (Yanagisako, 1985). It is erroneous to assume that cultural factors are not important in explaining the behavior of younger Japanese Americans, but differences between individuals of the same subculture should not be ignored.

An understanding of Japanese American culture must begin with the concept of self in Japanese American terms. Western concepts of self place the individual at the center with all other relationships arranged around the self. The Japanese concept sees the self as part of a set of interpersonal relationships of which the family system is the core. The individual learns to subordinate the self to a social unit, emphasizing solidarity and suppressing autonomy. Consequently, Japanese Americans find it difficult to stand out publicly as individuals, preferring to couch their individual achievements in the context of group accomplishment. Examples of this can be seen in their frequent reluctance to give speeches, to speak in meetings or classrooms, or to talk about themselves in casual conversations.

In Western society autonomy is prized and dependency is devalued. Japanese culture, on the other hand, fosters *amae* or interdependency, which is seen as enhancing group solidarity. Social relationships are based primarily on the preservation of harmony and suppression of conflict. Behavior oriented toward the group is strongly approved, and self-serving behavior is seen as disruptive to the group. When conflicts in relationships occur, they often take the form of ritualistic resistance. This involves the preservation of one's values while outwardly conforming to established behavior patterns.

On is a sense of obligation within the Japanese hierarchy. *On* forms the basis for reciprocal relationships between peers and within social networks. While *on* is taken for granted within the family, the Japanese frequently guard against accepting casual help from strangers because they want to avoid becoming entwined in a reciprocal relationship with unknown individuals. This behavioral form may be seen in the reluctance of elderly Japanese Americans to accept help from social service agencies.

Another example of *on* is the following. It is common for one member of a family to sacrifice his or her own educational goals to help finance his or her sibling's college education. In return, family members treat this person with the same reverence and respect accorded a parent. This sense of obligation is passed on to the children. As this person reaches old age, the family insures that he or she is cared for to the point of sacrificing their own financial stability.

H. L. Kitano (1976) suggests that the *enryo* syndrome explains a large part of Japanese behavior. *Enryo* emphasizes modesty, respect, and deference to others and has two components. *Hazu kashii* is the implicit fear of being ridiculed manifested by embarrassment and reticence. *Hige* is the denigration of self and others. Both concepts emphasize conformity to group norms and, if the individual accomplishes something of importance, minimization of the accomplishment to maintain the singular importance of the group. An example of *enryo* can frequently be seen when Japanese Americans achieve something of importance. Many a *Sansei* has experienced a *Nisei* parent's reaction to an outsider's praise. If someone praises a *Sansei* child—and by association the parents for their responsible socialization—the parents rarely accept the compliment but will deflect the praise with some disparagement about the child in a different area. If the child is praised for being well behaved or a good scholar or athlete, the parent will make a remark about his or her inability to keep his or her room clean or how the child "really" behaves at home. The parent is reacting in a Japanese cultural way—being modest about the child's accomplishments and teaching the child to be modest. The child, however, who is more socialized in individualistic American values, may feel denigrated or unappreciated by the parents. This may have psychological effects on the child who may desire a more straightforward American approach to praise and demonstration of love. Again, this example illustrates how generation leads to different levels of integration into Japanese and American cultural values and inter-pretations.

Gaman refers to the internalization and suppression of anger and emo-tion. During an unpleasant incident, the individual avoids confrontation and accepts the results of the negative social interaction. *Gaman* also means to bear up under adversity. Related to *gaman* is *shikata ga nai*— the notion that whatever has happened cannot be helped or nothing more can be done to improve the situation.

PROFILE OF SOCIAL AND PSYCHOLOGICAL PROBLEMS AND ISSUES

Help-Seeking Behaviors

While empirical studies on the help-seeking behavior of Japanese Americans are scant, two commonly reported observations are that Jap-anese Americans (a) generally do not seek or delay seeking professional help for their personal problems, and (b) generally do not complete treatment (Leong, 1986; Sue, 1977). Cultural and social factors seem to suggest several reasons for this help-seeking and treatment pattern.

Kitano (1969) speculates on possible reasons for the underutilization of mental health services by the Japanese: (1) the strength of the Japanese family and community to control and "hide" problem behavior, (2) dif-ferent cultural styles of expressing problems, (3) inappropriateness of current therapeutic organizations, and (4) lack of relevant connections to the therapeutic community. Other reasons that are offered include the lack of bilingual therapists, the inability of therapists to provide culturally responsive forms of treatment (Sue, 1977), community stigma due to emotional problems, crossethnic relationships involving racism, lack of service alternatives, and the poor reputation of the treatment system (Lee, 1982).

The stigma attached to emotional problems is a significant deterrent to seeking help from social service agencies within the Japanese Amer-ican community. For the Japanese, "craziness" is often traced to the family as (1) a hereditary trait running in the family line, (2) punishment for the past behavior of the family (similar to *karma*), or (3) a reflection of poor guidance and discipline by the family leader (Shon and Ja, 1982, p. 222). An individual or family may not seek services because of the anticipated disgrace. Japanese Americans frequently try to keep the per-son with the problem in the family unless the individual is acting out. *Gaman* and *shikata ga nai* can be mechanisms to deny a problem exists or to avoid dealing with it.

To talk about personal problems with an outsider is frowned upon because it incurs a loss of face for the group (family, church, community), which is viewed as having "failed" in its responsibility to the individual member. The shame and loss of face resulting from such culturally inappropriate actions are frequently used to reinforce adherence to a prescribed set of obligations in the Japanese American community since individuals may prefer to suffer personally than to have the group criticized. They may also fear that seeking professional help will make them stand apart from others in the group and that they will be denigrated or ridiculed for their inability to resolve problems on their own. One's character and one's health, whether physical or mental, are intimately intertwined. Weakness in health is viewed as weakness in character or will. To admit or submit to physical or psychological distress is to publicly display a character flaw.

On affects help-seeking behavior in several ways. First, Japanese Americans may hesitate to seek help because they feel they may become obligated to an outsider. Second, they may not seek professional services because they feel that their family or close friends will help them. Third, family members may feel it is necessary to take care of their own members. This sense of obligation is often seen in many lower- and middle-class Japanese families who overburden their financial and social resources to take care of an elderly parent or relative.

Problem Presentation

When Japanese Americans do seek help, they are likely to attribute their discomfort to somatic symptoms, thus expressing their distress only indirectly. A number of studies have found that Asian Americans, including the Japanese, tend to express symptoms via somatization (Leong, 1986; Marsella, Kinzie, and Gordon, 1973; Rahe, Looney, Ward, Tung, and Liu, 1978; Sue and Morishima, 1982). Physical dysfunction is a culturally accepted means of expressing emotional distress in Japanese culture. T. J. Tracey, F. T. Leong, and C. Glidden (1986) examined the nature of presenting complaints at a counseling center in Hawaii and found that Asian American clients are much more likely to perceive themselves as having educational and vocational concerns, in contrast to Caucasian clients who are more likely to endorse personal and emotional concerns. S. C. Kim (1985) suggests that these somatic, educational, or vocational problems should be taken seriously and accepted graciously, recognizing that they may be a culturally acceptable way for Japanese Americans to obtain help through therapy without "losing face."

Kitano (1970) notes that one of the first signs of mental distress leading to hospitalization among Japanese inpatients is difficulty at work (a demotion, being fired, or walking off the job). Given the primacy of work in the Japanese ethic, dysfunctional behavior in this particular area can be a significant marker of distress. It may be that Japanese Americans place a higher priority on the functional requisites necessary to survive in society so that the abilities to work hard, support the family, and provide food, shelter, and clothing are equated with mental health. Mental health professionals, in contrast, may tend to define mental health in terms of "quality of life, open relationships, sharing of feelings, and amount of psychological insight" (Kitano, 1982, p. 163).

SOCIAL SERVICE INTERVENTION

Principles of Practice

The accessibility of social services can be enhanced through community outreach and the use of bilingual and bicultural staff. The use of clinicians is not a familiar avenue of help-seeking for Japanese Americans, particularly *Issei* and *Nisei*, so that the inclusion of staff who can speak Japanese and who understand Japanese American culture may make services more accessible to them. Intervention for Japanese Americans does not begin with the patient initiating contact with the worker's office; community involvement and outreach are critical to familiarize Japanese Americans with this option. Since they are reluctant to express problems in their lives about which they need social service assistance, outreach is important in establishing social networks within the community. When service providers are an integral part of the community, they can make residents comfortable with the agency or individual worker.

Accurate assessment of the client's background and presenting problems is essential. In striving to provide culturally sensitive services to their Japanese American clientele, workers need to remember that it is possible to be "culturally sensitive" without being sensitive to the needs of a given individual. Careful assessment of the individual in the context of his or her Japanese American heritage is necessary before the appropriate culturally *and* individually sensitive treatment strategy can be formulated.

Treatment goals should reinforce the cultural expectations of effective intervention. These expectations are based on physical and behavioral changes necessary to resume life responsibilities, including the ability to work, maintain good health, and assume family roles. In order to appear acceptable, treatment goals should be defined in terms of problem-solving tangible outcomes on a short-term basis. Long-term goals, however, may be broken down into a series of interrelated short-term goals, presented as renegotiable with the family. The importance of insight, dynamics, and emotional expressiveness should not be ignored, but the individual and/or family must be engaged in the therapy before the therapist can offer other options and goals (Kim, 1985).

Conceptual Models of Intervention

Two models indigenous to Japanese culture, which focus on mental distress (*seishin ijo*), are Morita therapy and *Naikan* therapy. These models are compatible with many cultural values and behavioral norms and may be useful in conceptualizing social service intervention.

Morita therapy, founded by Dr. Shoma Morita, is derived from principles stemming out of Zen Buddhism (Murase and Johnson, 1974). It consists of four treatment periods undertaken in an inpatient setting. The first period consists of virtual bed rest and social isolation for up to a week or more. During this time, the patient is discouraged from indulging in self-recrimination or "destructive" introspection. The goal is to achieve a peaceful condition of both mental and physical rest. The second period marks the beginning of occupational therapy, where the patient is allowed to carry out a few simple tasks under the supervision of the therapist. Introspection, however, is still discouraged. During the third period, the patient is instructed to engage in heavier physical labor and is allowed to read selected books and have more contact with people in the environment. The work is designed to give the patient an opportunity to experience satisfaction and confidence in the accomplishment of simple physical tasks, as well as to produce a state of natural, physical tiredness. At the same time, the therapist meets briefly with the patient to make suggestions on how he or she may correct both his or her "thinking" and behavior. Finally, during the fourth period, the patient is encouraged to begin to accommodate to external reality and gradually to resume his or her activities in the outside world. Having achieved success through rest, light activities, and, finally, physical labor, the patient is ready to leave the hospital. The goals of therapy are met when the patient is no longer obsessed with doubts and "destructive self-consciousness" and is no longer experiencing neurasthenic and/or psychophysiologic symptoms. In positive terms, the patient has learned *arugamama*, that is, to accept philosophically "things as they are" (Murase and Johnson, 1974) and the ability to once again take up his or her social roles and responsibilities. Mental health from this perspective, then, can be viewed as the successful fulfillment of life roles and social responsibilities.

Naikan (literally, *nai* meaning "inside" or "within" and *kan* meaning "looking") was founded by a lay practitioner, Ishin Yoshimoto, and is a more introspective form of psychological treatment than Morita therapy. *Naikan* is a highly structured regime of self-reflection, rooted in the Jodo-shin sect of Buddhism. There are two related goals: (1) to rediscover personal guilt for having been ungrateful and irresponsible toward individuals in the past, and (2) to discover a positive gratitude toward individuals who have extended themselves on behalf of the client at some time in the past (Murase and Johnson, 1974). These particular attitudes of guilt and gratitude are part of the fundamental cultural assumptions that govern norms of social relatedness in Japan (Murase and Johnson, 1974) and are not considered to be dysfunctional individual attributes.

Both Morita and *Naikan* therapy sharply limit the boundaries of introspection. Free association would probably be viewed as undisciplined thinking and destructive. In Morita therapy, especially, the physical, mental, emotional, and spiritual aspects of the client are treated holistically, as fundamentally inseparable from each other. There is a clear emphasis on the functionality of emotions and behavior so that those cognitions, emotions, and behaviors that do not serve a clear purpose are part of the destructive "waste" that the individual should leave behind. Intrapsychic processes are largely ignored; instead, particularly in *Naikan* therapy, the client is instructed to focus on interpersonal relationships with significant others in a highly structured fashion. In fact, it is not inconceivable that much of the "psychologic insight" Western practitioners so highly prize would be reclassified as "destructive" introspection by Japanese therapists.

Specific Skills for Intervention

Skills Related to the Worker. In the Japanese language, the term "therapist" translates broadly into a title that encompasses both "doctor" and "teacher." Usage of this word reflects the expectation that the therapist is an authority who possesses a wide range of skills for assuming multiple roles, such as a teacher and guide (Kim, 1985). S. Sue and N. Zane (1987) clarify two dimensions of worker status: *Ascribed* status refers to the role assigned to the worker by others that is dependent on such factors as age and sex, while *achieved* status refers to the worker's skills and expertise. They suggest that lack of ascribed status may be the primary reason for the underutilization of service, while lack of achieved status may better explain premature termination of treatment.

An implication of this distinction is that a worker's behavior must provide clear social cues regarding ascribed status, or confusion about the worker's competence will result. Hence, workers should display all degrees, certificates, and other concrete indications of professional competence on the walls of their offices and often refer to themselves as an authority (e.g., using phrases such as "in my professional judgment" and "after seeing many similar cases"). The worker should not hesitate to be assertive in such matters as indicating who should speak first, how much they should speak, and what the topic of discussion should be. A directive style is especially critical in the initial visit since a passive approach would be viewed as a lack of knowledge, skill, or interest (Shon and Ja, 1982; Lee, 1982).

Gender-matching between the worker and client in individual treatment may also be important in establishing trust and rapport. This match may be especially significant for *Issei* and older *Nisei* for whom male and female roles may be distinctly marked (Yanagisako, 1985). However, whether these treatment approaches would be appropriate for a given Japanese American client would depend on such factors as level of acculturation, ethnic identity, involvement in the Japanese American community, and familiarity with the intervention process.

Skills Related to Communication. In Japanese culture, the content of communication largely depends on the characteristics of the persons involved. S. P. Shon and D. A. Ja (1982) note that such factors as age, sex, education, social status, family background, and marital status often influence specific behaviors such as who will bow lowest, initiate the conversation, speak more softly or loudly, change subjects, or look away first with eye contact. Depending on the attributes of the individuals and the nature of the relationship, even the structure of the language—including syntax, word endings, and terminology—will vary. Consequently, any role or status ambiguity in social situations is a source of great anxiety for fear that a social blunder in behavior or speech will be committed and the person will lose face. The acceptable response to this ambiguity is to withdraw into silence and watchfulness for cues that will indicate the appropriate pattern of interaction that is called for (Shon and Ja, 1982, p. 215). Thus, for example, a worker who does not provide specific cues about the nature of the worker-client relationship for subsequent interactions with the family will exacerbate the anxiety caused by this social ambiguity. Additionally, the worker may mislabel an individual's appropriate response to this ambiguity as resistance.

Not surprisingly, much of what is labeled as resistant behavior in Western treatment is a reflection of proper upbringing in Japanese culture. What is called "openness" in Western culture may be construed as a sign of immaturity and lack of self-control in Japanese cultures if it entails the premature disclosure of emotions to a stranger (Kim, 1985). Premature "openness" can even bring shame to the family. Reframing is a useful skill that can often prevent this shame. Reinforcing a family's worldview and protecting them from revealing secrets prematurely, for instance, effectively allows the worker to give the individual or family "permission" to temporarily withhold information (Kim, 1985). Japanese culture emphasizes controlling strong emotions as a prerequisite for maintaining mental health and as an indication of maturity and wisdom. Again, workers should be careful before labeling such emotional control as dysfunctional or as treatment resistance, instead acknowledging its cultural value and function (Lum, 1982).

Service providers must also be aware of body language—their clients' and their own. Since Japanese Americans may be indirect with their responses to questions, verbal statements should not be taken at face value. If the discussion is about the source of psychological distress, it is likely that delicate and successive urgings are needed during the intervention session. A common example of this process occurs in everyday life. When asked if he or she would like something to eat, a Japanese American is likely to respond in the negative. However, if the host does not persuade the person to eat, then the host may be seen as insensitive. A "good host" will make sure that the guest is not just being polite and will encourage the person to eat (Ishizuka, 1978). In much the same way, service providers must be equally sensitive to nonverbal cues to better understand and serve the client.

CONCLUSION

In this chapter, we provide a historical, social, and cultural context for service providers working with members of the Japanese American community. Several important variables such as generation, geographic location, and wartime experiences are useful in understanding the heterogeneity found among Japanese American clients. Knowledge of these variables help form the foundation for culturally sensitive services.

REFERENCES

Barringer, H., K. Takeuchi, and P. Xenos (1990). Education, occupational prestige, and income of Asian Americans: Evidence from the 1980 Census. *Sociology of Education* 63: 27–43.

Bonacich, E., and J. Modell (1980). *The Economic Basis of Ethnic Solidarity: Small Business in the Japanese American Community.* Berkeley: University of California Press.

Coffman, T. (1973). *Catch a Wave: Hawaii's New Politics.* Honolulu: University Press of Hawaii.

Culley, J. H. (1984). Relocation of Japanese Americans: The Hawaiian experience. *Air Force Law Review* 24: 176–183.

Glenn, E. N. (1986). *Issei, Nisei, War Bride: Three Generations of Japanese American Women in Domestic Service.* Philadelphia: Temple University Press.

Ishizuka, K. C. (1978). *The Elder Japanese.* San Diego: Campanile Press, San Diego State University.

Kim, S. C. (1985, Summer). Family therapy for Asian Americans: A strategic-structural framework. *Psychotherapy* 22 (supplement): 342–348.

Kitano, H. L. (1969). Japanese-American mental illness. In S. Plog and R. Edgerton (eds.), *Changing Perspectives on Mental Illness.* New York: Holt, Rinehart and Winston.

——— (1976). *Japanese Americans: The Evolution of a Subculture*, 2d ed. Englewood Cliffs, N.J.: Prentice-Hall.

——— (1982). Mental health in the Japanese-American community. In E. E. Jones and S. J. Korchin (eds.), *Minority Mental Health*. New York: Praeger.

——— (1970). Mental illness in four cultures. *Journal of Social Psychology* 80: 121–134.

Kotani, R. (1985). *The Japanese in Hawaii: A Century of Struggle*. Honolulu: Hawaii Hochi.

Lee, E. (1982). A social systems approach to assessment and treatment for Chinese American families. In M. McGoldrick, J. K. Pearce, and J. Giordano (eds.), *Ethnicity and Family Therapy*. New York: Guilford.

Leong, F.T.L. (1986). Counseling and psychotherapy with Asian-Americans: Review of the literature. *Journal of Counseling Psychology* 33 (2): 196–206.

Lum, R. G. (1982). Mental health attitudes and opinions of Chinese. In E. E. Jones and S. J. Korchin (eds.), *Minority Mental Health*. New York: Praeger.

Marsella, A. J., D. Kinzie, and P. Gordon (1973). Ethnic variations in the expression of depression. *Journal of Cross-Cultural Psychology* 4: 435–458.

Moriyama, A. (1984). *Imingaisha: Japanese Emigration Companies and Hawaii, 1894–1908*. Honolulu: University Press of Hawaii.

Murase, T., and F. Johnson (1974). Naikan, Morita, and Western psychotherapy: A comparison. *Archives of General Psychiatry* 31: 121–128.

Rahe, R. H., J. G. Looney, H. W. Ward, M. T. Tung, and W. T. Liu (1978). Psychiatric consultation in a Vietnamese refugee camp. *American Journal of Psychiatry* 135: 185–190.

Rogers, T., and S. Izutsu (1980). The Japanese. In J. F. McDermott, Jr., W. S. Tseng, and T. W. Maretzki (eds.), *People and Cultures of Hawaii: A Psychocultural Profile*. Honolulu: University Press of Hawaii.

Shon, S. P., and D. A. Ja (1982). Asian families. In M. McGoldrick, J. K. Pearce, and J. Giordano (eds.), *Ethnicity and Family Therapy*. New York: Guilford.

Sone, M. (1953). *Nisei Daughter*. Boston: Little, Brown.

Sue, S. (1977). Community mental health services to minority groups: Some optimism, some pessimism. *American Psychologist* 32: 616–624.

Sue, S., and J. K. Morishima (1982). *The Mental Health of Asian Americans*. San Francisco: Jossey-Bass.

Sue, S., and N. Zane (1987). The role of culture and cultural techniques in psychotherapy: A critique and reformulation. *American Psychologist* 42 (1): 37–45.

Taylor, A. (1945). Human rights in California. *Asia and the Americans* 45: 388–391.

Tracey, T. J., F. T. Leong, and C. Glidden (1986). Help-seeking and problem perception among Asian Americans. *Journal of Counseling Psychology* 33: 331–336.

U.S. Bureau of the Census (1988). *We, the Asian and Pacific Islander Americans*. Washington, D.C.: U.S. Government Printing Office.

U.S. Immigration Commission (1911). *Immigrants in Industries, Part 25: Japanese and Other Immigrant Races in the Pacific Coast and Rocky Mountain States*. Washington, D.C.: U.S. Government Printing Office.

War Relocation Authority (1947). *People in Motion.* Washington, D.C.: U.S. Government Printing Office.

———— (1946). *The Relocation Program.* Washington, D.C.: U.S. Government Printing Office.

Yanagisako, S. J. (1985). *Transforming the Past: Tradition and Kinship Among Japanese Americans.* Stanford, Calif.: Stanford University Press.

CHAPTER 5

Chinese Americans

KAREN HUANG

INTRODUCTION

In the present generation, the Chinese are frequently stereotyped as "model minorities" living quietly in neon-happy Chinatown. The reality, however, is quite different. Since the first arrivals in the late 1700s, Chinese have come to the United States from different parts of the world in their quest for something better. The experiences of this heterogeneous population have been varied since different Chinese have different cultural, political economic, and social circumstances. This chapter cannot address the unique circumstances and interventions for the diverse groups of the Chinese population; however, it does attempt to provide information on which to base hypotheses that can inform culturally sensitive interventions.

HISTORICAL BACKGROUND

Immigration

Chinese have immigrated to the United States in temporally distinct waves. The very first trickle of Chinese arrived in Hawaii as early as 1789 (Lum and Char, 1985). Their numbers remained small until 1876 when the United States and Hawaii passed a reciprocal trade agreement that led to a need for "importing Chinese workers." During the late 1840s, Chinese were also arriving on the U.S. mainland in increasing numbers (Zo, 1971). Many were drawn to America from Guangzhou Province because of a coincidence in history: economic and political disasters in China and the discovery of gold in California. The ease of passage and the promise of endentured jobs led to more than 300,000 Chinese emigrating to the United States between the 1850s and 1882. During this period, there was extreme gender imbalance with more than 100,000 Chinese men and only 8,848 Chinese women immigrating to the United States (Lyman, 1973).

In the wake of American economic crises in the 1870s, the Chinese suffered resentment, discrimination, and, finally, exclusion. The Exclusion Act of 1882 suspended immigration of skilled and unskilled Chinese laborers for ten years and forbid them from becoming naturalized citizens. This act was extended an additional ten years by the Geary Act in 1892 and was extended indefinitely in 1904. The result was a steady decline in the numbers of Chinese and a concomitant decrease in their participation in white society.

Unaffected by the 1882 exclusion laws, Chinese students continued to enter the United States. Particularly during the 1940s, when China needed trained professionals to rebuild the country after the Japanese invasion, it sent more students to the United States. Unlike the sojourners, these men were members of China's upper echelon who planned to return to China to help rebuild their country. With the Communist takeover in 1949, these students were stranded in the United States and eventually became an elite group of upper-middle-class Chinese who were generally accepted into American society (Kuo, 1982).

The 1965 Immigration Act radically reformed the immigration law as it applied to Chinese persons. The law abolished strict quotas and allowed Chinese to enter the United States based on the U.S. need for skills or upon the person's desire to reunite with family members still overseas. The result was a dramatic increase in immigration during the "golden years" between 1965 and 1974 and a slower, but sustained, increase in the 1980s. Chinese immigrants during this period had origins in Taiwan, Hong Kong, and China (Chyr, 1988).

Most recently, another distinct Chinese group, the ethnic Chinese refugees from Southeast Asia, have arrived in the United States in large numbers. The 1975 collapse of South Vietnam precipitated a mass exodus of merchant-class Chinese who were encouraged to flee by the Vietnamese government. A second wave was precipitated in 1978 following political upheaval, racial persecution, and starvation. This population includes the educated elite as well as the preliterate, all of whom have faced great adjustment problems and negative public attitudes in the United States (Mark and Chih, 1982; Starr and Roberts, 1982).

Integration and Isolation

While the bulk of the early Chinese immigrants resided in California (Tsai, 1986), many also went to Hawaii to work on sugar plantations.

Those in Hawaii were relatively more dispersed than those in California and were gradually integrated into the culture. In California, however, the Chinese were viewed as a threat to labor (see Lyman, 1973). Whites feared that Chinese would "swarm" over the whole nation and rob California of its mineral wealth by shipping gold to China. These sentiments led to legal efforts to limit Chinese participation in labor.

In 1879 there was an attempt by the California Constitutional Convention to prohibit all state, county, municipal, or other public works from employing Chinese. The Exclusion Act of 1882 excluded Chinese from becoming citizens and prevented them from purchasing land or forming corporations. By 1910, white labor had almost completely driven Chinese from the work force and forced many Chinese businesspeople into bankruptcy (Lyman, 1973).

Animosity toward the Chinese also resulted in mob violence, sometimes ending in loss of life and property. For example, on October 24, 1871, "several hundred whites shot, hanged and stabbed 19 Chinese to death" following the accidental killing of a white man who was trying to stop a fight between two Chinese (Tsai, 1986, p. 67; see also Lyman, 1973, for further examples).

Chinese Communities: From Chinatown Ghettos to the Suburbs

The first Chinese communities were composed of male sojourners who expected to return home to China. Due to seasonal unemployment and exclusionary laws, most of these men led transient lives and owned no property in the United States. As a result, the Chinese community lacked the traditional stabilizing elements (Mark and Chih, 1982). Ironically, the anti-Chinese movement forced the entrenchment of Chinatown ghettos, which in turn strengthened the controls of traditional Chinese associations, resulting in the establishment, rather than the destruction, of the Chinese community.

The major community institutions were mutual aid associations based on homeland affiliations; the *huiguan*, which were district-based agencies organized by merchants; and the Chinese Six Companies, which provided numerous social services (Mark and Chih, 1982).

During this time, the establishment of a second generation of Chinese was markedly delayed because of policies that prevented the establishment of Chinese families. Between 1882 and 1943, no alien wife of an alien Chinese immigrant laborer was legally admissible to the United States. In addition, a woman who married a Chinese alien automatically lost her U.S. citizenship even if she was a citizen by birth. Further, fourteen states outlawed miscegenation: Arizona, California, Georgia, Idaho, Mississippi, Missouri, Montana, Nebraska, Nevada, Oregon,

South Dakota, Utah, Virginia, and Wyoming (Harper and Skolnick, 1962).

After World War II, the Chinese community underwent dramatic changes. Highly visible portions of the population entered professional positions, and the number of Chinese scholars and scientists began to grow. For instance, the Chinese representation in professional/technical occupations grew from 2.8 percent in 1940 to 7.1 percent in 1950, 17.9 percent in 1960, and 26.5 percent in 1970 (U.S. Bureau of the Census, 1940; 1950; 1960; 1970). In this period there was also increased immigration of women and children. Chinese communities were gradually being transformed from bachelor societies into communities with families and women (Lee, 1982).

SOCIODEMOGRAPHIC OVERVIEW

Since 1950, the Chinese population in the United States has doubled each decade (Mark and Chih, 1982, p. 155). In 1980, 23.4 percent of the 3.7 million Asians in the United States were Chinese, making them the largest Asian ethnic group for the first time (U.S. Bureau of the Census, 1988). By unofficial estimates, there were over 1 million Chinese living in the United States in 1980 (Tsai, 1986).

The Chinese are concentrated in metropolitan areas on both the east and west coasts, with the largest proportion living in California (40.1 percent). A substantial number live in New York (18.1 percent), and smaller fractions live in Hawaii (6.9 percent), Illinois (3.6 percent), and Texas (3.3 percent) (U.S. Bureau of the Census, 1988). Projected growth indicates that by 1990, 350,000 Chinese will reside in the San Francisco Bay area.

The Chinese population averages about the same age as the national population (median age of 29.6 years for Chinese compared to 30 years for the nation). However, their family composition differs. The Chinese average a slightly larger family size (3.7 persons) than the national average (3.3 persons), partly because of a higher percentage of children living with both parents and elderly living with family members. In addition, they have a slightly higher rate of married couple families (87 percent) than the national average (83 percent) and a much lower divorce rate (Mangiafico, 1988, p. 131). Chinese women have a lower fertility rate than that of U.S. females (Mangiafico, 1988, p. 129), along with very low rates of unwed births (3.7 percent of the national total) and teenage births (1.1 percent of the national total) (U.S. Bureau of the Census, Social and Economic Statistics Administration, 1990).

Compared to the nation, a much larger percentage of Chinese are foreign born (63.3 percent of Chinese compared to 6 percent nationally). In 1980, over 80 percent of those Chinese persons age 5 or older spoke a language other than English at home (U.S. Bureau of the Census, 1988).

The Chinese have a higher than average rate of participation in the labor force (66.4 percent compared to 62 percent), many of them in business. In 1982, more than 2 percent of the 12 million U.S. firms (excluding large corporations) were owned by Asian and Pacific Islanders, with Chinese owning the most firms (52,839) and earning the highest total receipts (U.S. Bureau of the Census, 1988). The vast majority of these companies were sole proprietorships involved in service and retail trade, such as health and personal services, eating and drinking establishments, and food stores.

In 1980, with a higher median family income ($22,600) than the national median ($19,900), the Chinese population was thought to be economically better off than the national average. However, the poverty rate among Chinese (13.5 percent) was slightly higher than the national average (13 percent). In addition, since Chinese families averaged more workers per household who contributed to the median family income, and since the vast majority of Chinese lived in metropolitan areas with high costs of living, the median income may not have reflected a higher standard of living for this population.

In 1940, only 1.5 percent of all Chinese adult males 25 years or older had completed four or more years of college (Lyman, 1973). Two generations later, the Chinese are one of the best educated groups in the United States (see Mangiafico, 1988, pp. 132–133 for a detailed review). For persons 25 years old and older, 71.3 percent have graduated from high school. The national rate is 66 percent. In addition, 44 percent and 30 percent of Chinese men and women, respectively, have graduated from college. This far exceeds the national rates of 20 percent and 13 percent for men and women.

Despite the higher levels of educational attainment, socioeconomic analyses reveal that the Chinese do not benefit economically as much from it as other groups. For example, among college graduates, Chinese women earn less than black and white women. The discrepancy is even greater among women with postgraduate education (Fong, 1984).

Chinese employment has a bimodal distribution in terms of occupational success (Mark and Chih, 1982, p. 155). This is reflected by their occupational distribution largely into either the technical/professional fields (e.g., engineering or medicine) or the unskilled service industries (e.g., restaurant workers or garment factory workers). For example, while one-quarter of Chinese women are employed in professional or managerial positions, another quarter work in sewing factories. Those at the lower end of the occupational spectrum often reside in Chinatown ghettos, living in substandard, crowded housing.

VALUES AND BEHAVIORAL NORMS

A Holistic Worldview

The traditional Chinese worldview is rooted in the concept of inter-connections—between mind and body, between parent and child, be-tween neighbor and neighbor (Hsu, 1955; Lee, 1982). Along with this idea is a tremendous emphasis on maintaining harmonious interpersonal relations, which is reinforced by a socialization process that results in a self-consciousness in relation to others. Unlike the Western idea of striv-ing for autonomy and independence, the Chinese tradition values har-mony, togetherness, and unity. While many writers have pointed to Confucian roots for such beliefs, the daily hardships of agricultural so-cieties historically made such unity a necessity. In the United States, racist segregation, which forced Chinese into geographically bounded ghettos (i.e., Chinatowns), further reinforced a turning toward and unity with other Chinese.

The Family Unit

Within the family, relatedness is defined by the concept of *jen* or benevolence, which encompasses filial piety and fraternal love (Chai, 1959, p. 32). The group, rather than the individual, is the major unit of society. In addition, parent-child relationships often take priority over spousal relationships. The former tend to be characterized by a mutual obligation within a vertical power hierarchy. Virtuous parents are those who do what is appropriate for their children, even at the expense of personal needs. The original sojourners, for example, toiled long hours for a lifetime in order to support their families in China. In many in-stances, these men never enjoyed the fruits of their labor until after retirement, sometimes returning to children and wives whom they had rarely or never seen during the intervening years. While the nature of parental sacrifice and fulfillment of duty no longer takes this exaggerated form, Chinese culture continues to perpetuate a powerful pressure on parents to think of the family first.

Children repay parental sacrifice via filial piety. Ideally, children gladly engage in obligatory duties for the sake of their parents. Even in chil-dren's stories these themes are reinforced. For instance, the children's Chinese classics do not tell of fanciful tales of magic and romance like those in the United States. Instead, they contain twenty-four examples of filial self-sacrifice—for example, a child warming the father's mat with his own body, a child gladly playing the guinea pig and ingesting the parent's possibly toxic medicine first, or a child cutting his flesh to make a medicinal brew for his mother. Not only is this attitude and behavior expected, a child should behave in a filial manner without resentment or displeasure.

Role fulfillment is paramount in Chinese culture. Roles are generally prescribed according to gender, age, and birth order, with the first-born senior men possessing the most authority but also the greatest responsibilities. Associated with the rather rigid social roles and power hierarchies are the undirectional communication patterns (Hsu, 1955). Traditionally, parents speak and children listen. The latter, regardless of age, should never question parental authority. In addition, women and girls are subordinate to men and boys and are given little choice. The result is often a large degree of emotional distance between certain familial dyads, such as fathers and youngest children (Lee, 1982).

Shame

In combination with the group orientation, shame and loss of "face" are other cornerstones of traditional Chinese thought. Unlike a guilt-oriented culture, which emphasizes self-blame as a punishment, a shame-based culture emphasizes public disgrace as punishment. One feels bad in the context of significant social relationships. In addition, an individual's shame also affects his or her family's "face," or pride, as well. As a result, individual actions have wide implications and a constellation of meanings. One cannot simply "work through" the personal meaning of an act. Instead, the action is additionally subject to the meanings imposed by the social system. Due to its emphasis on the social system, the shame-based culture tends to lead to projection of fault onto others, particularly when shame is too great to be tolerated and face is lost.

Coping

T. T. Yee (1984) identifies four primary coping strategies in Chinese culture: endurance, look the other way, don't think too much, and activity. All of these coping patterns emphasize avoidance of direct confrontation. Problems are preferably dealt with indirectly, sometimes via the enlistment of third party assistance, either as direct intervention or advice. These forms of coping, however, can create additional stress for the individual (Ryan, 1985).

Mental Health Beliefs and Help-Seeking

In ancient China, madness was thought to originate from dog rabies. Those with psychological problems were considered maniacs, bizarre, or "gone haywire" (see T'ien, 1985, for further details). Today, others view emotional problems as an imbalance resulting from an irregular lifestyle or trauma, which is consistent with the concepts of *Yin* and *Yang*. Emotional problems tend not to be labelled as such but instead are spoken of in somatic terms (Kleinman and Lin, 1981; Lin, 1981). Also, the Chinese worldview emphasizes the interpersonal to such an extent that the Chinese look to their relationships with people instead of to themselves as the cause of their stress (Lin, 1958). In coping with mental health problems, Chinese are taught to avoid disclosing private concerns to outsiders (Hsu, 1981; Ryan, 1985). In addition, the Chinese culture does not believe in the utility of resolving problems by talking (Lin, 1985). As a result, instead of the usual long-term introspective process, most Chinese and Chinese Americans seek therapy only as a last resort, at times of crisis or severe depression. Typically, believing that they should and can control their own destiny and emotional state, they privately handle problems as long as they are tolerable.

PROFILE OF SOCIAL AND PSYCHOLOGICAL PROBLEMS AND ISSUES

In general terms, human distress usually derives from conflicts between the individual and society, between the individual and other people, and within oneself. For the Chinese in the United States, some issues have particular salience. With regard to external society, the immigration experience and its attendant stresses of culture shock, alienation, and racism are major issues. Interpersonally, familial conflict between generations is a frequent problem that can be further compounded by acculturation differences. Lastly, within the individual, feelings of depression, identity conflict, and powerlessness are notable in this population.

Societal Stresses for Chinese Immigrants

Racism toward Chinese has persisted since the earliest days of violent persecution. For example, in 1885, whites killed twenty-eight Chinese and ran hundreds out of town in what is known as the Chinese Massacre in Rock Springs, Wyoming (Crane and Larson, 1940). The hatred that spawned this incident still exists and continues to be a powerful source of persecution and psychological tension for many Chinese in the United States. As recently as 1982, a Chinese man, Vincent Chin, was brutally beaten to death with a baseball bat by two unemployed white auto workers who thought he was Japanese. In fact, hate crimes against Asians have been reportedly on the rise (Ng, 1990).

In its other forms, racist attitudes are reflected in acts of discrimination, devaluation, and negligence. These acts can affect well-being and self-esteem (Kuo, 1982; Sue, 1948), induce racial self-hatred (Sue, 1977), and impede economic success.

Chinese immigrants also often face grave disappointment in the United States, particularly with regard to socioeconomic achievement. Most immigrants left their homelands with high hopes, only to face the grim reality of unemployment or underemployment. These grave life disappointments and associated anger sometimes combine with beliefs that are lethal. In San Francisco, the Chinatown suicide rate is four times that of the rest of the city (Tom, 1968). Unlike the general population, more women than men succeed. This is a particular problem for women between the ages of 55 and 65, a time of midlife reevaluation. Indeed, the Chinese elderly have a high rate of psychological dysfunction, depression, and suicide (Kalish and Yuen, 1973).

Intergenerational Conflict

Intergenerational conflicts are inherent in any family's development. However, the process poses additional complications for the Chinese in the United States when there are intergenerational differences in acculturation and language proficiency. Frequently, the children have greater English facility and greater exposure to mainstream values and attitudes than their parents. The result is that the youth gradually depart from the traditional ways (Fong, 1973). In a culture that prizes child obedience, this can cause tremendous conflict. In addition, the differences in language proficiency can create a literal barrier to communication. Additionally, the parental need for control may be exaggerated because of the parent's own feelings of having little control in an alien culture. Many parents respond by trying to exert even greater control over their children, exacting achievement pressure that far exceeds traditional filial expectations. Traditional Chinese parents can sometimes respond in a manner akin to disownment. While this rarely occurs, the threats are clearly understood, and the children respond accordingly. Some children solve the problem by hiding the difference from their parents and pretending to obey (Fong and Peskin, 1969), while others become immobilized with depression (Bourne, 1975) or struggle under rigid expectations. A handful turn to suicide.

Two major points of intergenerational contention are dating and achievement. With both of these issues, the central conflict tends to be around choice. The traditional value is to make choices that benefit the family. This directly conflicts with the Western value of individual choice. Further, since children usually know that their parents have often put off their own choices for the children's sake, the latter can experience tremendous guilt, resentment, and a host of other complicated feelings in resolving the dilemma. P. Bourne (1975), for instance, writes that many Chinese women date Caucasian men against familial wishes and experience psychological conflicts, feelings of guilt, and that "something is wrong." He gives the following example:

E.L. was a 20 year old junior from Hong Kong who had little social life and became deeply involved with a Caucasian, but constantly expressed misgivings to Chinese friends that it was wrong. She became dependent on him and her behavior became increasingly erratic until she eventually decompensated to psychosis. (p. 276)

While decompensation into psychosis is the exception rather than the rule, the quality of the psychological conflict can be extraordinary nonetheless.

Acculturation Conflict

The process of acculturation necessitates the integration of Western and Chinese values, attitudes, and beliefs. Due to the sometimes extreme difference between the Chinese and mainstream U.S. cultures, the conflicts within an individual can be particularly intense. Consistent with the traditional preference for maintaining one's ethnic identity, many Chinese in the United States try to preserve the traditional ways despite culture clashes. This shift can lead to stressful confusion in value orientations, communication difficulties, psychological isolation, and increased uncertainty concerning oneself and one's relation to others. The consequence is sometimes serious. For example, the high rate of psychosis among Chinese, relative to other disorders, may be the result of the stress of shifting from one culture to another.

When the culture clashes are not extreme, they can still cause significant psychological pain, much of it resulting in social withdrawal and introversion. R. W. Scofield and C-W. Sun (1960), for example, found that immigrant Chinese college students were more withdrawn, shy, emotionally insecure, introverted, sensitive, suspicious, cold, and aloof than American college students. Similarly, other researchers have also noted the relative introvertedness of Chinese in the United States (Sue and Sue, 1971). Part of this is attributable to the incongruence between Western-valued verbal aggressiveness and Chinese-valued reserve and restraint (Toupin, 1980), but some is likely the result of feeling insecure, feeling unaccepted, and low self-esteem.

SOCIAL SERVICE INTERVENTION

In the most general sense, social service interventions aim to heal individuals in pain, to "alleviate distress, to reintegrate the client into the culture, and to enable him or her to respond to cultural roles and to meet cultural expectations" (Draguns, 1981). Regardless of the professional title or technique (e.g., the Feng Shui or the acupuncturist in Chinese culture or the psychotherapist in Western culture), five ingredients are essential (Torrey, 1972):

1. naming and explaining the disorder;
2. gratifying the need for acceptance and warmth;
3. exercising status and prestige;
4. communicating with the client; and
5. conveying one's understanding.

While these ingredients pertain across all cultures, E. F. Torrey argues that the particulars of the roles and the relationship can differ depending on the client's belief system and expectations. In working with Chinese clients, practitioners need to know the particulars about a client in order to facilitate a "good match." The following are general guidelines for practice that a practitioner can keep in mind when working with a Chinese client. Given the heterogeneous nature of Chinese in the United States, practitioners need to carefully assess the client's degree of acculturation, and the applicability of the following principles.

Principles of Practice

Naming and explaining the disorder: The practitioner, not the client, has the role of naming and explaining the disorder.

Whereas mainstream American psychotherapy assumes that the client identifies the problem and labels the disorder, Chinese clients often expect a rapid diagnosis and concrete solutions from the practitioner. For example, a traditional Chinese folk healer will pronounce a diagnosis and recommend a treatment simply after taking a patient's pulse. Analogous to this, the Chinese client receiving social service intervention may expect the practitioner to structure the interview, take charge, and identify a diagnosis without intrusive questioning. The client would also be likely to expect an explanation as to the nature of the process and structure of the therapeutic relationship (Tsui and Schultz, 1985; Root, 1985).

In naming their disorders, few Chinese Americans begin with the same assumptions that underlie Western psychotherapy principles. They generally enter treatment at a moment in which they no longer feel able to deny, suppress, or individually cope with their problems. As a result, the client seeks symptom removal and strategies for coping and effecting change, not introspection and self-reflection.

> *Exercising status and prestige: Rather than strive for an egalitarian relationship, the practitioner may need to establish authority and competence early on in order to attain status and prestige in the eyes of the client. This is important in enhancing the client's perception that the practitioner can provide competent healing.*

Chinese societies are hierarchical, and interpersonal exchanges are role based. As a result, Chinese culture socializes individuals to be very sensitive to formal cues for proper behavior. The practitioner/client transaction is no exception. This transaction is a complex feedback loop in which the client and practitioner influence each other in an interactive fashion.

Communicating status, prestige, and authority can take many forms. Most obviously, using formal titles and displaying documents can establish the practitioner's professional placement. More importantly, the interpersonal exchanges further contribute to the client's perception of authority. For example, if a practitioner designates a particular seat for the client, a white American client might interpret this as a show of bossiness, whereas a Chinese client might interpret it as an indication of authority and competence. The structure of the session can also convey a sense of authority. The client often reads from the practitioner's behavior how to act next. To receive a "blank screen" or neutrality flies in the face of this fundamental Chinese social rule (Tsui and Schultz, 1985). Chinese clients often complain, "We from Asia look for the cue, but don't find it, and misunderstandings do occur" (Fong, 1973). When a practitioner fails to act authoritatively or fails to provide the proper cues for behavior, polite silence ensues, generating anxiety in both parties. For example, in psychotherapy, a common interaction is the instance of the mainstream American practitioner waiting for the patient to assume responsibility for making use of the amorphous therapy structure. Meanwhile, the client, who has been culturally conditioned to avoid incurring shame by confronting the therapist, remains silent (Tsui and Schultz, 1985). Similarly, a Chinese client may perceive a practitioner who relies on open-ended questions, such as, "What brought you here?" or "Can you tell me a bit more about that?" as irresponsible and unconscientious (Tsui and Schultz, 1985). The consequence is a failure to establish the working alliance.

> *Gratifying the need for acceptance and warmth: Practitioners should be alert to a Chinese client's sense of fear, confusion, or apprehension about receiving social service intervention and should make every effort to convey that the client's problems are acceptable and do not indicate that he or she is "crazy," "weak," or "defective."*

Given that the majority of Chinese clients receiving outside intervention feel ashamed, apprehensive, and/or have mixed feelings about the interaction, the practitioner can convey acceptance and warmth by anticipating these concerns giving permission for the client to acknowledge such feelings rather than waiting for the client to mention them. By affirming that the client is not crazy, asking him or her about embarrassment in accepting help, and inquiring about the family's view of help-seeking, the practitioner can show a strong sensitivity to the client's experience.

Acceptance and warmth in Chinese culture are typically conveyed through action rather than words. In particular, "giving" actions can have significant import in indicating a practitioner's acceptance and warmth to a Chinese client (Sue and Zane, 1987). Giving can take on many forms, such as providing assistance with life tasks (e.g, filling employment forms or facilitating school placement). While these case management tasks may appear unclinical and outside of the bounds of the stated role of the practitioner, they are culturally appropriate and can send a powerful message that the practitioner is caring and capable enough to actually do something for the client.

Another important interaction that indicates warmth is the way in which practitioners answer direct personal questions. Failure to respond directly to personal questions is often interpreted as rude (Tsui and Schultz, 1985). It also establishes a boundary that implies a lack of acceptance on the part of the practitioner.

Finally, the experience of many Chinese in the United States has been one of exclusion, rejection, and discrimination. In addition, many are themselves or have ancestors who are illegal residents of the United States and have to be silent in order to avoid deportation (Ho, 1976). As a result, many Chinese have learned the value of silence and inconspicuousness and to be wary of "outsiders." In interventions, this may be manifested in a reluctance against trusting the warmth and acceptance offered by the practitioner, as well as caution toward self-disclosure. Rather than viewing this as resistance, these alternative interpretations can help the practitioner to be more accepting and patient.

> *Communicating with the client: Practitioners must learn the psychological language (i.e., the meaning of different verbal and nonverbal communications) and the metarules of communication in the Chinese culture.*

Two communication metarules stand out in Chinese culture: (1) The relationship between individuals (e.g., age, sex, education, occupation, social status, family background, marital status, and parenthood) determines what is communicated and how, and (2) individuals avoid emotional expressiveness, especially if it involves direct confrontation, which may lead to "loss of face" (Chang, 1985; Wu, 1982).

Communication between practitioner and client is often influenced by the roles perceived by the client. In Chinese culture, three figures are accorded unchallenged respect: the king, the father, and the teacher. Physicians and, to a lesser extent, other healers fall in the rank of teacher or parent. As a result, the Chinese client may have a very strong need to maintain face in the presence of a revered authority figure by communicating only the good things. On the other hand, the client is there out of pain and need and may strongly desire to regress and be taken care of by the practitioner.

Nonverbal communication is more important than verbal when working with many Chinese clients since Chinese people rely on nonverbal communication or symbolic figurative expression of emotion rather than verbal communication (Kinzie, 1978; Lin, 1985; Sue, 1977). Also, Chinese often use metaphors to convey meanings of emotions (Chang, 1985; Kleinman, 1980). For example, to speak of "heartache means intense sadness and a sense of loss for self or for others," and "headache means stress caused by difficult tasks" (Chang, 1987). Practitioners must learn to intuit the true meaning of the client's message.

> *Conveying one's understanding: A practitioner must develop empathy, or "vicarious introspection: the capacity to think and feel oneself into the inner life of another person" (Kohut, 1984), as well as the ability to convey it in a culturally appropriate manner.*

Empathic understanding is the essence of all psychotherapies (Patterson, 1986) and is key in all social service interventions. For many Chinese, empathy should be conveyed in a manner similar to that of a parent to a child. This is not to say that Chinese wish to be patronized. Instead, Chinese healers are expected to "guess" or understand the clients' intentions and feelings. This diverges from the Western emphasis on reflection of client feelings and the maintenance of practitioner neutrality.

Theoretical/Conceptual Models of Intervention

Given the heterogeneous nature of the Chinese population in the United States as well as the multiplicity of problems they face, no single theoretical or conceptual model of intervention can be identified. Rather than focus on a singular treatment modality, the practitioner should make an informed disposition after conducting a careful assessment of the client. This assessment should include: the individual's migration, social, economic, and familial circumstances; his or her psychological state (e.g., acculturation, interpersonal relations, and mental status); and his or her beliefs and expectations regarding intervention.

Specific Skills

Below are suggestions for increasing the appropriateness of social service interventions with Chinese clients:

1. Make services as accessible as possible (e.g., location, hours of operation, drop-in hours instead of appointments only, and appearance).
2. Conduct ongoing outreach to facilitate the service's acceptability by Chinese clients.
3. Have flexible processes for entry into the system (e.g., not requiring individuals to make appointments for themselves).
4. Hire Chinese staff and inform the community.
5. Use the client's preferred language.
6. Respect and work with the client's expectations and beliefs.
7. Emphasize specific behavioral goals, at least in the beginning stages of intervention.
8. Be sensitive to the client's ethnic identification.
9. Be aware of one's own ethnic identification and unfounded assumptions about Chinese clients.

CONCLUSION

As in all social service interventions, there is no simple recipe for change. While Chinese in the United States may share the same ethnic ancestry, they are a heterogeneous population with very divergent cultures and histories in the United States. Therefore, in working with Chinese clients, practitioners must be mindful of the social roles, stereotypes, and sociopolitical contexts with which their clients live. This chapter attempts to offer hypotheses rather than formulas that practitioners may keep in mind when encountering Chinese clients.

REFERENCES

Bourne, P. (1975). The Chinese student—acculturation and mental illness. *Psychiatry* 38: 269–277.

Chai, C. (1959). Chinese humanism: A study of Chinese mentality and temperament. *Social Research* 26: 32.

Chang, W. C. (1985). A cross-cultural study of depressive symptomatology. *Culture, Medicine and Psychiatry* 9: 295–317.

——— (1987). Empathy: A cross-cultural encounter. Conference proceedings from Interactive Forum on Transference and Empathy in Psychotherapy with Asian Americans, Boston, Mass.

Chyr, C. (1988, December 9, 10). Asians 1/4 of bay area by 1990, paper says. *Asian Week*, p. 14.

Crane, P., and A. Larson (1940, January). The Chinese Massacre. *Annals of Wyoming* XII, pp. 47–55 and 153–161.

Draguns, J. G. (1981). Cross-cultural counseling and psychotherapy: History, issues, current status. In A. J. Marsella and P. B. Pedersen (eds.), *Cross-cultural Counseling and Psychotherapy*. New York: Pergamon Press.

Fong, P. (1984). The current social and economic status of Chinese American women. In G. Lim (ed.), *The Chinese American Experience*. San Francisco: Chinese Historical Society of America and Chinese Culture Foundation of San Francisco.

Fong, S. (1973). Assimilation and changing social roles of Chinese Americans. *Journal of Social Issues* 29 (2): 115–127.

Fong, S.L.M., and H. Peskin (1969). Sex role strain and personality adjustment of China-born students in America: A pilot study. *Journal of Abnormal Psychology* 74 (5): 563–567.

Harper, F. V., and J. H. Skolnick (1962). *Problems of the Family*, rev. ed. New York: Bobbs-Merrill.

Ho, M. K. (1976). Casework with Asian Americans. *Social Casework* 57 (3): 196–201.

Hsu, F.L.K. (1955). *Americans and Chinese*. London: Cresset Press.

——— (1981). *Americans and Chinese: Passages to Differences*. Honolulu: University Press of Hawaii.

Kalish, R., and S. Yuen (1973). Americans of East Asian ancestry: Aging and the aged. In S. Sue and N. Wagner (eds.), *Asian-Americans: Psychological Perspectives*. Palo Alto, Calif.: Science and Behavior Books.

Kinzie, J. D. (1978). Lessons from cross-cultural psychotherapy. *American Journal of Psychotherapy* 32: 510.

Kleinman, A. (1980). *Patients and Healers in the Context of Culture: An Exploration of the Borderland Between Anthropology, Medicine and Psychiatry*. Berkeley: University of California Press.

Kleinman, A., and T. Y. Lin (eds.) (1981). *Normal and Deviant Behavior in Chinese Culture*. Hingham, Mass.: Reidel.

Kohut, H. (1984). *How Does Analysis Cure?* Chicago: University of Chicago Press.

Kuo, C-L. (1982). Perceptions of assimilation among the Chinese in the United States. In C. B. Marrett and C. Leggon (eds.), *Research in Race and Ethnic Relations*. Greenwich, Conn.: JAI Press.

Lee, E. (1982). A social systems approach to assessment and treatment for Chinese American families. In M. McGoldrick, J. K. Pearce, and J. Giordano (eds.), *Ethnicity and Family Therapy*. New York: Guilford Press.

Lin, K. M. (1981). Traditional Chinese medical beliefs and their relevance for mental illness and psychiatry. In A. Kleinman and T. Lin (eds.), *Normal and Abnormal Behavior in Chinese Culture*. Dordrecht, Holland: Reidel.

Lin, T. Y. (1985). Mental disorders and psychiatry in Chinese culture. In W. S. Tseng and D.Y.H. Wu (eds.), *Chinese Culture and Mental Health*. San Diego: Academic Press.

Lum, K. Y., and W. F. Char (1985). Chinese adaptation in Hawaii: Some examples. In W. S. Tseng and D.Y.H. Wu (eds.), *Chinese Culture and Mental Health*. San Diego: Academic Press.

Lyman, S. (1973). The Anti-Chinese movement in America, 1785–1910. *Chinese Americans*. New York: Random House.

Mangiafico, L. (1988). *Contemporary American Immigrants: Patterns of Filipino, Korean, and Chinese Settlement in the United States*. New York: Praeger.

Mark, D.M.L., and G. Chih (1982). *A Place Called Chinese America*. Dubuque, Iowa: Kendall/Hunt.

Ng, J. (1990, August 14). Senator Simon warns of rise in hate crimes. *Asian Week* 12 (3): 5.

Patterson, C. H. (1986). *Theories of Counseling and Psychotherapy*. New York: Harper and Row.

Root, M. P. (1985). Guidelines for facilitating therapy with Asian American clients. *Psychotherapy* 22: 349–356.

Ryan, A. S. (1985). Cultural factors in casework with Chinese-Americans. *Social Casework* 66 (6): 333–340.

Scofield, R. W., and C-W. Sun (1960). A comparative study of the differential effect upon personality of Chinese and American child training practices. *Journal of Social Psychology* 52: 221–224.

Starr, P. D., and A. E. Roberts (1982). Attitudes toward new Americans: Perceptions of Indo-Chinese in nine cities. In C. B. Marrett and C. Leggon (eds.), *Research in Race and Ethnic Relations*. Greenwich, Conn.: JAI Press.

Sue, D. W., and A. C. Frank (1973). A typological approach to the psychological study of Chinese and Japanese American college males. *Journal of Social Issues* 29 (2): 129–148.

Sue, S. (1984). Chinese American mental health. In G. Lim (ed.), *The Chinese American Experience*. San Francisco: Chinese Historical Society of America and Chinese Culture Foundation of San Francisco.

——— (1977). Psychological theory and implications for Asian Americans. *Personnel and Guidance Journal* 55: 381–389.

Sue, S., and D. W. Sue (1971). Chinese American personality and mental health. *Amerasia Journal* 1 (2): 36–49.

Sue, S., and N. Zane (1987). The role of culture and cultural techniques in psychotherapy: A critique and reformulation. *American Psychologist* 42 (1): 37–45.

T'ien, J. K. (1985). Traditional Chinese beliefs and attitudes toward mental illness. In W. S. Tseng and D.Y.H. Wu (eds.), *Chinese Culture and Mental Health*. San Diego: Academic Press.

Tom, S. (1968). Mental health in the Chinese community of San Francisco. Unpublished manuscript. Los Angeles: UCLA Asian American Studies Center.

Torrey, E. F. (1972). What Western psychotherapists can learn from witchdoctors. *American Journal of Orthopsychiatry* 42: 69–76.

Toupin, E.S.W.A. (1980). Counseling Asians: Psychotherapy in the context of racism and Asian-American history. *American Journal of Orthopsychiatry* 50: 76–86.

Tsai, S.S.H. (1986). *The Chinese Experience in America*. Bloomington: Indiana University Press.

Tsui, P., and G. L. Schultz (1985, October). Failure of rapport: Why psychotherapeutic engagement fails in treatment of Asian clients. *American Journal of Orthopsychiatry* 55 (4): 561–569.

U.S. Bureau of the Census (1940, 1950, 1960, 1970). *Characteristics of the Population: General Social and Economic Characteristics*. Washington, D.C.: U.S. Government Printing Office.

———— (1988). *We, the Asian and Pacific Islander Americans*. Washington, D.C.: U.S. Government Printing Office.

U.S. Bureau of the Census, Social and Economic Statistics Administration (1990). *Statistical Abstract of the United States*. Washington, D.C.: U.S. Government Printing Office.

Wu, D.Y.H. (1982). Psychotherapy and emotion in traditional Chinese medicine. In A. J. Marsella and G. M. White (eds.), *Cultural Conceptions of Mental Health and Therapy*. Boston: Reidel.

Yee, T. T. (1984). Family stress: Appraising and coping processes. In G. Lim (ed.), *The Chinese American Experience*. San Francisco: Chinese Historical Society of America and Chinese Culture Foundation of San Francisco.

Zo, K. Y. (1971). Chinese emigration into the United States. Ph.D. dissertation, Columbia University.

CHAPTER 6

Filipino Americans

JONATHAN Y. OKAMURA AND
AMEFIL AGBAYANI

INTRODUCTION

During the 1980s, Filipino Americans replaced Chinese as the largest Asian American group and increased their numbers to more than 1 million (East-West Population Institute, East-West Center and Operation Manong, University of Hawaii [EWPI and OM], 1985, p. 3). Such rapid growth and change in their population can be expected to result in a variety of social and economic problems and challenges for Filipino Americans, particularly recent immigrants. Population increase through ongoing immigration also has contributed to the marked social and cultural diversity of the Filipino American community. Filipinos differ amongst themselves in terms of language spoken, place of birth, generation, length of residence in the United States, degree of acculturation, ethnic identity, gender, and social class status. All of these factors, and not only those pertaining to cultural characteristics and influences, need to be taken into consideration in social services intervention with Filipino American clients.

It is also very important to distinguish Filipino Americans as a distinct group from other Asian American populations so that culturally responsive intervention techniques can be developed for working with Filipino American clients as Filipinos and not as Asians in general. This chapter represents an initial effort toward that objective. Given the paucity of research and training materials on social services intervention with Filipinos, it has been necessary to draw on the literature from the Philippines on culturally appropriate strategies. By taking into consideration the social status of Filipinos in the larger structural context of

American society, Philippine approaches may be applied to Filipino American clients, particularly immigrants who comprise a majority of the Filipino population in the United States.

HISTORICAL BACKGROUND

Filipino immigration to the United States began in 1906, when Filipinos immigrated to work on the sugar plantations in Hawaii. Immigration of labor from the Philippines differed from that of other countries since as "nationals" of the United States (the Philippines were annexed in 1898 following the Spanish-American War), Filipinos were allowed free entry into America. Between 1906 and 1946 about 127,000 Filipinos came to the United States via Hawaii under the auspices of the Hawaiian Sugar Planters' Association (Dorita, 1954, p. 131). The great majority of them were single young men from rural villages who had little or no formal education. Lack of education was a desired condition for labor recruitment since the plantations wanted docile workers who would not organize themselves for better working and living conditions. The ardent hope of most of the labor recruits was to accumulate sufficient savings from their three years of toil in order to buy some land upon their return to the Philippines (Cariaga, 1936, p. 23; Quinto, 1938, p. 73).

Filipinos in Hawaii remained concentrated in agricultural work during the 1920s and 1930s due to the lack of alternative employment opportunities, particularly during the Depression. In 1930 the overwhelming majority (90 percent) of employed male Filipinos were unskilled laborers, and four-fifths of this group were sugar plantation workers (Lind, 1980, pp. 82, 85). In that year, three out of every ten Filipinos in Hawaii, including children, were illiterate, and more than 50 percent of all Filipinos could not speak English (Fuchs, 1961, pp. 146–147).

In California, Filipinos were concentrated in three general types of work: agricultural "stoop" labor, domestic and personal services, and the fishing and canning industries, which extended from California to Alaska (Wallovits, 1966, p. 27). Given the seasonal nature of agriculture, Filipino laborers had to move regularly in search of employment, which precluded the development of stable communities. In the summer they went to work in the Alaskan salmon canneries; in the fall they labored on asparagus and lettuce farms in Salinas and Stockton, California; and in winter they traveled to the Imperial Valley east of San Diego to work on tomato, cantaloupe, and melon farms (Almirol, 1977, p. 53).

A notable aspect of the Filipino historical experience in California was the exclusion movement against their further immigration that was led by organized labor in the late 1920s and early 1930s. Various local and state organizations called for an end to Filipino immigration on the basis that they represented "unjust and unfair competition" to white workers in agricultural and domestic work (Wallovits, 1966, p. 38). Filipinos also were viewed as social "undesirables" because of their alleged "extreme unassimilability," frequent relationships with white women, "offensive personality traits and behavior," and tendency to be arrested (Wallovits, 1966, p. 42). This hostility against them was manifested in widely publicized "anti-Filipino race riots" in several California farming towns in 1929 and 1930. Similar racial attacks against Filipinos occurred in farming communities in Washington (1928), Oregon (1930), and Florida (1932).

Unlike other American immigrant groups, Filipinos had a much greater difficulty starting families in the United States because of their highly unbalanced sex ratio (five males to every female in the 1930s), which was the result of the labor recruitment focus on unattached men. Also, many Filipino workers with families in Hawaii sent their wives and children back to the Philippines because they were unable to support them on their low salaries. Thus, Filipino socioeconomic advancement in the United States was delayed due to the restricted development of their second generation, which traditionally has represented the first advance in social status mobility for American immigrant groups.

Philippine immigration to the United States in substantial numbers did not commence again until after 1965 with the passage of the present Immigration Act. This legislation was intended primarily to reunite families and to bring in skilled workers. Under the conditions of this law, Filipinos have immigrated to the United States through a process of "chain migration" with primary kinship relations providing the essential links of assistance and support in this chain.

In comparison to previous Filipino immigrants, the post–1965 group has far greater educational and professional qualifications (Keely, 1973; Medina, 1984, p. 137). For example, in 1970, professionals represented almost one-half of Filipino immigrants to the United States (Gupta, 1973). The post-1965 immigrants have come to the United States primarily to join their relatives and for economic advancement (Lasman, Buluran, Nolan, and O'Neil, 1971, p. 44; Okamura, 1984, p. 31). Their arrival has resulted in a sociocultural revitalization in Filipino languages, norms, and values and social activities in Filipino communities throughout the United States where they have settled. Thus, the Filipino American population can be said to be comprised of three main groups: "oldtimer" former plantation and farm laborers, the American-born (called "local" in Hawaii), and "newcomer" post-1965 immigrants.

SOCIODEMOGRAPHIC OVERVIEW

According to the 1980 Census, Filipino Americans numbered 781,894, which represented more than a doubling of their 1970 population of 343,060 (Hsia and Hirano-Nakanishi, 1989, p. 22). Indeed, Filipinos are the fastest growing of the various Asian American groups, and they comprise almost one-fourth (22.6 percent) of the total (U.S. Bureau of the Census, 1988b, p. 2). With an annual average of 50,000 Filipino immigrants entering the United States from 1985 through 1989 (Asian population in U.S. soars 70% since 1980, 1990, p. A–8), the 1990 Census will very likely indicate that Filipinos are the largest Asian American group with a population of well over 1 million. Furthermore, by the year 2000, Filipino Americans are expected to number more than 2 million (EWPI and OM, 1985, p. 3).

The 1980 Census provides basic sociodemographic information on Filipino Americans (U.S. Bureau of the Census, 1988a; 1988b). Over two-thirds (68.8 percent) of the Filipino American population is concentrated in the west with almost one-half (45.8 percent) of their total in California (358,378) and another one-sixth (16.9 percent) in Hawaii (132,075). Smaller numbers of Filipinos are found in Illinois (44,317), New York (35,630), Washington (25,662), and New Jersey (24,470). The Filipino American population is primarily urban with its greatest concentrations in the Los Angeles–Long Beach (100,894), San Francisco–Oakland (97,154), and Honolulu (96,421) metropolitan areas.

Given prior and ongoing Filipino immigration to the United States, it is not surprising to note that almost two-thirds (64.7 percent) of the Filipino American population is foreign-born. Nonetheless, a substantial majority (57.5 percent) of Filipinos 15 years old and over are American citizens. Possibly due to their substantial immigrant numbers, about two-thirds (67.4 percent) of Filipinos 5 years and older speak a language other than English at home.

Filipinos are among the highest ranked Asian American groups in terms of socioeconomic status. For example, with regard to occupational status, a majority of Filipinos are employed in technical, sales, and administrative support work (33.3 percent) and as managers and professionals (25.1 percent). Significant numbers of Filipinos also are employed as service workers (16.5 percent), operators, fabricators, and laborers (14.0 percent) and as precision production, craft, and repair workers (8.3 percent).

Among Asian Americans, Filipinos have the highest percentage (72.5 percent) of their population age 16 and over in the labor force, a proportion substantially greater than the national average (62 percent). Notably, more than two-thirds (68.1 percent) of Filipino women are employed, again the highest percentage among Asian Americans and considerably above the national figure (49.9 percent). Filipinos also have the highest proportion among Asian American groups of families with three or more workers (21.8 percent). These figures on high rates of employment are consistent with the Filipino self-perception, particularly in Hawaii, that they are a "hardworking" people (Okamura, 1983, p. 151).

Filipinos have the third highest median family income ($23,700) among Asian Americans, falling behind Japanese ($27,400) and Asian Indians ($25,000), and are somewhat above the national median ($19,000). However, in terms of female individual income, Filipinos ($8,300) are foremost among Asian Americans and are considerably above the national median ($5,300). Not surprisingly then, Filipinos (7.1 percent) have the second lowest poverty rate for individuals after Japanese (6.5 percent) and also have the second lowest family poverty rate (6.2 percent) among Asian Americans.

As for educational attainment, almost three-fourths (74.2 percent) of Filipinos 25 years old and over were high school graduates in 1980, which was significantly above the national rate (66 percent). Filipinos are unique among Asian Americans in having a greater proportion of female (75 percent) than male (73 percent) high school graduates. A similar situation prevails among Filipino female (41 percent) and male (32 percent) college graduates, which is again distinctive among Asian Americans and the country as a whole. Thus, Filipino women have the highest percentage of college graduates and the second highest proportion of high school graduates among Asian American females.

The above review of social and economic characteristics of the Filipino population in the United States indicates that they compare quite favorably to other Asian American groups and to national medians and rates. However, if appropriate adjustments are made for nonethnic factors, such as years of work experience, education, and generation, Filipinos may be shown to earn considerably less than their white counterparts (Suzuki, 1989, p. 15). Furthermore, substantial differences in socioeconomic status exist among Filipinos in the various states. In general, Filipinos on the continental United States, particularly in California, New York, and Illinois, have a higher socioeconomic status than Filipinos in Hawaii, which can be attributed to their different immigration histories and experiences with the larger society.

Filipinos in Hawaii are one of the most economically disadvantaged groups in the state by virtually all objective indices of socioeconomic status. This condition is especially evident in terms of occupational status where Filipinos have encountered the greatest resistance in their individual and collective efforts to advance themselves from their sugar plantation background. Both Filipino males (25.4 percent) and females (7.4 percent) have the highest percentage of workers employed at the lowest end of the occupational scale as farm and nonfarm laborers among the five major ethnic groups in Hawaii—Chinese, Filipinos, Japanese, native Hawaiians, and whites (Hawaii State Department of Health, 1981,

p. 11). Conversely, both male (8.5 percent) and female (9.9 percent) Filipinos have the lowest proportion of workers employed at the uppermost end of the occupational scale as professional and technical workers, managers, officials, and proprietors. While nationally a clear majority of Filipinos hold white collar positions, Filipino men in Hawaii are primarily employed as operators, laborers, service workers, and craft workers, while Filipino women generally hold clerical, sales, and service occupations (Okamura, 1990).

With regard to income, Filipinos have the second lowest median family income ($20,500) of the five major ethnic groups in Hawaii, which is considerably below their overall U.S. median ($23,700) (U.S. Bureau of the Census, 1982, p. 68). Filipino males ($9,500) rank lowest and Filipino females ($6,200) rank second to the lowest in terms of median personal income among Hawaii's major ethnic groups. These figures are again well below the national medians for males ($10,700) and females ($8,300).

As for educational attainment (for persons 25 years old and over), Filipinos in Hawaii have the lowest median number of years of schooling completed (12.1 years) of the major ethnic groups (U.S. Bureau of the Census, 1982, p. 54). They also have the lowest percentage of high school graduates (51.1 percent) and the second lowest proportion of college graduates (10.8 percent) of Hawaii's major ethnic groups (Okamura, 1990), percentages that are considerably below the national high school (74.2 percent) and college (37 percent) graduate figures for Filipinos. Thus, wide disparities in socioeconomic status occur among Filipino American communities.

PROFILE OF SOCIAL AND PSYCHOLOGICAL PROBLEMS AND ISSUES

The comparatively lower socioeconomic status of Filipinos in Hawaii as described above is indicative of some of the social and psychological problems that Filipino Americans encounter. In general, these problems affect immigrant Filipinos more so than American-born Filipinos, although the latter may share some of the same problems as their foreign-born counterparts.

Filipinos who have come to the United States after the 1965 changes in the immigration law have found employment problems particularly difficult. Many of these post-1965 immigrants are college graduates and held professional and other white collar positions in the Philippines before immigrating. However, upon seeking work soon after their arrival, they are shocked to learn that their previous education and employment experience in the Philippines are not highly evaluated or even recognized in the United States, and they find themselves being rejected for positions that they thought they were qualified to hold (Almirol, 1977, p. 125; Okamura, 1983, pp. 141–142). Such rejection has been especially disappointing and frustrating for Filipino immigrants since one of the primary reasons they have come to the United States is to enhance their economic circumstances, and most immigrants arrive with an exceptionally positive perception of America as a virtual economic "paradise" where jobs are easy to find and wealth can be quickly amassed (Okamura, 1983, p. 117).

Due to the necessity to support their families, Filipino immigrants settle for any job in order to be gainfully employed. Thus, former professionals and administrators in the Philippines experience occupational downgrading in the United States; that is, a certified public accountant must work as a bookkeeper, a teacher as an educational assistant, a registered nurse as a nurse's aide, and so on. Other former professionals and college graduates who are unable to obtain positions in their field of training may end up in service work as janitors, hotel room maids, or fast food workers, particularly in the tourist industry in Hawaii. Besides feelings of discouragement, this experience of downward occupational mobility results in a considerable loss of self-esteem on the part of the immigrants. However, there is no great stigma within the Filipino community attached to such loss of status since they are all aware of the nature of the problems that immigrants, especially college graduates, face in adjusting to their new lives in the "States." Close friends and relatives thus can be a useful resource in assisting Filipino immigrants, especially the newly arrived, to cope with their emotional difficulties in their adjustment to American life.

A significant factor in the occupational downgrading experienced by Filipino immigrants is the discrimination that they encounter in seeking employment (Okamura, 1983, p. 139). Since their arrival in America in the early 1900s as unskilled and undereducated agricultural laborers, Filipinos have been plagued by discrimination in employment, education, and other social areas. Such unequal and illegal treatment is a primary contributory factor in their relatively low socioeconomic status, especially in Hawaii where a survey of post-1965 immigrant Filipinos found that 42 percent believed that Filipinos were discriminated against in Hawaii (EWPI and OM, 1985, p. 9).

Many Filipinos in Hawaii consider another Asian American minority, the Japanese, rather than whites to be the principal perpetrators of discrimination in employment against them (Okamura, 1983, p. 146). From the Filipino perspective, the Japanese are able to discriminate against them because of their substantial numbers in positions of authority and influence, particularly in state and local government.

A sustaining element in the discrimination and prejudiced attitudes against Filipino Americans is the perpetuation of derogatory stereotypes that depict them as "uneducated" and "unintelligent" (Okamura, 1983, pp. 146–147). These stereotypes have their origins in the perceptions of the early agricultural workers as being "ignorant," "flashy," and "unpredictable" (Okamura, 1982, p. 229) and have continued to be applied to American-born Filipinos and particularly to the post-1965 immigrants.

In Hawaii, the involvement of some young Filipino immigrants in youth gangs and drug dealing has resulted in especially disparaging perceptions of the Filipino community. The police and both the local and national media have contributed to these negative stereotypes by portraying Filipinos as "dope entrepreneurs" who allegedly support their relatives in Hawaii and the Philippines with the profits from the sale of drugs, particularly crystal methamphetamine (Crystal meth called potential powder keg, 1989, p. A-1; The fire of "ice," 1989, p. 38). This connection made by the police between illicit drug monies and the primary Filipino value of maintenance of close family ties is especially offensive to Filipino Americans.

Another possibly problematic area for Filipino immigrants concerns family relationships. Unlike American families, the traditional Filipino household is basically egalitarian with a strong female bias. The income and education levels of the wife or husband are not relevant to increasing or decreasing their relative decision-making power within the family (Alcantara, 1990). However, the stronger American emphasis on individualism and male dominance may result in Filipino women and men seeking a change in their household position based on their income and public status. Filipino men may expect greater power in the family, and individual members may want to seek personal goals rather than to maintain the primacy of the family unit. Family stress also may arise if the husband/father experiences a decline in occupational status in the United States, such as from being a professional in the Philippines to being a service worker in the United States, or if the wife/mother becomes for the first time a significant contributor to the household budget. Conflict within the family also may occur if the children's traditional obedience to their parents declines due to their perception of their parents' lower social and economic status in the United States than in the Philippines.

It is very likely that the social and psychological problems of Filipino Americans described above will continue in the near future because of continuing discrimination against them, the perpetuation of disparaging stereotypes, and the ongoing arrival of new immigrants from the Philippines and their consequent adjustment difficulties.

VALUES AND BEHAVIORAL NORMS

Several well-known studies on Philippine values were conducted in the 1960s (Bostrom, 1968; Bulatao, 1962; Kaut, 1961; Lynch, 1961). These studies, which were written in English rather than a Philippine language, nonetheless focused in particular on the concepts of *hiya* (shame or embarrassment), *utang na loob* (debt of gratitude), *amor propio* (sensitivity to personal affront), and *pakikisama* (giving in or following the lead or suggestion of another), which were presented as especially distinctive of Filipino culture and behavior. Because of the encapsulating and facile way by which these few terms could be used to characterize Filipinos, it is not surprising that they soon made their way uncritically into the literature on Filipino values and behavioral traits published in the United States (e.g., Ponce, 1974; Orque, 1983). Furthermore, this literature has virtually ignored subsequent critical reviews in the Philippines or the studies conducted in the 1960s.

Criticism of both the methods used and the analyses made in the 1960s values studies has been advanced by both American and Filipino social scientists. An early and very harsh critic, R. Lawless (1967; 1969; as cited in Church, 1986, p. 116) maintains that concepts such as *hiya*, *utang na loob*, and *pakikisama* have been inappropriately generalized from vernacular terms associated with specific behaviors and situations into "all-pervading, organizing values and trait complexes" that have assumed an almost stereotypic character and have been accepted as valid by scholars, foreigners, and Filipinos in general.

V. G. Enriquez (1978) is perhaps the most outspoken critic of studies presented in English of Filipino values. His primary argument is that most of these studies employ "the colonizer's perspective and colonial language" as the medium of research and analysis rather than making use of indigenous concepts available in Filipino languages. He contends that the three primary concepts generally discussed in studies of Filipino values—that is, *hiya, utang na loob*, and *pakikisama*—represent only "surface values" in Philippine culture and that previous analyses of them have been somewhat superficial. He argues that all three values have as an essential prerequisite the "pivotal" value of *pakiramdam* ("shared inner perception," Enriquez, 1990). Without the latter, a person cannot have a sense of the other three values. Similarly, all four of the above values derive their significance from the "core" value of *kapwa* ("shared identity," Enriquez, 1990). Enriquez (1990) contends that *kapwa* is at the very heart of Filipino and indeed human values.

More recent studies on Filipino values have been presented that are more behavioral in orientation. The Philippine Senate commissioned a Task Force in 1988 to initiate a study on the strengths (positive behaviors/ traits) and weaknesses (negative behaviors/traits) of the Filipino character toward the development of a national moral recovery program (Ramos-Shahani, 1988).

The Senate study identified the following strengths of the Filipino character: *pakikipagkapwa-tao* (having a "regard for the dignity and being of others," Enriquez, 1978), family orientation, joy and humor, flexibility, adaptability, creativity, hard work and industry, faith and religiosity, and ability to survive (Ramos-Shahani, 1988). Each of these behaviors and characteristics is discussed briefly below (Ramos-Shahani, 1988).

Pakikipagkapwa-tao is manifested among Filipinos in their basic sense of justice and fairness and in their concern for others. They regard others with respect and deal with them as fellow human beings. Filipinos are open to and can empathize with others. Because of *pakikipagkapwa-tao*, Filipinos are very sensitive to the nature and quality of interpersonal relationships and are dependent on them insofar as they provide security and happiness.

The family orientation of Filipinos is evident in their possession of a deep and sincere love for not only spouse, children, parents, and siblings but also for other relatives such as grandparents, aunts, and uncles. Concern for one's family is expressed in the honor and respect bestowed on parents and older relatives, the care provided to children, and the sacrifices that one is willing to endure for the family. For Filipinos, the family is the source of one's personal identity and emotional and material support and is the focus of one's primary duty and commitment.

The Filipino sense of joy and humor is evident in their optimistic approach to life and its travails. Being able to laugh at themselves and their predicament is an important coping mechanism for Filipinos. The result is emotional balance, optimism, and a capacity to survive.

Filipino flexibility, adaptability, and creativity are manifest in Filipinos' ability to adjust to circumstances and to the physical and social environment. Unlike other Asian populations (Leong, 1986, p. 197), Filipinos have a tolerance for ambiguity that enables them to remain unperturbed by uncertainty or lack of information. Filipinos are resourceful, creative, and fast learners and can improvise and make productive and innovative use of whatever is available. These qualities are demonstrated in their capacity to adapt to living in any part of the world and in their ability to accept change.

Filipinos have the capacity for hard work and industry given the appropriate incentives and opportunities. This propensity for hard work is based on the desire for economic security and advancement for oneself and one's family.

Filipinos have a deep faith in God and an innate religiosity that enable them to accept reality in terms of God's will. This faith can be seen in their ability to accept failure and defeat without their sense of self being destroyed. Filipino faith is related to the concept of *bahala na*, which tends to be incorrectly equated with an "expression of fatalism" and "resignation to fate" (Bostrom, 1968). Instead, *bahala na* can be viewed more positively as a significant psychological basis for action in the face of uncertainty or stress to improve a problematic condition.

The Filipinos' ability to survive is evident in their capacity to endure despite difficult times and to get by on so very little. This ability is clearly related to other Filipino strengths, such as optimism, flexibility, adaptability, hard work, and a deep faith in God.

A review by A. T. Church (1986) of various studies on Filipino "personality values or ideals" yielded results consistent with the character strengths discussed in the Senate study. The values identified in Church's review include an emphasis on family ties, respect for authority, emotional control and self-control, courteous and friendly interactions, warm concern and sharing with others, industry, courage and endurance, and a desire for economic progress (Church, 1986, p. 9).

Apparent contrasts and conflicts between various Filipino values and between certain values and beliefs and observed behavior have been pointed out by L. V. Lapuz (1973, as cited in Church, 1986, p. 87). These incongruencies include *hiya* versus a predilection for status; *bahala na* attitudes versus a clear desire for economic security and mobility; in women, *hiya* and modesty versus strong achievement needs; and, in men, a tendency for dominance versus a tendency for abasement. Similar contrasts in values and behavior can be expected between immigrant and American-born Filipinos and among those of varying social class, generation, and degrees of acculturation and assimilation.

SOCIAL SERVICE INTERVENTION

Compared to other Asian American minorities, particularly Japanese and Chinese, there is very limited literature on providing culturally responsive services specifically for Filipino clients (see Leong, 1986). While there is an abundance of research and training materials on working with Asian Americans, this literature should not be assumed to be necessarily applicable to Filipinos because they are Asians. The Asian American population is quite diverse with subpopulations having unique historical experiences and varied cultures and socioeconomic statuses in the United States.

Based on his comprehensive review of the literature on counseling and psychotherapy with Asian Americans, in addition to noting the minimal attention given to Filipinos and other Asian American groups, F.T.L. Leong (1986, p. 200) points out that a majority of the studies were conducted by a "handful" of the same researchers. Furthermore, he notes that the samples were primarily from Hawaii and California, thus bringing into question the generalizability of the conclusions drawn and recommendations made for Asian Americans as a whole.

Intervention techniques proposed for Asian Americans in general have been largely based on clinical experience and research with Japanese and Chinese Americans. For this reason, they cannot be applied unilaterally to any particular group without some knowledge of its specific sociocultural and historical background. Significant social and cultural differences among Asian American groups should be assumed to exist and to necessitate distinct intervention approaches.

Individual Asian American groups themselves also are quite diverse. Filipinos, for example, differ in terms of being American- or Philippine-born, and the latter vary with regard to length of residence in the United States, degree of acculturation and integration into American society, age at immigration, and ethnic self-identification. As indicated above, Filipino Americans also differ markedly in terms of socioeconomic status. Because of the salience of such ingroup variations, particularly between the American- and Philippine-born, the intervention models, techniques, and skills discussed below should be understood as applicable primarily to post-1965 immigrant Filipinos who are more likely to follow Filipino cultural norms and values.

Principles of Practice

Intervention techniques for working with clients in the Philippines have been developed and can be applied to Filipino American clients, particularly post-1965 immigrants. It would be the immigrant population who is likely still to adhere to Filipino norms and values, especially those pertaining to interpersonal relationships. The following principles of practice primarily apply to this group of Filipinos.

In general, a directive counseling approach that involves a structured and authoritarian relationship, recommended specific courses of action, explanations and advice, and less emphasis on emotional disclosure has been found to be more appropriate for Filipinos than a nondirective style. The cultural basis for this approach is that Filipinos can be passive, modest, and restrained, particularly concerning the disclosure of their emotions. The practitioner may need to take a more direct and active role in the initial period of treatment (Bulatao, 1978; Cuizon and Zingle, 1968). While presenting oneself authoritatively as knowledgeable and competent, at the same time the practitioner may have to be more paternalistic and personable than when serving clients from other cultures since Filipinos have strong desires for acceptance and emotional closeness (Varias, 1963; Cuizon and Zingle, 1968).

Although current American counseling techniques specify a passive role for the therapist in an egalitarian relationship, an emphasis on emotional disclosure and reflection, and a focus on the individual, a nondirective practitioner may be perceived by Filipinos as detached and unconcerned (Bulatao, 1978). However, a nondirective style may be quite appropriate for American-born Filipinos or for immigrants who came to the United States at a very young age since they probably ascribe to

American interpersonal norms of behavior and individual achievement values.

It has been found that Filipinos believe that one's state of mental health is dependent on external pressures in the immediate environment (Arkoff, Thaver, and Elkind, 1966; Sechrest, Fay, Zaidi, and Flores, 1973). The significance of these external sources of stress requires interventions at the level of the community, from significant others and coworkers, in addition to the client (Valencia and Palo, 1979).

Since Filipinos tend to be family and small-group oriented, significant members of the family or group may have to be involved in the treatment process (Salazar, 1976; Varias, 1963). Such involvement on their part is understood as an expression of their obligatory concern for the client's well-being.

While Western approaches generally specify the individual as the locus of control for behavior change and decision making, this view may not be as appropriate for more group- and situation-focused cultures, such as Filipinos, in which the individual is defined less distinctly from the family and where a more "external orientation" is valued and accepted as indicative of positive personal adjustment (Church, 1986, p. 82). Thus, J. C. Bulatao (1978) maintains that Filipinos and Asians in general are freer to be themselves when in a supportive group of relatives and friends than in a one-to-one counseling situation. However, it has been noted that greater emphasis on directive counseling and on family- and group-centered approaches could reinforce dependency in some clients even though they may feel more comfortable with those techniques (Church, 1986, p. 86).

Intervention between practitioners and Filipino American clients should take into consideration the factors of professional credentials, age, and gender. Filipinos generally are uncomfortable and unaccustomed to discussing their problems, particularly personal, intimate problems, with others. This discomfort is increased if the other party is perceived as being of lower educational status, younger, or of the opposite sex. Filipinos are more willing to accept assistance and seek advice from persons with the appropriate educational and professional qualifications or ascribed credibility—for example, a therapist with an M.D. or Ph.D. degree rather than a peer counselor or a paraprofessional with no obvious academic qualifications. Similarly, age confers a significant degree of acceptance to Filipino Americans since they regard older people as having wisdom and authority. However, a young practitioner can overcome the age disadvantage by having the proper professional credentials. In terms of gender, both male and female practitioners are acceptable to Filipino clients, although a male counselor will have greater difficulty in obtaining the confidence and trust of a Filipino female client, and a female practitioner can expect similar problems in working with a Filipino male client. Intervention should be most effective when the counselor and client are of the same gender.

Conceptual Models of Intervention

S. Sue and N. Zane (1986) have emphasized the process of "credibility" and "giving" as especially relevant when working with Asian American clients. They define credibility as referring to the client's perception that the therapist is an effective and believable helper, while giving refers to the client's perception that some benefit was received from the treatment encounter (Sue and Zane, 1986, p. 160). They contend that culturally consistent counseling techniques for Asian Americans, such as assuming an authoritarian and directive role, do not necessarily result in effective treatment, but they do result in processes such as increased therapist credibility and/or expectations on the part of clients that then may lead to positive treatment (Sue and Zane, 1986, p. 176). Their argument is that establishing credibility is a more proximate intervention process than being authoritative and structured with clients, and therefore the former approach should be the focus of treatment efforts rather than the more "distal" latter techniques. However, it would seem that assuming authoritarian and directive roles, insofar as they are consistent with relationships among Asian Americans, are immediate rather than distant interactive techniques by which therapist credibility can be enhanced. Nonetheless, establishing credibility and giving provide more specific treatment guidelines than general admonishments to be culturally sensitive and responsive or to provide services in a culturally appropriate mode or manner. Based on their clinical experience, Sue and Zane (1986, p. 171) recommend minimizing problems in establishing credibility and maximizing giving as practical objectives in intervention with Asian American clients.

Both credibility and giving are relevant approaches for working with Filipino Americans since they are related to Filipino values and behavioral norms. The ascribed credibility of the therapist, or that which is based on expertise (Sue and Zane, 1986, p. 163), is enhanced through the authoritarian and directive role that Filipino clients expect of practitioners. On the other hand, a nondirective and unstructured counseling style might indicate detachment or even incompetence to a Filipino expecting immediate guidance and advice from an acknowledged expert in the field.

The process of giving also is especially relevant for Filipino American clients since they tend to expect some form of direct benefits of services from the practitioner. Giving also is consistent with the higher status of the practitioner from whom Filipinos would expect some assistance or advice. The established tendency of Asian Americans, including Filipinos, for premature termination of treatment may well be related to their perception that benefits and gains were not forthcoming to them and thus indicates the necessity of early if not immediate problem alleviating or solving "gifts." Furthermore, gift giving enhances the "achieved" credibility of the practitioner and his or her treatment. The types of benefits that can be provided early on to clients in mental health therapy include anxiety reduction, depression relief, cognitive clarity, normalization, reassurance, hope and faith, skills acquisition, coping perspective, and goal setting (Sue and Zane, 1986, p. 167).

Specific Skills for Intervention

The required clinical skills that have to be developed for working with Asian American clients are delineated by Sue and Zane (1986, pp. 172–173). These skills are organized around four clinical tasks that they regard as critical in the treatment of Asian Americans: problem conceptualization, means for problem solving, goals for evaluating progress, and gift giving.

The various intervention skills identified by Sue and Zane are appropriate in serving Filipino American clients and probably most ethnic minority clients insofar as application of the skills is based on specific, required types of knowledge of the cultural norms, values, attitudes, and behaviors of the client's ethnic group. Of the various clinical skills prescribed by Sue and Zane (1986, p. 173), a few are particularly important in working with Filipino Americans.

With regard to the clinical task of problem conceptualization, the necessary skill of "appropriate role observance" is especially relevant in intervention with Filipino clients given the generally structured nature of their social relationships. It is recommended above that practitioners assume an authoritarian and directive role with Filipinos. This role involves problem identification and evaluation by the practitioner for the client rather than a more egalitarian and introspective approach to the client's problem.

The clinical skill of "generation of an adequate number of treatment options" is significant in meeting the task of identifying appropriate means for problem solving when working with Filipino American clients because such a skill is necessary in establishing the practitioner's credibility. A Filipino client expects the therapist to recommend appropriate treatment strategies rather than have the two of them jointly develop a possible approach.

As for the task of establishing goals for evaluating progress, the required skill of "assessment of reinforcers and aversive stimuli in the environment" is particularly relevant in the treatment of Filipinos since, as noted above, they tend to believe more so than other Americans that one's mental health is dependent on pressures in the immediate environment.

In terms of gift giving, the clinical skill of "family mediation" is especially significant for Filipino Americans due to their close familial ties and to the recommendation noted above that family members be directly involved in the treatment process.

Since a majority of the Filipino American population consists of immigrants who speak a language other than English at home, appropriate language skills are important in intervention with immigrants. If a client does not speak English fluently, a practitioner who is able to speak his or her Filipino language clearly can develop a closer relationship (Church, 1986). The practitioner can then also promote more precise expression and emotional experiencing on the client's part. However, since it is more likely that practitioners in general will lack such language ability, intercultural skills and familiarity with Filipino cultural values and behavioral norms become very significant in establishing personal credibility with clients. In particular, given the salience of interpersonal interactions among Filipinos, being able to adhere to their norms of behavior such as *pakikipagkapwa-tao* (having regard for the dignity of another) will facilitate the development of a personable relationship.

CONCLUSION

The 1990 U.S. Census will confirm that Filipinos represent the largest Asian American group with a population in excess of 1 million. This development has critical implications for research and training for social services intervention for Filipino Americans. Since Filipinos will comprise the largest Asian American population, the validity and applicability of intervention models and techniques ostensibly designed for Asian Americans in general but based primarily on clinical experience and research with Chinese Americans and Japanese Americans need to be reconsidered. Furthermore, it is imperative that intervention and treatment approaches intended specifically for working with Filipino American clients be continually enhanced. At a minimum, the particular differences in intervention with Filipinos in contrast to other Asian Americans should be emphasized.

We have mentioned the comparative paucity of materials, at least outside the Philippines, on culturally responsive intervention strategies for Filipinos. One reason for this absence in the literature is the relative lack of Filipino professional practitioners and of non-Filipino practitioners who have developed an expertise in serving a Filipino American clientele. There is a clear and urgent need for the training of both Filipinos and non-Filipinos on culturally appropriate intervention with Filipino Americans. The critical necessity for such trained professionals is

directly related to the growing and changing Filipino American population and their consequent problems as they seek to establish themselves in the United States.

REFERENCES

Alcantara, A. (1990). Gender differentiation: Public vs. private power in family
decisionmaking in the Philippines. Ph.D. dissertation, University of
Hawaii.
Almirol, E. B. (1977). Ethnic identity and social negotiation: A study of a Filipino
community in California. Ph.D. dissertation, University of Illinois at
Urbana-Champaign.
Arkoff, A., F. Thaver, and L. Elkind (1966). Mental health and counseling ideas
of Asian and American students. *Journal of Counseling Psychology* 13 (2):
219–223.
Asian population in U.S. soars 70% since 1980 (1990, March 2). *Honolulu Star-
Bulletin*, pp. A-1, A-8.
Bostrom, L. C. (1968). Filipino *bahala na* and American fatalism. *Silliman Journal*
15 (3): 399–413.
Bulatao, J. C. (1978, July 24–29). An Asian approach to transpersonal counseling.
Paper presented at the Convention of the Association of Psychological
and Educational Counselors in Asia, Hong Kong University.
——— (1962). Philippine values: The Manileno's mainsprings. *Philippine Studies*
10 (1): 48–81.
Cariaga, R. R. (1936). The Filipinos in Hawaii: A survey of their economic and
social conditions. Master's thesis, University of Hawaii. Reprinted by R
and E Research Associates, San Francisco, 1974.
Church, A. T. (1986). *Filipino Personality, A Review of Research and Writings*. Manila: De La Salle University Press.
Crystal meth called potential powder keg (1989, April 19). *Honolulu Star-Bulletin*,
pp. A-1, A-8.
Cuizon, E. A., and H. W. Zingle (1968). A rational approach to counseling. *The
Guidance and Personnel Journal* 3 (1): 92–100.
Dorita, Sister Mary (1954). Filipino immigration to Hawaii. Master's thesis, Uni-
versity of Hawaii.
East-West Population Institute, East-West Center and Operation Manong, Uni-
versity of Hawaii (1985). Filipino immigrants in Hawaii: A profile of recent
arrivals. Honolulu.
Enriquez, V. G. (1978). Kapwa: A core concept in Filipino social psychology.
Philippine Social Sciences and Humanities Review 42: 1–4.
——— (1990). Personal communication.
The fire of "ice" (1989, November 27). *Newsweek*, pp. 37–40.
Fuchs, L. H. (1961). *Hawaii Pono—A Social History*. New York: Harcourt, Brace
and World.
Gupta, M. L. (1973). Outflow of human capital—high level manpower from the
Philippines with special reference to the period 1965–1971. *International
Labor Review* 10 (3): 167–191.

Hawaii State Department of Health (1981). Population characteristics of Hawaii, 1980. *Population Report*, no. 13.

Hsia, J., and M. Hirano-Nakanishi (1989, November/December). The demographics of diversity, Asian Americans and higher education. *Change*, pp. 20–27.

Kaut, C. R. (1961). *Utang na loob*: A system of contractual obligation among Tagalogs. *Southwestern Journal of Anthropology* 17 (3): 256–272.

Keely, C. B. (1973). Philippine migration: Internal movements and emigration to the United States. *International Migration Review* 10 (3): 177–187.

Lapuz, L. V. (1973). *A Study of Psychopathology*. Quezon City: University of the Philippines Press.

Lasman, L., O. J. Buluran, J. Nolan, and L. O'Neil (1971). A study of attitudes of Filipino immigrants about Hawaii. Master's thesis, University of Hawaii.

Lawless, R. (1969). *An Evaluation of Philippine Culture-Personality Research*. Quezon City: University of the Philippines Press.

——— (1967). The foundations for culture and personality research in the Philippines. *Asian Studies* 5 (1): 101–136.

Leong, F.T.L. (1986). Counseling and psychotherapy with Asian-Americans: Review of the literature. *Journal of Counseling Psychology* 33 (2): 196–206.

Lind, A. (1980). *Hawaii's People*. Honolulu: University Press of Hawaii.

Lynch, F. (1961). Social acceptance. In F. Lynch (ed.), *Four Readings on Philippine Values*. Quezon City: Ateneo de Manila University Press.

Medina, B.T.G. (1984). The new wave: Latest findings on Filipino immigration to the United States. *Philippine Sociological Review* 32 (1–4): 135–143.

Okamura, J. Y. (1982). Ethnicity and ethnic relations in Hawaii. In D.Y.N. Wu (ed.), *Ethnicity and Interpersonal Interaction: A Cross-Cultural Study*. Singapore: Maruzen Asia.

——— (1990). Ethnicity and stratification in Hawaii. *Operation Manong Resource Paper*, no. 2. Honolulu: Operation Manong, University of Hawaii.

——— (1983). Immigrant Filipino ethnicity in Honolulu, Hawaii. Ph.D. dissertation, University of London.

——— (1984). Kinship and community: Filipino immigrants in Honolulu. *Dialogue* 20 (1): 27–43.

Orque, M. S. (1983). Nursing care of Filipino American patients. In M. S. Orque, B. Bloch, and L. S. Monrroy (eds.), *Ethnic Nursing Care, A Multicultural Approach*. St. Louis, Mo.: C. V. Mosby Co.

Ponce, D. (1980). The Filipinos. In J. F. McDermott, Jr., W. S. Tseng, and T. W. Maretzki (eds.), *People and Cultures of Hawaii: A Psychocultural Profile*. Honolulu: University Press of Hawaii.

Quinto, D. (1938). Life story of a Filipino immigrant. *Social Process in Hawaii* 4 (1): 71–78.

Ramos-Shahani, L. (1988, May). *A Moral Recovery Program: Building a People—Building a Nation*. Report submitted to the Committee on Education, Arts and Culture and the Committee on Social Justice, Welfare and Development, Manila, Philippines.

Salazar, Z. (1976). Some bases for a Filipino psychology. In L. F. Antonio, E. S. Reyes, R. E. Pe, and N. R. Almonte (eds.), *Report on the First National*

Conference on Filipino Psychology. Pambansang Samahan sa Sikolohiyang Pilipino.

Sechrest, L., T. Fay, H. Zaidi, and L. Flores (1973). Attitudes toward mental disorder among college students in the United States, Pakistan and the Philippines. *Journal of Cross Cultural Psychology* 4: 342–360.

Sue, S., and N. Zane (1986). Therapists' credibility and giving: Implications for practice and training in Asian-American communities. In M. R. Miranda and H. L. Kitano (eds.), *Mental Health Research and Practice in Minority Communities: Development of Culturally Sensitive Training Programs.* Rockville, Md.: National Institute of Mental Health.

Suzuki, B. H. (1989, November/December). Asian Americans as the "model minority," outdoing whites? Or media hype? *Change,* 13–19.

U.S. Bureau of the Census (1988a). *Asian and Pacific Islander population in the United States: 1980.* Section 1, Tables 1–47.

——— (1982). *Census of Population: 1980, General Social and Economic Characteristics, Hawaii.*

——— (1988b). *We, the Asian and Pacific Islander Americans.* Washington, D.C.: U.S. Government Printing Office.

Valencia, L. B., and E. M. Palo (1979). Community responses to mental illness and utilization of traditional systems of medicine in three selected study sites in metro-Manila: some implications for mental health planning. *Philippine Sociological Review* 27 (2): 103–115.

Varias, R. R. (1963). Psychiatry and the Filipino personality. *Philippine Sociological Review* 11 (3–4): 179–184.

Wallovits, S. E. (1966). The Filipinos in California. Master's thesis, University of Southern California. Reprinted by R and E Research Associates, San Francisco, 1972.

CHAPTER 7

Vietnamese Americans

JON K. MATSUOKA

INTRODUCTION

The fall of Saigon in 1975 spelled the end of decades of American military involvement in Southeast Asia. Continuing into the 1990s, the effects of warfare continue to plague those who were involved. Posttraumatic stress disorder afflicts American Vietnam veterans who remain psychologically unprepared to integrate the atrocities and horror they witnessed during their combat experience. Amerasian children, pariahs of Vietnamese society, await immigration and hopes of unification with their natural fathers and a better life in America. Vietnamese refugees face the hardships associated with adjustment to a new culture and lifestyle. Each of these groups has suffered from the debilitating effects of the war, and social and political efforts are underway to ameliorate or mitigate their problems.

Theoretically, the Vietnamese refugee experience crosses into two major areas. First, they are a refugee population resembling other refugee groups (e.g., Cubans and Hungarians) who were forced to leave their homelands and settled in the United States. Second, their resettlement experiences are similar in many ways to those of other Asian immigrant groups in this country. The interaction of the two sets of experiences has predisposed this population to major mental health problems.

This chapter focuses on Vietnamese refugees, with specific emphasis placed on the problems and issues they experience during their ongoing transition to American life. Problems related to postwar resettlement and issues such as culture change, acculturation stress, and intergenerational conflict are addressed. A discussion of these issues provide a basis for an examination of appropriate social service intervention.

HISTORICAL BACKGROUND

The experiences of the first wave of Vietnamese refugees are characterized by three major historical factors: the war, relocation camps, and sponsorship programs. The experiences of successive waves of refugees leaving Vietnam are different in many respects although there are commonalities associated with the trauma of evacuation and resettlement.

The refugees already endured the debilitating effects of decades of warfare before coming to the United States. With the onslaught of Communist forces, they were forced to leave their homeland in fear of persecution. In the mass confusion of evacuation, many of the refugees had no sense of who might be able to evacuate and who might be left behind. Some individuals found themselves swept into the evacuation process without any serious consideration of the outcome.

Upon leaving their homelands, the Vietnamese refugees were relocated to temporary camps in the United States while sponsorship and other arrangements were made for their resettlement. Confusion and chaos characterized the mental state of refugees during this internment period (Chu, 1983). They had no notion of what the future would hold for them. Refugees were then placed with individuals or organizations willing to assume responsibility for their welfare. Large families were encouraged to split up so that they would be easier to manage. Few of them realized that this would lead to the scattering of family members across the entire country.

The sponsorship program was a plan devised by resettlement personnel at the federal level. The purpose of this program was to promote economic self-sufficiency among the refugees. It was thought that short-term, localized private funding by sponsors could be combined with existing federal and state employment training programs to result in the rapid achievement of self-sufficiency (Skinner and Hendricks, 1979). Following the initial policy decision to disperse the refugees, prescriptions for the refugees' adaptation fell into place. An underlying tenet was the "melting pot" ideology. Refugees were encouraged to achieve economic self-sufficiency, adopt American ways of life, and blend in.

The factors that influenced the basic outline of the resettlement policy appear to be political and financial and not social or psychological. Proponents of the dispersal policy expressed concerns that refugees, left to their own devices, would resettle in large concentrations in select geographic areas. A large and sudden influx of refugees in certain locales would conceivable disrupt the finely balanced economies. From a more altruistic perspective, the resettlement program provided Vietnamese refugees with American social contact and economic security unknown to earlier Asian immigrants. The sponsorship period provided refugees with basic survival needs (i.e., food, clothing, and shelter). This simplified the resettlement process as it absolved the Vietnamese from primary survival concerns and allowed them to focus on secondary matters such as job training and learning the English language. Critics of this program claimed that the government's objective of low-visibility resettlement militated against the development of Vietnamese enclaves. Policymakers were thought to have neglected the historical value of communities settled by a single ethnic group. The dispersal of the Vietnamese inadvertently hindered the emergence of refugee-organized associations that could develop programs and social networks conducive to the maintenance of traditions and psychological well-being (Skinner and Hendricks, 1979).

SOCIODEMOGRAPHIC OVERVIEW

In June 1975, United Press International reported that 131,000 refugees had entered the U.S. system of control. According to a demographic study conducted by the U.S. Department of Health, Education, and Welfare (1976), these refugees were almost equally divided between males and females (51 percent and 49 percent respectively). The refugees were a relatively young population with 43 percent being children age 17 and under. A total of 37 percent were between the ages of 18 and 34. Only 7 percent fell between 45 and 62 years of age, and less than 5 percent were 63 or older.

The Vietnamese refugees were relatively well educated and considered to be the educated elite in South Vietnam. Based on a sample of 124,457 respondents, nearly 50 percent of the heads of households had at least a high school education, and more than 25 percent were college graduates (U.S. Department of State, 1976). In terms of occupation, 24 percent of the heads of households had professional, technical, or managerial skills. The next largest category (17 percent) was jobs related to transportation. The other occupations were distributed over a broad range of categories.

After three years of living under the new Communist regime, another mass exodus of Vietnamese began. The group that came to be known as the "boat people" fled by sea after the regime decided to nationalize the business operations of the bourgeois tradesmen (Atkinson, 1979). The ethnic Chinese, who had dominated retail trade for generations, were forced to turn over their businesses. Seeing no future for themselves in Vietnam, they risked the dangers of the open sea. Thousands drowned or starved to death. Many of the survivors were granted asylum in the United States. Chronic economic and political instability has perpetuated the steady flow of thousands of Vietnamese from their homelands. Many continue to be admitted to the United States on humanitarian grounds.

The 1980 Census counted 245,025 Vietnamese living in the United States, 90.5 percent of whom were born in foreign countries (U.S. Bureau of the Census, 1988). The median age of Vietnamese Americans was relatively young at 21.5 years, and compared to other Asian and Pacific Islander American (APIA) groups they had the largest family size, tied with Samoans, of 5.2 persons per family. In 1980, 57.3 percent participated in the labor force, which was the lowest of all APIA groups and lower than the national average of 62 percent. They were also substantially below the national median family income level ($12,800 compared to $19,000 nationally) and had a poverty rate that was approximately three times higher than the national average (35.5 percent compared to 12 percent nationally). The income statistics are ostensibly related to the unexpected nature of evacuation and the difficulties associated with adjusting to a new society. As Vietnamese adapt to life in America and engage in entrepreneurial activities, their standard of living will predictably rise.

VALUES AND BEHAVIORAL NORMS:
COPING STRATEGIES

Since the resettlement phase, many refugees have made strong efforts to unify family members. With passing time, social networks are being built and gradually repaired. W. T. Liu, M. Lamanna, and A. K. Murata (1979) state that Vietnamese refugees yearn for the companionship of their country people and appear to be following the route taken by earlier Asian immigrant groups. The migration of Vietnamese refugees has been underway since 1976 as extended families are reunited and are settling in areas with higher concentrations of Vietnamese (Montero, 1979).

The formation of enclaves provides a comfortable base for common customs, language, and culture. Like those who came before them, the Vietnamese have repeated the old pattern of joining together in mutual assistance associations. D. Bui (1983) reported that more than 500 mutual assistance associations have developed within the Indochinese refugee communities since 1975. These groups serve their community in many different ways. Some of them are more oriented toward culture, religion, and politics; others serve more social and supportive functions. These groups provide a range of educational, professional, and language services to their communities. Some of them are also involved in resettlement activities.

The secondary migration of Vietnamese refugees throughout the United States did not occur without major problems. Federal officials frowned upon this movement because it differed from their resettlement plans. Refugees who migrated to another state were not reassigned sponsors and had to seek employment opportunities themselves. Consequently, many became heavily dependent upon public assistance. Although the migration of refugees implied otherwise, preliminary evidence (Liu et al., 1979) indicates that some Vietnamese refugees had become apprehensive about living in close proximity to other Vietnamese. A large amount of mutual suspicion existed among Vietnamese refugees. Much of this mistrust could be attributed to economic competition, class differences, and an unequal distribution of resources originally made available to refugees. Enmity and mutual suspicion also grew out of a political situation in Vietnam in which one was unsure of who was an informer and who was not (Ishisaka, 1977). There also appears to be a substantial amount of intrafamilial conflict as younger cohorts are anxious to exercise their newly found freedom.

Refugees separated from their families in Vietnam were forced to rely upon different means for developing ethnic support systems. K. M. Lin and M. Masuda (1983) describe the creation of "pseudo-families" where unaccompanied refugees band together into mutually supportive units. Young individuals are able to draw desperately needed emotional support from these makeshift families. These units serve to ease the process of working through grief and loneliness for loved ones. To compensate for feelings of guilt and despair associated with leaving behind family members, many of these lone refugees mail material goods home. This is done in spite of their own poor financial status. This form of self-sacrifice gives them a sense of connectedness with loved ones they miss. Home sharing is another strategy employed by refugees to increase income and decrease living expenses. Through collective efforts and a common income pool, refugees are able to sustain a desired lifestyle. The practice of home sharing has value from the viewpoints of economics and social support.

PROFILE OF SOCIAL AND PSYCHOLOGICAL PROBLEMS AND ISSUES

Acculturation Stress

Voluntary and involuntary migrations of people may result in acculturation stress and its sequel—mental disorders. The changes set in motion when different cultures come into contact and the stressors evoked within an individual because of demands for new adaptive responses have been considered to have very pernicious effects on mental health (Spindler, 1968).

Sudden changes in the environment that disrupt ordinarily daily activity may be especially relevant to the experiences of Vietnamese refugees. For some refugees their situation appeared to change overnight. One story describes how a young refugee couldn't even figure out how he arrived in the United States. He recounts, "I walked into a hole and then I walked out of a hole and here I am." He had left Thailand at night, walking down a corridor into a 747. He sat down and fell asleep. When he awoke, he was taken down another corridor, arriving in the United States (Asian, Inc., 1983). Although it is difficult to evaluate the adjustment status of the Indochinese in the United States, due to the large size and heterogeneous nature of this population, isolated reports have documented a significant incidence of depression, anxiety, and psychosomatic complaints among segments of the various Indochinese subgroups (Harding and Looney, 1977; Lin, Tazuma, and Masuda, 1979; Rahe, Looney, Ward, Tung, and Liu, 1978; Smither and Rodriguez-Giegling, 1979). For the most part, these studies examined refugees soon after they arrived in America. Reactive disorders are ostensibly related to events that occurred prior to arrival. The impact of current stressors upon Vietnamese refugees has yet to be ascertained. Until now, their adjustment has been studied as if it were totally a product of their wartime experiences. However, the Vietnamese refugees are also faced with the task of finding a comfortable alignment between their old and new cultures. As demonstrated, this in itself may have negative effects upon mental health. The resettlement experiences may interact with the background of the Vietnamese refugees and have a profound effect upon adjustment. Studies on other populations have shown that current life events can create or exacerbate existing stress responses (Fontana, Marcus, Noel, and Rakusin, 1972; Pearlin and Lieberman, 1979; Vinokur and Selzer, 1975).

Another source of stress involving the past and present is the disruption of the family. For persons raised in a cultural system that places enormous emphasis on family life, the lack of family must be seen as a critical factor. News from the family left behind has a strong effect on those who are separated from their families (Matsuoka and Ryujin, 1989/1990; Ishisaka, 1977). Even a minimally adequate lifestyle in the United States may result in guilt when refugees hear of extreme poverty, illness, or death of family members left behind. The inability to respond to family needs may produce feelings of apprehension and failure. For example, many refugees may feel depressed and anxious at mealtimes because of fears that their loved ones in their native land are going hungry.

Still another source of stress relates to ethnic identification. Ethnic identification emerges from, and is shaped by, the adaptational patterns of immigrants to a new environment (Matsuoka, 1990; Skinner and Hendricks, 1979). The original decision to disperse Vietnamese refugees throughout the United States precluded the development of ethnic enclaves, which serve to reinforce ethnic values and identification. Policymakers anticipated that the diffusion of refugees would accelerate the assimilation process. Refugee families and individuals had little choice but to accommodate themselves to an alien culture as rapidly as possible.

Although Vietnamese enclaves are forming as refugees migrate to be near their country people, their still remain countless numbers of isolated families across the United Sates. Without the means of adequately preserving cultural practices outside of the family, structural and marital assimilation may occur within the next generation of Vietnamese in America.

There is no available research that compares differential rates of acculturation and ethnic identity of Vietnamese refugees by geographic location. It seems likely that those residing in areas with sparse populations of other Vietnamese would acculturate at a faster pace than those residing in areas sustaining large populations of Vietnamese. This condition has significant psychological implications. Those entering a new culture should have available to them a familiar culture by which to define themselves, at least until the new culture is learned. This allows a much broader knowledge base by which to identify. Individuals who prematurely forgo their culture in favor of another may be more vulnerable to crisis (Maykovich, 1972).

The Family System and Role Relationships

The radical shift from one culture to another may result in the loss of traditional age-related roles that members of the family once occupied. These roles become critical in terms of how individuals view themselves. Among the Vietnamese, the process of evacuation and resettlement may result in the displacement of the multiplicity of social roles occupied by refugees prior to evacuation.

The following discussion examines aspects of the traditional family system and how role loss becomes problematic among acculturating individuals. J. K. Matsuoka (1990) proposes several generalizations that can be made among three major age groups: elderly, adults, and youth.

The Elderly. In traditional Asian cultures, the elderly are considered the most respected members and an integral part of the family system. They receive deferential treatment and contribute advice to the family and community. They perceive growing old as a blessing, as a period in life when they can sit back and enjoy the fruits of their labor while the family members seek their advice on important issues and in decision making. Many of these traditional expectations brought over by the first generation have been subject to change in the American context. Several authors address the issue of Asian elderly who possess a traditional set of expectations about growing old and the consequent problems they encounter (Ishikawa, 1978a; 1978b; Ishizuka, 1978; Cheng, 1978; Chen, 1979). These studies find that Asian elderly feel a sense of familial dis- location, a lack of respect by the younger generations, that customs of helping are breaking down, and a lack of concern for the future.

The problems faced by elderly Vietnamese are similar to those of other elderly Asian Americans. These problems, however, are compounded by the hardships of resettling. Many are exhausted from the journey to the United States and from old age itself. Perhaps the greatest difficulty in adjusting to American lifestyle is their loss in status (Asian, Inc., 1983). While other family members are preoccupied with meeting sur- vival needs, the elderly are often left in a state of isolation. Dislocation and culture change work to deprive them of the age-appropriate amen- ities that they would expect to receive in their native environment. Sen- sing that they are of no instrumental value, they may become apathetic and lack concern for their future.

Adults. In Vietnamese tradition, there is a strong emphasis on social order and the need for loyalty to social units beginning with one's family. H. Ishisaka (1977) claims that the authority pattern implicit in Confu- cianism and Buddhism emphasizes an individual's position in a struc- tured hierarchy. The individual is expected to defer to the goals of the family and to the head of the household in all matters dealing with family welfare and continuity. The father is the head of the household and is expected to support his dependents adequately. He is viewed as the full authority on all matters inside the family. The mother is generally responsible for everything inside the house and is expected to maintain a somewhat subservient role to her husband.

As Vietnamese refugees enter American society, they are confronted with new role behaviors for men and women. The situation in America is generally more equitable between men and women. For the first time, Vietnamese women are able to join the work force in order to contribute to family income. Other family members are then required to make structural modifications to accommodate to this change. Changing stan- dards of socialization and evaluation inevitably lead to changes in in- dividuals and may lead to problems if it occurs out of sequence with the rest of the family.

Problems concerning role loss arise as Vietnamese adults attempt to adjust to American society. The rapid movement of families to the new land sometimes involves the loss of the father's ability to support his dependents. Persons who find themselves underemployed and working in menial capacities may experience a dramatic loss of self-esteem. Sim- ilarly, the type of work in which an individual is involved has meaning in Asian cultures. There is a clear ranking of work positions that parallels ancient values regarding differences in importance of occupational sta- tus. Loss of occupational status, in addition to its financial implications, must be seen as having serious psychological and emotional significance to the individual and the family (Ishisaka, 1977).

Youth. Youth, especially adolescents, come to the United States at a very vulnerable period in their development. They are faced with problems concerning learning a new language, getting accustomed to new patterns of behavior, and understanding and accepting conflicting values. Coupled with these adjustment difficulties, they have to accomplish a number of developmental tasks brought on by sexual maturity and the flood of new feelings that follow.

To an American adolescent, personal identity is a developmental need that is met through strong identification with people of the same age. In Vietnamese culture, there is greater emphasis on achieving one's identity and sense of worth through close relationships with family adults and being a member of an established lineage and extended family system. However, the disruption and separation of many families, coupled with exposure and socialization in an age-segregated society, increases the importance and influence of peers. Vietnamese youth, as they encounter different norms of behavior, may become more peer-oriented and refuse guidance from their parents.

Another area of concern was the flight of 44,000 unaccompanied minors to the United States in 1975. Theses were children who were entrusted to friends and relatives who could leave Vietnam. Parents felt that their children's chances for a good life would improve in another country and placed them in the custody of others. Liu et al. (1979) reports that at Camp Pendleton, California, these children were identified and transferred to the unaccompanied children's quarters. In these separate quarters, they began to exhibit signs of deep depression, sleeplessness, somatic disorders, and suicidal tendencies. Many of these children were never reunited with their surrogate families but became pawns of the juvenile court system. They were placed in foster homes until they turned 18. At that time they are terminated from social services and financial aid. More than any other subgroup, this population of unaccompanied minors has been traumatized by the dissolution of the family system, culture conflict, and racism. Many of them have resorted to delinquent activities in their communities (Asian, Inc., 1983).

SOCIAL SERVICE INTERVENTION

Principles of Practice

The design of social service programs serving immigrant populations must first consider some basic principles of practice.

An essential aspect to helping is the ability to communicate in terms of language and to understand the basic values underlying behaviors and coping patterns. In this respect, it is imperative to have bilingual and bicultural workers assisting Vietnamese clients. Without the assistance of someone who can understand what they are going through or who can communicate with them, the refugees settlement process can be confusing, and services may not even address their central needs. Bilingual and bicultural workers can provide refugees with information regarding the nature of social services and assist the refugee client in obtaining them. The workers can also serve to interpret the refugee's point of view to agency personnel and act in behalf of the client to insure quality services.

The worker's role should go beyond that of a traditional social worker by serving the didactic function of teaching clients about American systems. This would minimize the degree of confusion experienced by those refugees who cannot comprehend Western ways. The development of "culturation" programs would also be instrumental in teaching refugees about American culture and serve to reduce their frustration by enhancing their understanding.

Conceptual Model of Intervention

The difficulties experienced by the Vietnamese refugees when they arrive point to the need for services designed to enhance their adjustment. Shortly after their initial arrival, numerous programs were established to teach the refugees English and job skills and to provide health services, mental health treatment, and social services. Each of these services was provided through its own traditional service delivery system. For example, English language courses were contracted out to the community colleges and public schools, employment to state and private employment agencies, and mental health services to mental health agencies. This model of intervention was probably the quickest and most cost-efficient means of getting the services to the refugees. However, the problem with this form of service provision was that services were divided into categories and lodged in agencies that traditionally had not worked together.

The maze of services offered in many refugee communities needs to be coordinated in order to reduce the confusion of refugees and support service agencies. A more ideal model of intervention would be a centralized agency that would provide a wide range of services to refugees. These services should include social service assessment, financial assessment, health and mental health screening, vocational training, and information referral. The development of referral protocols would serve to improve service delivery efficiency. The coordination of services would also enable those involved to identify problem areas and gaps in service delivery and develop ways of resolving them.

Another feature of an ideal model of intervention would be its geographic accessibility to Vietnamese refugees. The development of ethnic enclaves reflects the desire of Vietnamese refugees to live in close proximity to each other. This condition promotes economic development, community organization, and political strength in the larger society. Furthermore, the formation of geographic communities creates an environment where refugees can practice indigenous ways and begin to interrelate new and old cultural material. The emergence of churches, temples, and social organizations within the community provides refugees with a major source of social and emotional support and possibly compensates for the loss of family members. For example, senior citizen programs can be developed and lodged in churches to serve a variety of functions ranging from recreational activities to health services. Thus, maintaining a centralized agency within a geographic community would enhance accessibility and encourage participation.

Specific Skills for Intervention

On the practice level, many of the issues previously discussed have specific implications for mental health treatment. Refugees who experience guilt or depression over lost loved ones need to be treated before they are able to move ahead to other concerns. The worker should use skills that focus on reliving, analyzing, and working through the events contributing to feelings of client guilt or depression. The objective is to allow the client to accept the conditions or to aim toward a reconceptualization of the events that took place in order to reduce the possible feelings of self-blame. From there the client should be encouraged to move away from the stressful events and the associated thoughts.

The concepts of control or perceived control over one's environment may be essential in promoting the mental health of Vietnamese refugees who experience a significant degree of fatalism and helplessness. In these cases, an instructive, behavioral approach to treatment may allow clients to realize their domain of control over situations. The client is encouraged to set a realistic goal and then advance along a series of short, attainable steps toward the goal. Skill-building techniques and assertiveness training may also be useful for those clients who believe that life events are unchangeable and beyond their control.

The close-knit organization of the Vietnamese family warrants the use of family therapy whenever possible or appropriate. In cases where the family is experiencing turmoil due to structural realignments, the worker is required to make extensive assessments before intervention can take place. Problems stemming from the wife working can be addressed by encouraging a more equitable division of household labor so that she is not overburdened with responsibilities. Cognitive therapy techniques can be used to allow the husband to make situational attributions and not internal ones that reflect upon his inability to support his family. The building of confidence and self-esteem is especially important in cases where occupational changes have resulted in the underemployment of the husband. The husband must be able to see the value of new role behaviors that assign him more responsibilities in terms of child-rearing and household tasks.

Family members who have no economic value because of age restrictions that keep them out of the labor market are often at risk. Children and the elderly are often neglected by the working members of the family, and this condition may lead to "acting-out" or delinquent behavior by children and withdrawal or depression by the elderly. In such cases, intervention should aim to reintegrate displaced members into the family system so that they feel as though they contribute to its welfare. For example, the feelings of rolelessness and displacement expressed by the elderly may be alleviated by assigning them the role of family consultant. Although they may not be qualified to give advice on matters concerning Western culture, their general wisdom concerning life matters has many redeeming qualities.

Another potentially problematic situation stems from the pressures placed on children to succeed. Such pressures may lead to high anxiety and feelings of failure and guilt when expectations are not met. Intervention should emphasize an examination of different cultural norms, and parents may need to be reminded that their American-socialized children may have ideas and interests that may not coincide with their own. In this regard, they must realize that their children are entitled to their own pursuits and refrain from imposing their own self-interests upon them.

CONCLUSION

As carriers of an old culture enter a new one, reliable alignments need to be made before they can proceed. The merging of two cultures provides for complex, yet predictable, results. Characteristics of the old culture can be matched against those of the new, and predictions can be made as to what might ensue.

The significance of this chapter lies in the implications for providing culturally sensitive services to a growing refugee population and more specifically to provide practitioners with a context for understanding the conditions that constitute the Vietnamese American experience. Many lessons can be learned from policy errors made during the resettlement phase. Efforts to disperse the Vietnamese have proved futile as refugees follow the path of previous immigrant groups by forming their own communities. As future refugees arrive in the United States, policymakers need to be aware of this natural tendency and perhaps use their monies to enhance community development instead of discouraging it.

The study of special populations has just begun. As culturally trained personnel emerge, the development and reformulation of theories and models is the first move toward a better understanding of these groups. Conceptual knowledge is a requisite to responsible planning. Too often in the past, policies and practices have been based on ignorance and stereotypes, and a great deal of research and program development is needed to rectify the situation.

REFERENCES

Asian, Inc. (1983). Southeast Asian mental health conferences executive summary, University of San Francisco.

Atkinson, B. (1979). *Background Information on Refugees.* Olympia, Wash.: Bilingual Task Force.

Bui, D. (1983). The Indochinese mutual assistance associations. In Special Service for Groups (ed.), *Bridging Cultures: Southeast Asian Refugees in America.* Los Angeles: Special Service for Groups.

Chance, N. (1965). Acculturation, self-identification, and personality adjustment. *American Anthropologist* 67: 372–393.

Chen, P. N. (1979). A study of Chinese American elderly residing in hotel rooms. *Social Casework* 60 (2): 89–95.

Cheng, E. (1978). *The Elder Chinese.* San Diego: Campanile Press, San Diego State University.

Chu, J. (1983). The trauma of transition: Southeast Asian refugees in America. In Special Service for Groups (ed.), *Bridging Cultures: Southeast Asian Refugees in America.* Los Angeles: Special Service for Groups.

Fontana, A. F., J. L. Marcus, B. Noel, and J. M. Rakusin (1972). Prehospitalization coping styles of psychiatric patients: The goal-directedness of life events. *Journal of Nervous and Mental Disorders* 155: 311–321.

Harding, R. K., and J. G. Looney (1977). Problems of Southeast Asian children in a refugee camp. *American Journal of Psychiatry* 134: 407–411.

Ishikawa, W. H. (1978a). *The Elder Guamanian.* San Diego: Campanile Press, San Diego State University.

———— (1978b). *The Elder Samoan.* San Diego: Campanile Press, San Diego State University.

Ishisaka, H. (1977). Audio-training tapes focused on the mental health of Indochinese refugees. Seattle: Department of Health, Education, and Welfare Region X and the Asian Counseling and Referral Service.

Ishizuka, K. C. (1978). *The Elder Japanese.* San Diego: Campanile Press, San Diego State University.

Lin, K. M., and M. Masuda (1983). Impact of the refugee experience: Mental health issues of Southeast Asian refugees. In Special Service for Groups (ed.), *Bridging Cultures: Southeast Asian Refugees in America.* Los Angeles: Special Service for Groups.

Lin, K. M., L. Tazuma, and M. Masuda (1979). Adaptational problems of Vietnamese refugees. *Archives of General Psychiatry* 35: 955–961.

Liu, W. T., M. Lamanna, and A. K. Murata (1979). *Transition to Nowhere*. Nashville, Tenn.: Charter House Publishers.

Matsuoka, J. K. (1990). Differential acculturation among Vietnamese refugees: Implications for social work practice. *Social Work* 35 (4): 341–345.

Matsuoka, J. K., and D. Ryujin (1989/1990, Fall/Winter). Vietnamese refugees: An analysis of contemporary adjustment issues. *Journal of Applied Social Sciences* 14 (1): 23–45.

Maykovich, M. K. (1972). *Japanese American Identity Dilemma*. Tokyo: Waseda University Press.

Montero, D. (1979). *Vietnamese Americans: Patterns of Resettlement and Socioeconomic Adaptation in the United States*. Boulder, Colo.: Westview Press.

Pearlin, L. I., and M. A. Lieberman (1979). Social sources of emotional distress. In R. Simmons (ed.), *Research in Community and Mental Health*. Greenwich, Conn.: JAI Press.

Rahe, R. H., J. G. Looney, H. W. Ward, M. T. Tung, and W. T. Liu (1978). Psychiatric consultation in a Vietnamese refugee camp. *American Journal of Psychiatry* 135: 185–190.

Skinner, K., and G. Hendricks (1979). The shaping of ethnic self-identity among Indo-Chinese refugees. *Journal of Ethnic Studies* 7 (3): 25–41.

Smither, R., and M. Rodriguez-Giegling (1979). Marginality, modernity, and anxiety in Indochinese refugees. *Journal of Cross-Cultural Psychology* 10 (4): 469–478.

Spindler, G. D. (1968). Psychocultural adaptation. In E. Norbeck, D. Price-Williams, and W. M. McCord (eds.), *The Study of Personality: An Interdisciplinary Appraisal*. New York: Holt, Rinehart and Winston.

Sue, S., and D. W. Sue (1971). Chinese American personality and mental health. *Amerasia Journal* 1 (2): 36–49.

U.S. Bureau of the Census. (1988). *We, the Asian and Pacific Islander Americans*. Washington, D.C.: U.S. Government Printing Office.

U.S. Department of Health, Education, and Welfare (1976). HEW Refugee Task Force, Report to the Congress, Washington, D.C.: U.S. Government Printing Office.

U.S. Department of State (1976). Interagency Task Force on Indochina Refugees, Report to the Congress, Washington, D.C.: U.S. Government Printing Office.

Vinokur, A., and M. L. Selzer (1975). Desirable versus undesirable life events: Their relationship to stress and mental distress. *Journal of Personality and Social Psychology* 32: 329–337.

CHAPTER 8

Kānaka Maoli: Indigenous Hawaiians

KEKUNI BLAISDELL AND NOREEN MOKUAU

INTRODUCTION

Contemporary *kānaka maoli*, or indigenous Hawaiians (Blaisdell, 1989b), are no longer culturally one people as were their ancestors prior to the arrival of the first foreigners in 1778. Since that fateful time, *kānaka maoli* have become increasingly heterogeneous (Kanahele, 1982; Blaisdell, 1988; Andrade, 1989). Such differences include degree of *kānaka maoli* ancestry; range of traditional Hawaiianness in thought and behavior; Western educational and economic status; *'ohana* (family) relationships; housing, land, and ocean access; religious attitudes and political views; health needs; and related psychosocial variables. Much of the variation is the result of the impact of two centuries of Western exploitation with resulting conflict by the dominant *haole* (white) society (Young, 1980; Andrade, 1989; Blaisdell, 1989b).

Thus, overall *kānaka maoli* in the 1990s find themselves a minority at the bottom of a multiethnic hierarchy in their homeland (Native Hawaiian Study Commission, 1983; Thompson, 1983; Alu Like, 1985; Wegner, 1989). Still on top are the *haole* foreigners, while the Japanese, Chinese, Koreans, Filipinos, and Samoans are the other major later ethnic immigrants presently sharing the natural resources of the native host people.

Social service providers, in working with individual or groups of *kānaka maoli* clients, must take into account the variations within the culture. Providers also need to be aware, however, that in spite of the tragic plight of *kānaka maoli*, a growing number of these natives have begun to revitalize their culture. This resurgence, coupled with reempowerment of themselves as the first people of Hawaii, has come to be known as the Hawaiian Movement (Trask, 1984–1985).

This chapter presents information on history, sociodemographics, cultural values, and presenting problems of *kānaka maoli* and proposes intervention that may enhance the provision of social services to them. A glossary of Hawaiian terms appears at the end of the chapter.

HISTORICAL ORIGINS

Kānaka maoli ancestors were 1 of 50 widely dispersed Pacific Oceanic societies later called Polynesians by Westerners (Kirch, 1985). About A.D. 100, these seafaring voyagers, numbering perhaps 100, left their earlier South Pacific island home, now believed to be the Marquesas, to settle in a new homeland to the north, subsequently termed Hawaii. Having survived over 2,000 miles of open sea in double-hulled sailing canoes, they proliferated and formed a new nation.

Apparently, these voyagers also continued their north-south ocean journeys until 1200 A.D. and settled on other islands, including Tahiti (Fornander, 1969 [1878–1885]; Emory, 1959; Green, 1974). Thereafter, they remained in complete isolation for about 500 years. In these most secluded of islands, they attained a self-sufficient population of perhaps 1 million and refined a civilization that continues to fascinate the Western world (Stannard, 1988; Mitchell, 1982; Bushnell, 1990).

The subsequent 1778 chance arrival of the first foreigners, Captain James Cook and his crew, unleashed five devastating interrelated forces still evident today (Beaglehole, 1967; Blaisdell, 1989c): depopulation; foreign exploitation; cultural conflict; adoption of harmful foreign ways; and neglect, insensitivity, and malice from the ruling establishment.

Depopulation

Hawaii was rapidly depopulated from the estimated 1 million islanders to a nadir of 40,000 in 1893, the time of the United States' armed landing and overthrow of the Hawaiian kingdom (Stannard, 1988; Schmitt, 1977; Nordyke, 1989). Initially this decline was mainly due to introduced contagious infections to which the natives lacked immunity (Schmitt, 1969; Bushnell, 1990). By 1893, the 40,000 *kānaka maoli* were also outnumbered by 50,000 foreigners—20,000 whites and 30,000 Asians (Schmitt, 1977). More Asian laborers, imported by the ruling whites, were to follow (Fuchs, 1961; Daws, 1968; Nordyke, 1989). A slow upturn in the native population began about 1900 due to a rise in the birth rate; however, the high infant mortality and death rates continued the progressive decline of the population. Today there are less than 8,000 *piha kānaka maoli* (pure Hawaiians) remaining (Ikeda, 1987).

Foreign Exploitation

Many outsiders came, and continue to come, to Hawaii, not to live as *kānaka maoli* with *kānaka maoli* but to take from the native people and their natural resources. This began at the time of Cook with the replacement of the island subsistence-sharing economy with the for-profit barter and later money economy (Beaglehole, 1967; Trask, 1984–1985). Firearms, sandalwood, lumbering, whaling, cattle-ranching, Western military threats, and later sugar-growing supplanted the economic control of the ruling *ali'i* (chiefs), and these chiefs quickly became indebted to greedy *haole* merchants (Trask, 1984–1985; Daws, 1968; Bushnell, 1990).

Western legalized theft of native lands started with the *haole*-designed Mahele of 1848, which created private ownership of land (Kelly, 1980; Kame'eleihiwa, 1986). Within a generation, most of the private lands had passed into *haole* control for their capitalist business ventures. The *'āina* (land) was no longer a sacred trust for all but rather a commodity to serve immediate individual gratification. Loss of the *'āina* and access rights by natives led to disruption of the *'ohana* system and their alienation from the planting, fishing, and gathering ecosystems of their traditional *ahupua'a* (socioeconomic unit and extension of land extending from the ocean to the inland mountain ridge and including at least one valley) (Handy, Handy, and Pukui, 1972; Kame'eleihiwa, 1986; Kelly, 1989).

To these dislocations was added suppression of *kānaka maoli* religion, language, art, dance, music, the lunar calendar, education, and health care. This suppression came about through the influence of the New England Christian missionaries on the ruling *ali'i* after their arrival in 1820 and later through their occupation of key positions in the government that they designed (Kelly, 1988; Stueber, 1982; Tagupa, 1981). Dismantling of the *'ohana* and *kāhuna* (priest) on-the-job-training systems and their replacement by de-Hawaiinizing American classroom methods did not educate *kānaka maoli* for leadership but for subservience to *haole* rule in an un-Hawaiian, and often anti-Hawaiian, society (Fuchs, 1961; Stueber, 1982).

American imperialism culminated in 1893 with the U.S. military invasion of the independent kingdom of Hawaii and toppling of the native constitutional government (Blount, 1893). The new *haole* Provisional Government and the succeeding antidemocratic, self-proclaimed Republic of Hawaii denied voting rights to *kānaka maoli* and other nonwhites based on their alleged racial inferiority (Castle, 1981). The illegal annexation of Hawaii to the United States in 1898 was by congressional resolution rather than by treaty and statute, without the consent of or compensation to *kānaka maoli* and with the further taking of 2 million acres of native lands and their treasury (Native Hawaiian Study Commission, 1983; Trask, 1984–1985). Exploitation continued after the U.S.

establishment of the territory of Hawaii under the Organic Act of 1900 and with the establishment of statehood in 1959 because both situations occurred without the expressed approval of the native people.

Cultural Conflict

The pain of cultural conflict was immediately felt by the *kānaka maoli* who met the Cook expedition. The *kānaka maoli* were in conflict because of their attraction to firearms, other metal instruments, large sailing ships, the wheel, leather, clothing textiles, books, and freedom from the punishment of *kapu* (sacred law) violations. In 1819, despairing because the *kapu* were no longer effective, the ruling *ali'i* themselves formally abolished these official sacred laws, which had protected the natural resources and regulated human relationships for the common good (Kame'eleihiwa, 1986; Bushnell, 1990).

Cultural conflict was also evident in the eagerness with which some *ali'i* pursued material luxury by exploitation of *maka'āinana* (commoner) labor in sandalwood and other trade with Westerners (Kame'eleihiwa, 1986). Collaboration with foreigners on their terms invariably resulted in conflicting cultural values (Stueber, 1982). This clash of values resulted in loss of *kānaka maoli* identity and self-esteem. For many, this precipitated feelings of despair and a loss of willingness to live and further contributed to self-destructive behaviors (King, 1987; Andrade, 1989; Blaisdell, 1989c).

Adoption of Harmful Foreign Ways

Besides the vexing antitraditional attitudes described earlier, too many *kānaka maoli* have too eagerly embraced unwholesome Western lifestyles (Alu Like, 1985). These included consumption of tobacco, alcohol, and other toxic substances as well as diets containing saturated fat, cholesterol, sugar, and salt. Along with the consumption of unhealthy foods has come a decrease in concern for physical fitness. Adoption of other foreign ways has brought about an increasing disrespect for the environment, which has manifested itself in urban crowding, waste, pollution, and destruction of natural resources. Finally, *kānaka maoli* have become less able to cope with their stresses and to rely more heavily on government welfare and support (Blaisdell, 1989c; Andrade, 1989).

Neglect, Insensitivity, and Malice from the Ruling Establishment

The dominant Western society has been generally indifferent to the squalor of *kānaka maoli* and sometimes even hostile toward their culture and practices. Some examples are cited below.

- Since their arrival in 1820, Christian missionaries have regularly denounced the native religion and healing methods (Kame'eleihiwa, 1986; Bushnell, 1990).
- In 1859, the Queen's Hospital was chartered by the government of the Kingdom to save the *kānaka maoli* race by providing free medical care to "indigent sick and disabled Hawaiians." This service was to be supported by a hospital tax and private subscriptions (Greer, 1969). However, in 1909, eleven years after U.S. annexation, a minority of the all-white hospital board secretly deleted the terms "indigent" and "Hawaiians" from the hospital charter and ended government responsibility for needy and sick natives (Houston, 1950).
- Mounting pressure from *kānaka maoli* in 1922 led the U.S. Congress to set aside 200,000 acres of "ceded" lands for homesteading by natives with 50 percent or more *kānaka maoli* ancestry. The program failed because mostly third-class raw lands were awarded without adequate infrastructure and financing for housing. Most of the usable lands were commercially leased to non–*kānaka maoli* for income because no government funds were provided for administration of the program. In addition, many of the most suitable lands were transferred for other government purposes without payment of rent to the legal native beneficiaries (McGregor, 1990a).
- In 1985 a health study revealed that *kānaka maoli* had the worst health profile since annexation in 1900 (Alu Like, 1985). Top administrators of the State Department of Health were asked: "What are you doing about this?" Their response was: "Our department is color and race blind. . . . If Hawaiians choose not to use our services, the fault is not ours" (Bell, 1985).

These five interrelated historical factors continue in modulated form in the 1990s and contribute to the decline of *piha kānaka maoli* and the social and psychological problems that confront the people.

SOCIODEMOGRAPHIC OVERVIEW

The majority of *kānaka maoli* (204,000 or 68.6 percent) reside in Hawaii, while an estimated 90,000 (31.4 percent) live abroad in the continental United States, with a large number (50,000) residing in California (Barringer and O'Hagan, 1989). The following sociodemographic data reflect the circumstances of *kānaka maoli* in Hawaii in 1986. When useful, comparisons between *kānaka maoli* and other ethnic groups residing in Hawaii, including white, Japanese, Chinese, Filipino, and Samoans, are made. Comparisons are occasionally drawn between *piha kānaka maoli* and *hapa kānaka maoli* (part Hawaiian). Unless otherwise noted, most of the information is taken from Herbert Barringer and Patricia O'Hagan's (1989) *Socioeconomic Characteristics of Native Hawaiians*.

Population Census

In 1986, *kānaka maoli* in Hawaii were estimated to number 204,000. This represented 20 percent of the total state population of 1.024 million

(Ikeda, 1987). This population, however, was mostly comprised of *hapa kānaka maoli* (196,400 or 96.2 percent), while *piha kānaka maoli* continued to decline to less than 8,000 (3.8 percent, Ikeda, 1987).

Distribution

Distribution of *kānaka maoli* by island, in descending order, was: Oahu, 137,500 (67 percent); Hawaii, 33,000 (16 percent), Maui, 18,800 (9.3 percent); Kauai, 10,700 (5.4 percent); Molokai, 4,100 (2 percent); Lanai, 200; and Niihau, 200 (State of Hawaii, Department of Health, 1988). Island distribution by proportion of *kānaka maoli*, in descending order was: Niihau, 99 percent; Molokai, 60 percent; Hawaii, 30 percent; Maui, 22 percent; Kauai, 22 percent; Oahu, 17 percent; and Lanai, 10 percent (State of Hawaii, Department of Health, 1986). The highest proportion of all island ethnic groups, 21 percent of *kānaka maoli*, tended to reside in rural areas.

Gender and Age

Gender distribution of *kānaka maoli* since 1950 has been about equal. Only above age 65 do women outnumber men.

When comparing *kānaka maoli* with other ethnic groups, they have the youngest age distribution, with a mean age of 24.8 years. However, this younger age distribution reflects the *hapa kānaka maoli* inasmuch as the *piha kānaka maoli* show a mean age of 45.3 years.

Health

In comparison to other ethnic groups in Hawaii, the birth rate for *kānaka maoli* in 1985 was the highest at 31.5/1,000 births. However, this rate represented the first decline since 1970 when there were 50.9/1,000 births. The overall death rate for *kānaka maoli* in 1985 was the greatest of all ethnic groups at 5.6/1,000. It is noteworthy that *piha kānaka maoli* showed the lowest birth rate (0.8/1,000) and the highest death rate (20/1,000).

Mortality rates continued to be highest for *kānaka maoli* for the major causes of death, namely heart disease, cancer, stroke, accidents, diabetes, and infections (Alu Like, 1985; U.S. Congress, Office of Technology, 1987; Wegner, 1989). Rates for *piha kānaka maoli* were higher than for *hapa kānaka maoli*. Infant mortality was also highest for *kānaka maoli* in comparison with all other ethnic groups in Hawaii.

Life expectancy at birth in 1980 for *kānaka maoli* was 74 years, the shortest compared to the other ethnic groups (Gardner, 1980; 1984).

Family and Household

Kānaka maoli households were larger (3.4 persons per household) than those of whites and Japanese but slightly smaller than for Filipinos (3.6 per household). They also had the lowest rate of male householders (56 percent) and the highest rate of female householders with no husbands (21.3 percent). A consistent pattern since 1950, the rate for *kānaka maoli* men marrying non–*kānaka maoli* was the highest (56.5 percent) when compared with men of other ethnic backgrounds. The divorce/annulment rate when compared with other groups was the lowest, in overall rates (11.5 percent) and within-group rates (47 percent). The owner-occupied housing rate for *kānaka maoli* was 47 percent, ranking after whites, Japanese, Filipinos, and Chinese and just ahead of Samoans.

Education

When compared with other ethnic groups in Hawaii, overall educational levels were the lowest for *kānaka maoli*; high school completion, 44.8 percent; some college education, 18.2 percent; college degree, 5.6 percent; and doctoral level completion, 0.8 percent.

Occupations

Kānaka maoli in 1980 had less representation (8 percent) in high-prestige, high-salary managerial and professional jobs compared to other ethnic groups. They had greater representation in service positions, such as truck and bus drivers. *Kānaka maoli* ranked highest (35 percent) for proportion not in the labor force and for unemployed (7 percent). Finally, the lowest percentage of privately owned businesses (1.6 percent) was attributed to *kānaka maoli* ownership.

Data on income revealed *kānaka maoli* to have the lowest average incomes; mean personal income of $12,300, mean household income of $19,501, mean family income of $19,800, and mean female household income of $12,000. They had the highest rate of poverty (14.3 percent) when compared with other ethnic groups in Hawaii.

Interestingly, the 1980 Census data for the continental U.S. *kānaka maoli* were similar to those for island Hawaiians (Barringer and O'Hagan, 1989). This is surprising because migration from Hawaii to the continent is usually associated with better job opportunities. However, it appears that migration to the continental United States did not result in better incomes inasmuch as both personal and household incomes in Hawaii and the continental United States were the same.

WORLDVIEWS AND BEHAVIORAL NORMS

Traditionally, *kānaka maoli* trace their origins to Kumulipo* (dark source), with the mating of Wākea, the sky father, to Papa, the earth mother, from which everything in the cosmos was born and continues to be derived (Johnson, 1982). Great men became chiefs, and great chiefs became gods (Buck, 1939). But then, even honored *kūpuna* (ancestors or elders) of *maka'āinana* became *'aumākua*, or ever-present family guardian gods. Countless spiritual forces appeared as *kinolau* (many forms), not only as departed or present *kānaka* but as plants, animals, rocks, rain clouds, and winds. Indeed, the entire cosmos was living, conscious, and communicating (Malo, 1951; Kamakau, 1964; Handy, 1927; Handy and Pukui, 1958; Luomala, 1989). Because of common parentage from Wakea and Papa, the *kānaka maoli* considered the individual *lōkahi* (united) with all in the cosmos.

Gods by definition had greater inherent *mana* (specific quantifiable energy) than *kānaka*. The *ali'i* had greater *mana* by birth than *maka'āinana*. However, even *maka'āinana* could acquire *mana* by developing the skills of a master navigator, fierce warrior, productive fisherman, talented chanter, or effective healer (Handy and Pukui, 1958; Pukui, Haertig, and Lee, 1972; Pukui, Haertig, Lee, and McDermott, 1979).

Pālua (dualism) of complementary opposites was also recognized, such as sky and earth, day and night, sun and moon, male and female, right and left, fire and water, material and spiritual, health and illness, good and evil, and life and death (Handy, 1927; Luomala, 1989). *Pono*, or proper order or harmony of these interacting, cyclic, and opposing forces, required conscious effort of each individual *kānaka*. Thus, continuous informal communication with self, one's *'aumākua*, and all of nature was punctuated by daily formal rituals (Handy, 1927; Handy and Pukui, 1958).

Kapu, established by the *kāhuna* (priest specialists), sanctioned by the ruling *ali'i*, and enforced by all, was society's way of preserving *pono* for the common good (Handy, 1927; Pukui et al., 1979; Kame'eleihiwa, 1986).

Imbalance of *mana* or loss of *pono* accounted for misfortune, such as illness, sparse catch of *i'a* (fish), or crop failure (Handy, 1927; Pukui et al., 1972; Pukui et al., 1979). While there was collective *lōkahi* and interdependence with self, others, and all of nature, nevertheless, individual self-reliance was expected (Pukui et al., 1972; Pukui et al., 1979).

Each child was a precious *pua* (flower) assuring perpetuation of the race. *Mākua* (adults) were the providers, and the *kūpuna* were esteemed.

---

*The name of a chant thought to be composed about A.D. 1700, but not recorded until 1881 and first translated into English by Queen Lili'uokalani in 1897.

Death after a meaningful life was welcomed as a reunion with one's departed *kūpuna* in the eternal spiritual *ao* (realm). Death also signified the completion of a recurring cycle of rebirth and transfiguration into *kinolau* or reincarnation into other human forms (Kamakau, 1964; Pukui et al., 1972; Pukui et al., 1979). Thus, the *kānaka* considered the self during his or her *ola* (individual physical existence) as part of a continuum extending from the *kūpuna* to the present *'ohana* and nature, and to the *kamali'i* (offspring) and *mamo* (succeeding generations). An individual alone, without these relationships, was "unthinkable" (Handy and Pukui, 1958).

The traditional law of the land was *aloha 'āina* or *mālama 'āina* (love and care for the land) (Handy and Pukui, 1958; Kame'eleihiwa, 1986; McGregor, 1990b). The resources of the *'āina* nurtured *kānaka maoli*, and thus it was the responsibility of *kānaka maoli* to care for the *'āina* for future generations. *Kānaka* were stewards, not private owners, of the *'āina*. Their subsistence economy required mutual *mālama* (caring). The fisherman provided his catch not only for himself but for everyone in the *ahupua'a*. Similarly, the taro planter shared the harvest, and the *mauka* (upland) forester supplied wood for fellow *ahupua'a* residents (Handy and Pukui, 1958; Handy et al., 1972). To intentionally harm others or anything in nature was to harm oneself.

This ideal of pursuing harmonious relationships (*pono*) amongst themselves and all in their environment was manifest in the temperament of the natives as recorded by the earliest writers. Cook's journals describe the disposition of the islanders in a positive manner as hospitable, friendly, and cheerful (Beaglehole, 1967). Samuel M. Kamakau, a pioneer native historian, referred to pre-Western *kānaka maoli* as "a strong and hard-working people, skilled in crafts and possessed of much learning. In hospitality and kindness they excelled" (Kamakau, 1961, p. 237).

Contact with the non-*kānaka* world beginning in 1778 shattered the foregoing holistic views and practices of the island natives. Cultural conflict with Western domination and exploitation led to rapid discarding of many of the old beliefs and ways previously described. Thus, today, few modern *kānaka maoli* are familiar with many of the traditions sketched in historical accounts (Pukui et al., 1972; Pukui et al., 1979). Nevertheless, every *kānaka maoli* who identifies as one, and especially the rural native who has been able to remain close to the *'āina*, retains some remnants of the old concepts in his or her bones, although the ability to articulate these concepts may be lacking.

Cultural conflict results in a daily struggle within the self. Traditional values call for group affiliation, sharing with others, caring for nature, working together within the *'ohana* system for common goals, spiritual oneness with the land, and respect for the inherent value of everything in the cosmos. In contrast, the necessity for survival in the dominant

Western world demands individual competitive assertion for personal power, exploitation of others, materialism, commercialization of native culture, waste pollution, and destruction of the *'āina* and other natural resources (Trask, 1984–1985; Aluli, 1988; McGregor, 1990b).

The constant pressure by the dominant Western society on *kānaka maoli* to assimilate always carries the guilt of betrayal to the ways of native ancestors (Kanahele, 1990). Cultural pluralism, so popularly promoted in the communications media and Western schools, with its promise of "equal opportunity," has a hollow ring when it demands compliance to the *haole*, not *kānaka maoli*, frame of reference. The tragedy becomes amplified with the recognition that forced assimilation occurs in the *kānaka maoli's* own homeland. Non–*kānaka maoli* in Hawaii have their ethnic roots in their homelands elsewhere. *Kānaka maoli* have no other homeland than Hawaii. Yet, in their native land they are compelled to behave as non-*kānaka* Westerners in order to survive (Kame'eleihiwa, 1986; Blaisdell, 1989a; 1989b).

The varying intensities of cultural conflict account for three main, yet sometimes overlapping, subsets of modern *kānaka maoli* (Blaisdell, 1988):

1. One is the growing assortment of assimilated *kānaka*-Americans. Many of these people are ashamed and afraid to be *kānaka maoli*. They admit to being *kānaka* only when it is convenient. Mostly urban, including many in the continental United States, they are so de-Hawaiianized and Westernized that they are usually indistinguishable from *haole* in thinking and behavior. Looking to the continental United States as their ideal, they seem oblivious of the injustices to, and the resulting agony of, the majority of their fellow *kānaka maoli*.

2. Second is a large category of *kānaka maoli* pluralists. That is, those bicultural *kānaka maoli* who perceive themselves as another of the several minorities with "equal opportunity" in Hawaiian multiracial society. However, they do not seem to realize that opportunities are really *not* equal because the governing system is Western, not *kānaka maoli*, and indeed it continues to be anti-*kānaka*.

3. Third is a recently expanding, loose coalition of *kānaka maoli* by ancestry and conviction. These are *kānaka maoli* nationalists. Many are rural; others are college educated. Joined by some non–*kānaka maoli* supporters, they are revitalizing their traditional culture and empowering themselves to relieve the suffering of their people.

PROFILE OF SOCIAL AND PSYCHOLOGICAL PROBLEMS AND ISSUES

The historical and other background information cited in the previous sections has remained little known and only as scattered fragments until recently. This information was largely hidden from public awareness because of the official policy of the dominant Western society to promote assimilation of *kānaka maoli* and other nonwhite islander minorities (Fuchs, 1961; Daws, 1968; Stueber, 1982; Trask, 1984–1985). However, *kānaka maoli* unrest in the 1980s resulted in several published assessments on the status of *kānaka maoli*. One of these, the 1985 E Ola Mau Mental Health Task Force Report, identifies six major problems in the psycho-social profile of the native islanders: alcohol and other substance abuse, family violence, crime, school alienation, psychological disorders, and suicide (Alu Like, 1985; Takeuchi, Higginbotham, Marsella, Gomes, Kwan, Ostrowski, Rocha, and Wight, 1987).

While multiple causal factors underlie these problems, public attention has increasingly focused on cultural conflict and resulting despair as the genesis of such problems in *kānaka maoli*. Recommendations for culturally sensitive, trained personnel and programs represent a new direction that has increasingly drawn greater support (Mokuau, 1985; 1987; 1990a; 1990b; Andrade, 1989; E Ola Mau, 1990). Supporting data on problem areas experienced by *kānaka maoli* are uneven; the following sections profile three problems, on which some data are available, commonly associated with this population.

Family Violence: Child Abuse

In 1987, children of *kānaka maoli* ancestry had the highest number of cases per year of confirmed abuse and neglect cases (621, 25 percent) when compared with children of other ethnicities in Hawaii (State of Hawaii, Department of Human Services, 1988). However, when controlling for population size, *kānaka maoli* rank second to Samoans for cases of abuse and neglect. In an earlier study by G. W. Starbuck, N. Krantzier, K. Forbes, and V. Barnes (1984), it was reported that associated risk factors for child abuse and neglect included young maternal age and low socioeconomic status. These factors suggest stressful home factors and a lack of *'ohana* network to provide support in child-rearing (Dubanoski, 1982).

Severe child abuse is at variance with traditional *kānaka maoli* practices (Pukui et al., 1972; Pukui et al., 1979). The few reported studies in modern rural communities indicate that discipline of children is viewed as an *'ohana* duty of the adults. Once beyond toddlerhood, a child is expected to behave well, tend to assigned responsibilities, and respect elders. While harsh physical punishment may occur for serious infractions, this is unusual, is done openly, and may be performed by any adult in the *'ohana*. Thus, the discipline tends to be mitigated, and serious injury is rare (Korbin, 1990).

Family health education, such as the Kamehameha Schools Kupulani Demonstration Project in Honolulu may provide data to enhance childcare in a culturally appropriate way (Kaaa, 1982). The project assists *kānaka maoli* in nurturing adaptive learning skills and attitudes in their children beginning in pregnancy. The project emphasizes affective as well as cognitive learning, cultural relevance in prenatal and infant care, and continuity.

Crime

In 1979, although *kānaka maoli* were *not* overrepresented in police pre-trial arrests, with a rate of 15 percent, they had the highest rates for felon conviction and imprisonment (31 percent, Kassebaum, 1987). The more serious the crime or lengthy the incarceration, the higher the percentage of *kānaka maoli. Kānaka maoli* were also less likely to be transferred out of prison for psychiatric services, compared to other ethnic groups. More recent data suggest an increase in arrests during the 1980s: *Kānaka maoli* juveniles have the highest rates of arrests in terms of larceny, theft, burglary, assault, and vandalism, and *kānaka maoli* adults have arrest rates second only to whites (State of Hawaii, Department of Attorney General, 1988). Low socioeconomic status combined with unemployment, school impairment, and substance abuse are usually linked with crime.

The design and development of criminal justice programs with culturally appropriate intervention is long overdue. One example of a culturally designed program is Ho'ulu Kuahiwi (Let the Mountains Produce), a wilderness program developed and operated by the John Howard Association in Honolulu (Reardon, 1990). The program serves' adjudicated youth, primarily of *kānaka maoli* ancestry, and is based on a premise that intervention that is rich in cultural values and traditions best serves the rehabilitation of the youth. Cultural elements that are incorporated into the program include: (a) the focus on the youth in context of the family, (b) appreciation of the *'āina,* and (c) use of *ho'oponopono* (to make right), an indigenous form of dispute resolution.

Suicide

Beginning in 1958, *kānaka maoli* males had the highest suicide rate—for the 1978–1982 period, the rate was 29.2 per 100,000—when compared to other ethnic groups in Hawaii and in the continental United States (Chiu, 1979; State of Hawaii, Department of Health, 1986). Suicide was especially prominent among males ages 20 to 24, with a rate of 25.8 per 100,000, during the years from 1973 to 1987 (Tseng, Shu, Omori, and McLaughlin, forthcoming).

The continued high rate of suicide among young *kānaka maoli* males is disturbing. School dysfunction, unemployment, illicit drugs, crime, and lack of proper access to the land and sea for self-support may be significant factors. Psychosocial problems have been analyzed as arising when behavior in the process of conforming to, or deviating from, common cultural values results in maladaptation or ineffective social interactions (McDermott, Tseng, and Maretzki, 1980; Marsella and White, 1982). This pattern of progressive increase in suicide in young males has also been observed in other Pacific Islanders, most notably Micronesians and Samoans (Hezel, Rubinstein, and White, 1985).

Evolution of Culturally Sensitive Services

A separate issue aggravating *kānaka maoli* psychosocial problems is the inadequate availability, accessibility, and acceptability of social and related services for *kānaka maoli* peoples. Throughout most of Hawaii's post-Western contact history, government and social services have followed Western patterns, even though most of the clients or beneficiaries have been *kānaka maoli* (Catton, 1959; Kamakahi, 1989). In addition, white, Western-educated professionals have been recruited to manage these organizations, and they have done so without regard to local cultural needs (Catton, 1959; Higginbotham, 1987; Sanders, 1986).

An encouraging exception occurred during the years 1914 to 1928 when *kānaka maoli* leaders in Honolulu attempted to meet the pressing needs of indigent Hawaiians by founding Ahahui Pu'uhonua (Hawaiian Protective Association) (McGregor, 1990b). Alarmed by the open homelessness, hunger, illness, disability, and drunkenness of *kānaka maoli* in the city's streets, Ahahui Pu'uhonua engaged mainly Hawaiian church-going volunteers to provide health education and family social services for the indigent. Despite the strong motivating factor of ancestral pride of *lōkahi* as a people, Ahahui Pu'uhonua withered away because of a lack of financial support.

A more effective turning point came much later in the 1960s. Political activism of the 1960s served to identify the problems of *kānaka maoli*, renew a sense of cultural pride, and increase demands for improved and appropriate services. Initially fueled by the disenchantment of rural *kānaka maoli* communities with the booming tourist industry and the continual demand for more land for resorts, several concerted efforts occurred from the 1960s to the 1980s. These changes are suggestive of an evolution of culturally appropriate services.

• In 1962, the Queen Lili'uokalani Children's Center collaborated with other organizations to initiate anthropological and psychological field research on *kānaka maoli*. The results included: (a) the provision of training for staff members in culturally sensitive strategies; (b) several publications, especially the best-selling two-volume *Nānā I Ke Kumu*, with noted authorities Mary Kawena Pukui and E. W. Haertig as senior authors; and (c) an increased awareness among the *kānaka maoli* community on the impact of Western culture on their ancestral values and traditions.

- In 1974, the University of Hawaii, School of Social Work, with support from the Queen Lili'uokalani Children's Center, developed a Hawaiian Learning Program. This program was intended to provide culture-specific training to specially recruited *kānaka maoli* students. During a six-year period, the program graduated forty-eight social worker students with masters degrees in social work (Oda, 1974; Apoliona and Keanu, 1976; Higginbotham, 1987).

- Also in 1974, Alu Like, a nonprofit organization eligible to receive federal and other funds for *kānaka maoli* "economic and self-sufficiency," was established.

- In 1978, as a result of a class suit against the State of Hawaii Department of Health for inadequate services to non-English-speaking residents, an Ethno-cultural Task Force was established. It recommended that "services be delivered on the basis of people's cultural needs, and not on the basis of what is convenient for the institution and the service providers" (Higginbotham, 1987).

- During the 1980s, ferment in *kānaka* communities continued. Three reports were to augment the momentum toward reform: (a) The 1983 Native Hawaiian Educational Assessment Project of the Bishop Estates/Kamehameha Schools documented the roles of low socioeconomic status, crosscultural tensions, and ill health of *kānaka maoli* students; (b) the 1983 Native Hawaiian Study Commission Report to the U.S. Congress boldly proposed correction of historical injustices by return of stolen lands to *kānaka maoli* (Native Hawaiian Study Commission, 1983); and (c) the 1985 E Ola Mau Native Hawaiian Health Needs Study provided a comprehensive description of the impoverished health status of *kānaka maoli* (Alu Like, 1985).

Two significant events occurred in the mid- and late 1980s that have had implications for culturally sensitive services. One was the founding in March 1986 of E Ola Mau, an organization of *kānaka maoli* health workers committed to the health of their people. Second was the participation of E Ola Mau and other organizations and individuals in the passage of the Native Hawaiian Health Care Act of 1988 (U.S. Congress, 1988). The key provisions, detailed in the sections to follow, were: (a) incorporation of traditional Hawaiian cultural values and practitioners; and (b) empowerment by "maximum participation of Native Hawaiians" in planning and implementing health promotion, disease prevention, and primary health care programs for *kānaka maoli*.

SOCIAL SERVICE INTERVENTION

Principles of Practice

Five related principles of practice provide broad guidelines for practitioners working with *kānaka maoli* clients.

1. Assessment of psychosocial problems confronting *kānaka maoli* must go beyond conventional variables. The worker must also investigate evidence of persistent exploitation, cultural conflict, and neglect or abuse by the establishment in each case. This requires awareness and a special body of knowledge and skills that matches the unique needs of the group.

2. In order for intervention to be effective for all *kānaka maoli*, it must operate on at least three levels: (a) with the individual in a one-to-one worker/client relationship; (b) with the identified individual in context of his or her *'ohana*, other concerned parties in the client's social milieu, and relevant community resources; and (c) with the community in terms of the eradication of institutional racism and oppression. This means launching new and effective programs for and by *kānaka maoli* to assure that such services are available, accessible, and acceptable (Alu Like, 1985; Wegner, 1989).

3. Promotion of, support for, and participation in the revitalization of traditional *kānaka maoli* culture are necessary (Young, 1980; Chang, Durante, Nāhulu, and Wong, 1980). This is essential to bolster native self-image and to instill a sense of self-confidence that will help *kānaka maoli* cope with life's stresses and in particular to facilitate the resuming of wholesome thinking and ways of their ancestors and to discard self-destructive foreign ways (Alu Like, 1985; Wegner, 1989; E Ola Mau, 1990).

4. Empowerment of individual *kānaka maoli* clients and their *'ohana* in their problem-solving and of *kānaka maoli* community groups in the planning and implementation of culturally competent programs must be fostered. This requires special training of *kānaka maoli* personnel (Alu Like, 1985; Wegner, 1989; U.S. Congress, 1988).

5. Programs must be targeted where the needs are greatest, such as in underserved Hawaiian homestead communities and in urban *kānaka maoli* ghettos (Alu Like, 1985; Wegner, 1989). This requires more effective use of resources originally designated for *kānaka maoli*, including private and public trusts (Native Hawaiian Study Commission, 1983; Alu Like, 1985; Wegner, 1989) and recent legislation (U.S. Congress, 1988; 1990).

Conceptual Models

No single model can be expected to meet the needs of *kānaka maoli* because of the diversity of the people. Rather, models should be individualized depending on the problem, the client, the setting, and the degree and nature of cultural conflict. With these factors in mind, three general models are proposed.

Western Assimilation Model. Assuming that assimilation into the dominant Western mode is the ideal for ethnic minorities, the current American social service system is promoted. Based on professional ideology, with centralized bureaucratic authority, control of resources, and standardization of procedures, the system is staffed by Western-trained, English-speaking workers who expect clients to conform regardless of their cultural heritage (Higginbotham, 1987). Such an approach may be appropriate for Western-acculturated *kānaka maoli*. A limitation of this model is that it is not appropriate for many *kānaka maoli* clients who maintain traditional cultural perspectives (Alu Like, 1985; Andrade, Blaisdell, Forman, Leung, Matsumoto, and Takeuchi, 1987; E Ola Mau, 1990).

Indigenous Model: Hale Ola. Hale Ola Ho'opakolea healing resource center was designed and established in 1981 to serve the *kānaka maoli* of the Nanakuli-Wai'anae community (Nāhulu, 1990). Based on the premise that "people heal themselves through their own cultural patterns," Hale Ola features: (a) traditional *kānaka maoli* holistic cultural values and practices interfacing, as appropriate with the modern Western system; (b) a staff of Western-trained but culturally competent *kānaka maoli* professionals and paraprofessionals and a referral system of traditional healers; and (c) a community-controlled entity with support from private and government sources (Higginbotham, 1987; Nāhulu, 1990). Such a model may be appropriate for traditional or bicultural *kānaka maoli* clients. Major limitations of this model include overwhelming community needs, inadequate financial resources, and limited trained personnel.

Health System Model: Native Hawaiian Islandwide Health Model. The U.S. Congress Native Hawaiian Health Care Act of 1988 advocates the raising of the health status of *kānaka maoli* to the highest possible level and encourages maximum participation of *kānaka maoli* to achieve this objective (U.S. Congress, 1988). The health system model calls for: (a) nine islandwide community-based health systems established by *kānaka maoli* organizations; (b) incorporation of traditional healing concepts and practitioners; and (c) coordinated administration, planning, training, and evaluation by a five-member board called Papa Ola Lōkahi. Major limitations of this model include a lack of trained *kānaka maoli* personnel and insufficient funds to assure success and long-term commitment (E Ola Mau, 1990).

Specific Skills

Relationship Development. Knowledge and skills in the broad spectrum of contemporary *kānaka maoli* thinking and behavior are basic. This begins with "entry etiquette." Many *kānaka maoli* are generally sensitive to pretense, "phoniness," and attempts to set oneself apart and above. Appearance should be simple and modest. This type of modesty may be reflected by female workers by wearing no hats, no heels, and no excessive makeup or jewelry. For men, this may translate to no coats, no ties, and no fancy automobiles (Chang et al., 1980; Nāhulu, 1990).

While the initial appointment by telephone may succeed with Western acculturated *kānaka maoli*, going to the client's home to "talk story" enhances rapport with many *kānaka maoli* in need of social services. Talk story is informal dialog that may involve the use of Pidgin (Hawaiian-Creole-English) words, joking, personal disclosures, folk tales, and verbal play to promote shared feelings (Howard, 1974; Boggs, 1985). Through this medium, the client tests the worker's degree of appreciation of ancestral *kānaka maoli* values that persist in modern times. These include *'ohana* and *lāhui* (nation, race) affiliation, respect for elders, assigned *kuleana* (responsibilities) for each member of the *'ohana*, affection for infants, sharing, equality and freedom among peers, and spiritual attachment to the *'āina*, including the sea and, indeed, all of nature (Pukui et al., 1972; Pukui et al., 1979; Ito, 1987). Spiritualism may involve communicating with *'aumākua* (departed ancestral deities) who may reappear as *kinolau*, such as the wind, the lizard, or human reincarnations. Communication may be through omens, visions, dreams, voices, or just "feelings" (Pukui et al., 1972; Pukui et al., 1979; Rocha, 1985).

Familiarity with common *kānaka maoli* expressions is essential; however, mastery of the Hawaiian language is rarely necessary at the present time. Very few *kānaka maoli* speak their mother language. It is important to note that a new generation of preschoolers is learning the mother tongue in culture-language immersion programs (Kimura, 1989), and in the near future bilingual workers may be more important.

Problem Assessment and Intervention. Problem assessment calls for skills in identifying the underlying factors responsible for the presenting problem, and intervention requires the formulation of an effective plan with the client and *'ohana* for dealing with these factors. Skill in probing in culturally acceptable ways, skill in dealing with traumatic cultural conflict, and skill in devising realistic, constructive steps toward resolution usually involve two kinds of changes. First, the client and *'ohana* may need to conform in order to cope with the dominant Western system. Second, the established system must be made to respect the basic right of the native people to live their own way in their own homeland, as long as it is not harmful to themselves and others. Thus, the worker must simultaneously use his or her skills as a patient teacher or coach with skills of an activist and advocate.

Indigenous healing methods, such as *ho'oponopono* or structured family sessions, *kāhea* (calling for a response), *lā'au* (medicinal herbs), *lomilomi* (massage), and *hāhā* (palpation), may be helpful. In such instances, specially trained resource persons may be engaged (Pukui et al., 1972; Pukui et al., 1979; Mokuau, 1990a; 1990b).

CONCLUSION

Kānaka maoli, when compared to other ethnic groups in their own homeland, continue to have the worst overall profile of socioeconomic and health needs. This painful status is largely the outcome of native depopulation, beginning over 200 years ago, followed by foreign over-population, exploitation, cultural conflict, native acquisition of harmful foreign ways, and negligence and sometimes malice by the dominant society. The major presenting problems and issues demand social service intervention that is undergirded by an awareness of the historical origins of many problems, a promotion of culturally appropriate solutions, and the empowerment of *kānaka maoli* clients. In addition to the treatment of problems that already exist, the social service provider must also address prevention efforts designed to stop and reverse the effects of institutional racism and exploitation. Such recommendations are ambitious and formidable, but they represent a challenge to the *kānaka maoli* who have already begun to mobilize in partnership with social service providers to enhance services in the 1990s and beyond.

GLOSSARY

Hawaiian	English
ahupua'a	socioeconomic unit; extension of land from the ocean to the mountain
'āina	land
ali'i	chiefs
aloha 'āina	love for the land
ao	realm
'aumākua	family gods
hāhā	palpitation
haole	white
hapa kānaka maoli	part Hawaiian
ho'oponopono	to make right
i'a	fish
kāhea	calling for a response
kāhuna	priest
kamali'i	offspring
kānaka maoli	native Hawaiian(s)
kapu	sacred law
kinolau	many forms
kuleana	responsibilities

kūpuna	ancestors/elders
lā'au	medicinal herbs
lāhui	nation, race
lōkahi	unity
lomilomi	massage
maka'āinana	commoner
mākua	adults
mālama	care, caring
mamo	succeeding generations
mana	energy/power
mauka	upland
'ohana	family
ola	individual physical existence
pālua	dualism
piha kānaka maole	pure Hawaiian
pono	proper order or harmony
pua	flower

REFERENCES

Aluli, N. E. (1988, July). Interview by B. Uprichard. *Honolulu Magazine* 23 (1): 42.

Alu Like (1985). *E Ola Mau Native Hawaiian Health Needs Study*. Honolulu.

Andrade, N. N. (1989). Native Hawaiian Mental Health Research Center. Proposal submitted to National Institute of Mental Health from University of Hawaii, Honolulu.

Andrade, N. N., K. Blaisdell, S. Forman, D. Leung. S. Matsumoto, and D. Takeuchi (1987, June 9). *Service Utilization of VA Health Care Facilities: A Summary of Cross-Cultural Issues*. Honolulu: University of Hawaii.

Apoliona, H., and E. I. Keanu (1976). The development of a scale measuring degrees of Hawaiianness through cultural knowledge. Master's thesis, University of Hawaii School of Social Work, Honolulu.

Apoliona, H., A. Nāhulu, H. Chang, N. Minton, and K. Isaacs (1990, September 5–8). *Native Hawaiian Traditional Practitioners' Forum*. Honolulu: E Ola Mau.

Barringer, H., and P. O'Hagan (1989). *Socioeconomic Characteristics of Native Hawaiians*. Honolulu: Alu Like.

Beaglehole, J. C. (ed.) (1967). *The Journals of Captain James Cook on His Voyages of Discovery, The Voyage of the Resolution and the Discovery, 1776–80*, volume 3. London: Cambridge University.

Bell, B. Z. (ed.) (1985, November). *E Ola Mau Native Hawaiian Health Needs Study Conference Proceedings*. Honolulu: Alu Like.

Blaisdell, K. (1988, January 3). After Ho'olako predictions. *Sunday Star-Bulletin Advertiser*, p. B-1.

——— (1989a, February 21). Hawaiians are still the state's landless. *Star-Bulletin.*

——— (1989b). "Hawaiian" vs. "Kanaka Maoli" as metaphors. In D. Chenoweth (ed.), *Hawaii Review* (Board of Publications, University of Hawaii Mānoa) 13 (3): 77–79.

——— (1989c). Historical and cultural aspects of Native Hawaiian health. In E. L. Wegner (ed.), *Social Process in Hawaii* 32: 1–21.

Blount, J. (1893). *Report to U.S. Congress: Hawaiian Islands.* In Executive Document No. 46, 53rd Congress, Washington, D.C.

Boggs, S. T. (1985). *Speaking, Relating and Learning.* Norwood, N.J.: Ablex Publishing.

Boggs, S. T., and M. Naea Chun (1990). Ho'oponopono: A Hawaiian method of solving interpersonal problems. In K. A. Watson-Gegeo and G. M. White (eds.), *Disentangling Conflict Discourse in Pacific Societies.* Stanford, Calif.: Stanford University Press.

Buck, P. H. (1939). *Anthropology and Religion.* New Haven: Yale University.

Bushnell, O. A. (1990). *The Sliding Way of Death: The Effects of Introduced Infectious Diseases Upon the Social History of Hawai'i.* Honolulu: University of Hawaii Press.

Castle, A. L. (1981). The Dole-Burgess letters. *Hawaiian Journal of History* 15: 24.

Catton, M.M.L. (1959). *Social Service in Hawaii.* Palo Alto, Calif.: Pacific Books.

Chang, L., K. Durante, L. Nāhulu, and R. Wong (1980). The Hawaiians. In N. Palafox and A. Warren (eds.), *Cross-Cultural Caring: A Handbook for Health Care Professionals in Hawaii.* Honolulu: Transcultural Health Care Forum.

Chiu, D. (1979). Suicide in Hawaii, 1908–1972. *Research and Statistics Report,* no. 26. Honolulu: Hawaii State Department of Health.

Daws, G. (1968). *Shoal of Time: A History of the Hawaiian Islands.* New York: Macmillan.

Dedman, P. (1988). *Kapu Ka'ū.* Video by Ka 'Ohana O Ka Lae and Nā Maka O Ka 'Āina.

——— (1989). *Pele's Appeal.* Video by Pele Defense Fund and Nā Maka O Ka 'Āina.

Dubanoski, R. A. (1982). Child maltreatment in Europeans and Hawaiian-Americans. *Child Abuse and Neglect* 5: 457.

Emory, K. P. (1959). Origin of the Hawaiians. *Journal of the Polynesian Society* 68 (1): 29–35.

E Ola Mau (1990). *Principles to Improve Health Care for Native Hawaiians.* Honolulu: E Ola Mau.

Forbes, K., N. Potapohn, A. Lenzer, and C. A. Sumarnap (1990). *The Native Hawaiian Elderly Needs Assessment Report.* Honolulu: Alu Like.

Fornander, A. (1969, 1878–1885). *An Account of the Polynesian Race: Its Origins and Migrations.* Rutland, Vt.: Tuttle.

Fuchs, L. H. (1961). *Hawaii Pono—A Social History.* New York: Harcourt, Brace and World.

Gallimore, R., J. W. Boggs, and C. Jordan (1974). *Culture, Behavior and Education: A Study of Hawaiian-Americans.* Beverly Hills, Calif.: Sage Publications.

Gardner, R. W. (1980). Ethnic differentials in mortality in Hawaii, 1920–70. *Hawaii Medical Journal* 39: 221.

———— (1984). Life tables by ethnic group for Hawaii, 1980. *Research and Statistics Report*, no. 47. Honolulu: Hawaii State Department of Health.

Green, R. C. (1974). Tahiti-Hawaii A.D. 1100–1300: Further comments. *New Zealand Archaeological Association Newsletter* 17: 206.

Greer, R. A. (1969). The founding of the Queen's Hospital. *Hawaiian Journal of History* 3: 110.

Handy, E. S. Craighill (1927). Polynesian religion. *Bernice P. Bishop Museum Bulletin* 24.

Handy, E. S. Craighill, E. G. Handy, and M. K. Pukui (1972). Native planters in old Hawai'i. *Bernice P. Bishop Museum Bulletin* 126.

Handy, E. S. Craighill, and M. K. Pukui (1958). *The Polynesian Family System in Ka'ū, Hawai'i.* Wellington, New Zealand: Polynesian Society.

Hezel, F., D. Rubinstein, and G. White (1985). *Culture, Youth and Suicide in the Pacific: Papers from an East-West Center Conference.* Honolulu: East-West Center, University of Hawaii.

Higginbotham, N. (1987). The culture accommodation of mental health services for Native Hawaiians. In A. B. Robillard and A. J. Marsella (eds.), *Contemporary Issues in Mental Health Research in the Pacific Islands.* Honolulu: Social Science Research Institute, University of Hawaii.

Houston, V.S.K. (1950, December 18–27). The Queen's Hospital. *Honolulu Advertiser*, p. 6.

Howard, A. (1974). *Ain't No Big Thing: Coping Strategies in a Hawaiian-American Community.* Honolulu: University Press of Hawaii.

Ikeda, K. (1987). *Demographic Profile of Native Hawaiians: 1980–1986.* Honolulu: University of Hawaii Department of Sociology.

Ito, K. L. (1987). Emotions, proper behavior (hana pono) and Hawaiian concepts of self, person, and individual. In A. B. Robillard and A. J. Marsella (eds.), *Contemporary Issues in Mental Health Research in the Pacific Islands.* Honolulu: Social Science Research Institute, University of Hawaii.

Johnson, R. K. (1982). *Kumulipo.* Honolulu: Topgallant.

Kaaa, H. K. (1982). *Kupulani Program Summary 1981–82.* Honolulu: Kamehameha Schools/Bishop Estates.

Kamakahi, J. J. (1989). The crown-based health care legacies: A brief history. In E. L. Wegner (ed.), *Social Process in Hawaii* 32: 22–31.

Kamakau, S. M. (1964). Ka Po'e Kahiko. *Bernice P. Bishop Museum Special Publication* 51.

———— (1961). *Ruling Chiefs of Hawaii.* Honolulu: Kamehameha Schools Press.

Kame'eleihiwa, L. (1986). Land and the promise of capitalism: A dilemma for the Hawaiian chiefs of the 1848 Māhele. Ph.D. dissertation, University of Hawaii.

Kanahele, G. S. (1982). The new Hawaiians. In B. Hormann and A. Lind (eds.), *Social Process in Hawaii* 29: 21.

Kanahele, P. K. (1990). *Pele's Appeal.* Video by Pele Defense Fund and Nā Maka O Ka 'Āina, Honolulu.

Kassebaum, G. (1987). The offender-patient: Penal code authorization of mental health services for Native Hawaiians. In A. B. Robillard and A. J. Marsella (eds.), *Contemporary Issues in Mental Health Research in the Pacific Islands.* Honolulu: Social Science Research Institute, University of Hawaii.

Kelly, M. (1989). Dynamics of production intensification in precontact Hawai'i. In S. van deLeeuw and R. Torrence (eds.), *What's New? A Closer Look at the Process of Innovation*. London: Unwin Hyman.

——— (1988, November). *Early Mission Impact on Hawaiians and Their Culture*. Honolulu: Church of the Crossroads.

——— (1980). Land tenure in Hawaii. *Amerasia Journal* 7: 57.

——— (1982). Some thoughts on education in traditional Hawaiian society. In A. L. Pickens (ed.), *To Teach the Children: Historical Aspects of Education in Hawai'i*. Honolulu: Bernice Pauahi Bishop Museum.

Kimura, L.L.K. (1989). The revitalization of the Hawaiian language. In D. Chenoweth (ed.), *Hawaii Review* (Board of Publications, University of Hawaii Mānoa) 13 (3):74–76.

King, P. N. (1987). Structural changes in Hawaiian history: Changes in the mental health of a people. In A. B. Robillard and A. J. Marsella (eds.), *Contemporary Issues in Mental Health Research in the Pacific Islands*. Honolulu: Social Science Research Institute, University of Hawaii.

Kirch, P. V. (1985). *Feathered Gods and Fishhooks: An Introduction to Hawaiian Archaeology and Prehistory*. Honolulu: University of Hawaii.

Korbin, J. E. (1990). Hana 'ino: Child maltreatment in a Hawaiian-American community. *Pacific Studies* 13: 7.

Luomala, K. (1989). Polynesian religious foundations of Hawaiian concepts regarding wellness and illness. In L. E. Sullivan (ed.), *Healing and Restoring: Health and Medicine in the World's Religious Traditions*. New York: Macmillan.

Malo, D. (1951). Hawaiian antiquities. Translated and edited by N. B. Emerson. *Bernice P. Bishop Museum Publication*, no. 2.

Management Planning and Administration Consultants (MPAC) (1984). *Final Report of the External Evaluation of Hale Ola O Ho'opākōlea*. Honolulu: Alu Like.

Marsella, A. J. (1985). Culture, self, and mental disorder. In A. J. Marsella, G. DeVoss, and F.L.K. Hsu (eds.), *Culture and Self: Asian and Western Perspectives*. New York: Tavistock.

Marsella, A. J., and G. M. White (eds.) (1982). *Cultural Concepts of Mental Health and Therapy*. Boston: Reidel.

McDermott, J. F., Jr., W. S. Tseng, and T. W. Maretzki (eds.) (1980). *People and Cultures of Hawaii: A Psychocultural Profile*. Honolulu: University Press of Hawaii.

McGregor, D. P. (1990a). 'Aina ho'opulapula: Hawaiian homesteading. *Hawaiian Journal of History* 24: 1.

———. (1990b). Kūpa'a I Ka 'Āina: Persistence on the land. Ph.D. dissertation, University of Hawaii.

Mitchell, D.D.K. (1982). *Resource Units in Hawaiian Culture*, 2d ed. Honolulu: Kamehameha Schools.

Mokuau, N. (1985). Counseling Pacific Islander-Americans. In P. Pedersen (ed.), *Handbook of Cross Cultural Counseling and Therapy*. Westport, Conn.: Greenwood Press.

———. (1990a). A family-centered approach in Native Hawaiian culture. *Families in Society: The Journal of Contemporary Human Services* 71 (10): 607–613.

————— (1990b). The impoverishment of native Hawaiians and social work change. *Health and Social Work* 15 (3): 235–242.

—————. (1987). Social workers' perceptions of counseling effectiveness for Asian American clients. *Social Work* 32 (4): 331–335.

Murakami, S. R. (1985). An epidemiological survey of alcohol, drug and mental health problems in Hawaii: A comparison of four ethnic groups. Paper presented at the Epidemiology of Alcohol Use and Abuse Among U.S. Minorities Conference, Bethesda, Md.

Nāhulu, A. G. (1990, November 22–23). Hawaiian cultural healing at Hale Ola. Cross Cultural Implications in Holistic Healing Workshop, National Association of Social Workers Hawai'i Chapter Conference, Honolulu.

Native Hawaiian Study Commission (1983). *Report on Culture, Needs and Concerns of Native Hawaiians.* Pursuant to Public Law 96–585, Title III. Honolulu: Native Hawaiian Study Commission.

Nordyke, E. C. (1989). *The Peopling of Hawai'i,* 2d ed. Honolulu: University of Hawaii.

Oda, J. S. (1974). *Hawaiian Learning Program.* Honolulu: University of Hawaii School of Social Work.

Paglinawan, L. K. (1972). *Ho'oponopono Project II: Development and Implementation in a Social Work Agency.* Honolulu: Queen Lili'uokalani Children's Center.

Pukui, M. K., E. W. Haertig, and C. A. Lee (1972). *Nānā I Ke Kumu,* vol. 1. Honolulu: Hui Hānai.

Pukui, M. K., E. W. Haertig, C. A. Lee, and J. F. McDermott (1979). *Nānā I Ke Kumu,* vol. 2. Honolulu: Hui Hānai.

Reardon, G. (1990, November). Personal communication.

Rocha, B. A. (1985, November). Mental Health Task Force report. In B. Z. Bell (ed.), *E Ola Mau Native Hawaiian Health Needs Study Conference Proceedings.* Honolulu: Alu Like.

Sanders, D. S. (1986). *A Short History of the School of Social Work, University of Hawai'i at Mānoa, 1936–1986.* Honolulu: School of Social Work.

Schmitt, R. C. (1969). Catastrophic mortality in Hawaii. *Hawaiian Journal of History* 3: 66.

—————. (1977). *Historical Statistics of Hawaii.* Honolulu: University Press of Hawaii.

Stannard, D. E. (1988). *Before the Horror: The Population of Hawai'i on the Eve of Western Contact.* Honolulu: University of Hawaii.

Starbuck, G. W., N. Krantzier, K. Forbes, and V. Barnes (1984). Child abuse and neglect on O'ahu, Hawai'i: Description and analysis of four purported risk factors. *Journal of Development and Behavioral Pediatrics* 5: 55.

State of Hawaii, Department of Attorney General (1988). *Crime in Hawai'i.* Honolulu: Hawaii Criminal Justice Data Center.

State of Hawaii, Department of Health (1986). Health Surveillance Program. Honolulu.

————— (1988). Health Surveillance Program. Honolulu.

State of Hawaii, Department of Human Services (1988). *A Statistical Report on Child Abuse and Neglect in Hawai'i 1980–87.* Honolulu: Program Development, Family and Adult Services Division and Planning Office.

Stueber, R. K. (1982). An informal history of schooling in Hawai'i. In A. L.

Pickens (ed.), *To Teach the Children: Historical Aspects of Education in Hawai'i*. Honolulu: Bernice Pauahi Bishop Museum.

Tagupa, W.E.H. (1981). Education, change and assimilation in nineteenth century Hawai'i. *Pacific Studies* 5: 57.

Takeuchi, D., N. Higginbotham, A. J. Marsella, K. Gomes, L. Kwan, Jr., B. Ostrowski, B. A. Rocha, and K. Wight (1987). Native Hawaiian mental health. In A. B. Robillard and A. J. Marsella (eds.), *Contemporary Issues in Mental Health Research in the Pacific Islands*. Honolulu: Social Science Research Institute, University of Hawaii.

Thompson, M. B. (Chair) (1983). *Native Hawaiian Educational Assessment Project*. Honolulu: Kamehameha Schools/Bishop Estates.

Trask, H. K. (1984–1985). Hawaiians, American colonization, and the quest for independence. In G. Sullivan and G. Hawes (eds.), *Social Process in Hawaii* 31: 101.

Tseng, W. S., J. Shu, A. Omori, and D. McLaughlin (forthcoming) "Suicidal Behavior in Hawai'i." In *Suicidal Behavior in Asia and the Pacific*. Singapore: Singapore University Press.

U.S. Congress (1988, October 12). Congressional Record. Washington, D.C.: U.S. Government Printing Office.

——— (1990, October 27). Congressional Record. Washington, D.C.: U.S. Government Printing Office.

U.S. Congress, Office of Technology Assessment (1987, April). *Current Health Status and Population Projections of Native Hawaiians Living in Hawaii*. Washington, D.C.

Wegner, E. L. (1989). Recommendations for more effective health care. In E. L. Wegner (ed.), *Social Process in Hawaii* 32: 149–167.

Young, B.B.C. (1980). The Hawaiians. In J. F. McDermott, Jr., W. S. Tseng, and T. W. Maretzki (eds.), *People and Cultures of Hawaii: A Psychocultural Profile*. Honolulu: University Press of Hawaii.

CHAPTER 9

Samoans

NOREEN MOKUAU AND NATHAN CHANG

INTRODUCTION

Samoans are a Polynesian group who migrated to the United States as
recently as the 1950s. They brought with them distinctive cultural values
and lifestyle practices reflecting and emphasizing the importance of the
family. For the most part, these traditional values and customs are still
prevalent among Samoan communities in the United States, yet the
degree to which an individual or family adheres to these traditional ways
varies with the level of acculturation.

Social service providers working with Samoan populations enhance
their effectiveness by being informed about cultural background. This
type of information provides the background from which to assess and
treat a broad array of social and psychological problems and issues.
Samoans, with their richness in cultural tradition, are considered to be
one of the most "disadvantaged" minority groups of color in the United
States based on such indicators as poverty and unemployment.

This chapter seeks to address social services for Samoans by describing
major variables that are a part of the cultural context. The cultural context
may be conceptualized as comprising such variables as history, sociodemographic data, worldviews, behavior norms, and a profile of problems and issues. In light of such information, ideas and recommendations for social services are then described.

HISTORICAL BACKGROUND

The first major period of Samoan migration to the United States occurred in 1951 as a result of the closing of the U.S. naval base in American

Samoa. The naval base represented the principal economic resource of American Samoa (Pirie, 1970), and with its closing came high unemployment and inadequate market conditions to sustain the community. Robert Franco (1978) suggests that this first migration can be considered a forced migration in that high unemployment rates combined with the country's high birth rate necessitated immigration movement for economic opportunities. The first wave of immigrants, then, were primarily Samoan naval personnel and their dependents who transferred to the Pearl Harbor Naval Base in Hawaii. In addition, this group of immigrants also included Samoan nationals who sought economic opportunities not only in Hawaii but in key "gateway cities" on the west coast of the United States.

With the closing of the naval base, the administration of American Samoa was relinquished by the Navy and replaced by the U.S. Department of the Interior and its civilian staff. An influx of American administrators, the initiation of several government programs, and the opening of the tuna cannery industry contributed to improved economic and employment conditions from 1954 through 1963 (Franco, 1985, p. 167). These changes, in turn, contributed to a slowing down of immigration of Samoans to the United States in the same time period (Pirie, 1970, p. 496).

Influenced by legislation such as the 1965 Amendments to the U.S. Immigration and Nationality Act, which lifted immigration restrictions on quota systems (Thompson, 1972), and the open policy of the Department of the Interior allowing American nationals to migrate to the United States (Alailima, 1972), immigration has undergone periodic increases since the mid–1960s. The second major group of immigrants from Samoa consists of persons who are members of extended families, students, and those who are attracted to the American lifestyle and economic opportunities. For example, fifty Samoans in Hawaii responded to survey questions about their motivations for coming to Hawaii (Franco, 1985, p. 318). Nearly half the respondents gave a kinship-related reason such as "to visit a kinsman," "to care for a relative," or "to visit parents"; a second answer that was frequently offered was education (p. 318). This second group of immigrants includes persons from American Samoa as well as persons from Western Samoa, an independent nation.

The motivations for and experiences of immigration to the United States becomes clearer when viewed as part of major historical events in the Samoan islands. Samoans are descendants of Polynesians who were believed to have migrated to the islands over 2,000 years ago (Brigham Young University, Language and Intercultural Research Center, 1977). The Samoan islands were first introduced to Western culture in 1722 by the Dutch navigator Jacob Roggeveen, and by 1830 the London

Missionary Society and other Christian missionaries converted islanders to their teachings. International competition for Pacific Island military bases by the United States, England, and Germany resulted in the Samoan islands being divided into two parts in 1900: Western Samoa and American Samoa. Western Samoa, comprised of several islands including Upolu and Savaii, was under German administration from 1900 to 1914, New Zealand administration from 1914 through 1961, and gained independence in 1962 (Franco, 1985). American Samoa, which includes the islands of Tutuila and Manua, was secured by the United States and administered by the Navy from 1900 through 1951 and then by the Department of the Interior from 1951 to the present. American Samoa is an unincorporated territory of the United States, and its citizens are U.S. nationals. In being influenced by different administering nations, Western Samoa and American Samoa have been subject to different forms and varying rates of development (Pirie, 1970).

Both Samoas have, historically, been agrarian cultures producing mainly coconuts, cocoa, bananas, and taro. Western Samoa in the 1990s is still a predominantly agriculturally based nation with a low per capita income; however, American Samoa has a higher per capita income, is considered a cash-based economy, does not produce enough agricultural products for consumption, and is thus greatly dependent on agricultural exports. The change in economic development for American Samoa can be attributed to American influence, which has emphasized government financial support and nonagrarian employment. Both Samoas have increasing birth rates and a lack of employment opportunities to meet population needs.

While the economic development of Western Samoa and American Samoa are different, sociocultural traditions are similar. Both countries have had their traditional values and customs challenged by the introduction of Western cultures, and while there may be some degree of transition of values and customs, overall there is still a strong belief in and adherence to traditional norms. In particular, there is a continued emphasis on the church, the family system, and interpersonal relations.

Samoans who migrate to the United States in the future will bring with them a motivation for economic achievement as well as a desire to maintain values and norms of traditional Samoan culture. The challenge for Samoans, as well as all newly arrived immigrants, will be to successfully integrate new ways with traditional ways.

SOCIODEMOGRAPHIC OVERVIEW

Of the 260,000 Pacific Islanders residing in the United States, the 1980 Census indicates that approximately 40,000 (15 percent) are Samoans (U.S. Bureau of the Census, 1988). Samoans are the second largest group of Pacific Islanders, after native Hawaiians, to reside in the United States. Most of the Samoan population are American citizens or American nationals from American Samoa, but a significant number of Samoans (36 percent) are foreign-born and are primarily from Western Samoa. The population of Samoans in the United States is said to be larger than the estimated population of 34,000 Samoans in American Samoa (Territory of American Samoa, Office of the Governor, 1990, p. 1). Furthermore, the estimate of 150,000 Samoans in the United States in 1990 (Territory of American Samoa, Office of the Governor, 1990, p. 1) suggests an overwhelming increase in migration since 1980 and/or a severe under-counting of Samoans in the 1980 Census. The Samoans in the United States reside primarily in California (46 percent) and Hawaii (36 percent) (U.S. Bureau of the Census, 1988). Specific cities with a high-density Samoan population include San Francisco and Compton, California, Ka-lihi-Palama and Laie, Hawaii.

Other sociodemographic information on Samoans from the 1980 Census hints at the difficulties that Samoans may be having in their adjustment to American culture. The youngest population among all Asian and Pacific Islander American (APIA) groups with a median age in 1980 of 19 years, Samoans have slightly more males than females (51 percent) and the largest family size, along with Vietnamese, with an average of five persons per family. The majority (77 percent) of Samoans are bilingual and tend to speak their native language at home. In general, APIA groups have a higher percent (33 percent) of persons who are college graduates when compared with the total population of the United States (16 percent). Paradoxically, however, Samoans, with only 7 percent of their population having college degrees, rank significantly below the median scores of both the APIA and national populations.

Perhaps the most revealing statistics on adjustment difficulty relate to income, poverty status, employment rates, and home ownership. In each of these categories, Samoans tended to have lower median scores than other APIA groups. The median family income for APIA families at $23,000 was higher than the national median of $20,000. However, for Samoans, the median family income was $14,000, second lowest of all APIA groups. With such a low median income, poverty status for Samoans is not a surprise. Samoans experienced the second highest poverty rate among APIA groups with 30 percent of the population below the federally defined poverty level. This poverty status rate is compared with the median rate of 13 percent for all APIA populations and the median rate of 12 percent for the total U.S. population. Employment statistics further affirmed the financial difficulties for Samoans: 67 percent of APIAs participated in the labor force as compared with 62 percent of the national population; however, only 60 percent of Samoans were employed. The most frequently held positions included laborers, fabricators, operators, and technical, sales, and administrative support. Finally, the majority of Samoans did not claim home ownership, with only 29 percent maintaining owner-occupied residences (U.S. Bureau of the Census, 1988).

VALUES AND BEHAVIORAL NORMS

The historical influence of Germany, New Zealand, and the United States in the Samoan islands altered ideas on economic development but did not significantly erode the values and behavior norms that constitute the "Samoan way of life" (*fa'a Samoa*). Traditional values and behaviors are still being maintained and are shared by Samoans in American Samoa, Western Samoa, and the United States. The durability of a culture in perpetuating its customs is highly dependent on that culture's ability to be flexible and to adapt to changes and transitions in context of its values and norms. "No system is perfect, but if it is flexible, then its values will be perpetuated. The behavioral manifestations of values may change, but the values will be maintained. In Samoan culture, the umbilical cord is never cut" (Tuiasosopo, 1990).

Samoans, in sharing the same cultural values, may differ in the degree to which they subscribe to these values. For example, in a study focusing on a small Samoan community in Oxnard, California, it is reported that Samoans differed in their participation in cultural activities and that the difference was a function of economic security and prestige (Rolff, 1978, p. 5). The persons who were more in need of economic support and those who received prestige through participation were more likely to stay involved in traditional ways than those who were economically independent or who had gained access to prestige in mainstream American culture. Even though Samoans may vary in the degree to which they subscribe to traditional values and norms, there is a strong consensus on those values and behaviors that are the most prevalent (Franco, 1985; Markoff and Bond, 1980; Fiatoa and Palafox, 1980; Gratton, 1948).

Dominant values and behavioral norms in Samoan culture focus on the family, communal relationships, and the church. The family (*aiga*) is the basic unit of Samoan culture and is also the primary transmitter of values and behavioral norms. "If western civilization has focused on the individual as the primary unit of experience, Samoan culture has always seen the family as the most important agency of human interactions" (Territory of American Samoa, Office of the Governor, 1990, p. 19). In Samoan culture, the concept of family extends beyond the nuclear family unit to include extended family members (*aiga potopoto*) who may be related by blood, marriage, or adoption. Thus, an entire village may also be conceptualized as an extended family when there are several nuclear families who are related to one another (Markoff and Bond, 1980). One family may contain several hundred people (Fiatoa and Palafox, 1980). Members of the family experience a true sense of communal relationships because there is a sharing of roles and responsibilities that ultimately promote the family title. Mere Betham (1972) suggests that the single most important belief and practice that has contributed to the perpetuation of the family can be captured in a Samoan phrase, which translates, "the way to the family title is through loyal and faithful service to the family" (p. 18).

Due to such a broad conceptualization of the family, the structure of the leadership of the family is somewhat complicated. Each village is headed by a senior chief (*matai*) who has the overall responsibilities for the welfare of all the related families in the village. The chief's major duty is the leadership and care of the family under his or her control and, in reciprocity, is entitled to the service of all members of the family (Gratton, 1948, p. 10). The respect and deference afforded to a family by other families are related to the family title that is maintained by the senior chief. Each nuclear family within the village also has a chief who has direct responsibilities for that particular unit. The various chiefs participate in a village council (*fono*), which exercises authority in matters pertaining to the entire village. This village council is usually headed by the *matai* of the village.

Within the traditional Samoan family structure there are clearly identified roles and expectations related to men, women, and children. All values and behavioral norms within the family structure promote and perpetuate service to the family. Men function as providers of food; women operate in their own committees to perform caretaking roles related to children and household chores; and older children are often responsible for younger children. "In Samoa, old age has status over young people, titled people over untitled, men over women, and men and women over children" (Brigham Young University, Language and Intercultural Research Center, 1977, p. 5). Such hierarchical delineation of roles and responsibilities highlights the importance of social control and obedience. In a service-oriented culture, measures of social control and discipline are direct and overt and include physical punishment and public exposure (Markoff and Bond, 1980).

The roles and activities of the family are reinforced by the church. Religion in Samoan culture has served to affirm the structured and communal nature of the family. F.J.H. Gratton (1948) states that a review of Samoan society must include some discussion of church life since the influence of the church extends into every phase of Samoan life (p. 126). Churches are supported by the contributions of the village families, and missionaries and pastors of all denominations are highly respected. The behavioral practices of Samoan people include: observation of the Sabbath day, daily prayer in the home in the mornings and evenings, a ceasing of all work during prayer, and total participation of all family members under the leadership of the chief (Brigham Young University, Language and Intercultural Research Center, 1977).

The influence of the church is as strong in the United States as it is in the Samoan islands. Adele Satele (1978) reports that 95 percent of 410 Samoan families interviewed in southern California attended church at least once a week and that 97 percent said they felt religion was very important (p. 268). Fay Calkins (1962) states that the church is the most important gathering place for first-generation Samoans and that the church serves to support traditional values of mutual assistance and social control. The pastors and ministers of the churches are often the most important leaders in the Samoan communities in the United States.

The relationship of traditional values and behavior norms to the Samoan community's adjustment to American ways is somewhat ambiguous. On the one hand, traditional values and norms have facilitated the Samoan community's adjustment to the United States by providing a familiar network and support system. On the other hand, however, in keeping the ways of Samoa strong, the maintenance of these values and norms has also inhibited acculturation. Cultural emphasis on the family, communal relationships, and the church is associated with several social and psychological issues confronting Samoans in the United States.

PROFILE OF SOCIAL AND PSYCHOLOGICAL PROBLEMS AND ISSUES

"Growing up in Samoa is not an effective preparation for life in Hawaii" (Markoff and Bond, 1980, p. 190) and, it can be generalized, for life in other parts of the United States. The strong cultural emphasis on the extended family and sharing through communal living contrasts with the American emphasis on the individual and clear rules of individual ownership and privacy. In addition, language differences compound problems of adjustment. In the relatively short period of time that Samoans have been in the United States, a profile of social and psychological problems have been identified, including child abuse, mental health disorders, financial difficulties and unemployment, poor educational performance, teenage pregnancy, and substance abuse. Selected problems that are especially prevalent are discussed below.

Child Abuse

The functioning of the Samoan family system is dependent on participation by all members. Members of the family have different responsibilities based on such factors as their titles, gender, and age. Children, while loved and cherished, are at the bottom of the social hierarchy and are required to provide service and be obedient to their chiefs and other titled persons, their parents, and other older persons.

To assure children's participation in this type of family system, there is a reliance on mechanisms of external control such as physical discipline. "In some Samoan families, spankings, whippings and beatings with instruments like two-by-fours or pipes are common practice" (Territory of American Samoa, Office of the Governor, 1990, p. 46). Samoans do not readily place their trust in Western convictions of internalized self-control and believe that the replacement of physical discipline with verbal disciplinary techniques would only encourage disorder (Territory of American Samoa, Office of the Governor, 1990). Justification for the use of physical discipline is further captured in the biblical saying, "spare the rod, spoil the child" (Tuiasosopo, 1990).

In the United States, the problem of child abuse among Samoan families has become increasingly more visible. For example, it is reported that child abuse in the state of Hawaii occurs at a much higher rate per capita among Samoans than among other major ethnic groups (Bishop Estates/Kamehameha Schools, 1983, p. 64). Samoans constitute approximately 1.5 percent of the state population, yet Samoan children account for almost 5 percent of the confirmed reports of child abuse (State of Hawaii, Department of Human Services, 1988, p. 33).

Financial Difficulties

The financial difficulties that many Samoan families experience in the United States might be largely attributed to their basic belief and practice in the extended family and communal living. Communal ownership has far greater credibility than private ownership, and so materials and money within one's home belong to the entire family. When relatives from the Samoan islands join established Samoan households in the United States, they receive financial assistance and support from their relatives. In the Samoan islands, this would not present a problem because of the availability of communal lands and the abundance of the extended family; however, in a predominantly cash-based economy such as the United States, it is often difficult for Samoans to meet the financial needs of their huge families.

A special issue related to financial difficulties is that of remittances. Remittances are the income that Samoans in the United States send back to their relatives in the Samoan islands. Paul Shankman (1978) estimates that in 1974 as much as half of the personal income of most Western Samoans and large sums of money of American Samoans were from migrant remitters overseas (p. 120). A large portion of remittances are used to reinforce the cultural tradition of service to the family through obligation and reciprocity. In particular, there is a ritualized practice of mutual support during lifecycle events (Franco, 1985), often perceived as "trouble" (*fa'alavelave*), to support the family's involvement in major events such as weddings, the building of churches, christening of newborns, or funerals (Calkins, 1962, p. 67). The greater the contribution, the higher the esteem accorded to the family. The desire to maintain a financial commitment to the extended family may partially explain the extremely high poverty levels of Samoan families in the United States.

Another issue that may exacerbate financial problems relates to high levels of unemployment. In a major study by Franco (1985), employment profiles of Samoans in the United States were delineated, and culturally distinctive work perceptions were identified. In general, he notes that approximately 10 percent of all Samoans in the American labor force were unemployed, with the Samoan unemployment rate in California being 1.5 times greater than the statewide average (p. 281) and the rate in Hawaii being the highest for the entire Samoan civilian labor force than any other APIA group (p. 314). Employment difficulties are attributed to language barriers and inadequate training, but, more importantly, they may be associated with cultural traditions that emphasize the activities of the family more than the value of money. For example, the Samoan who chooses to participate in the numerous family activities of *fa'alavelave* will risk loss of job because of unscheduled absences.

Mental Health Disorders

Most of the problems identified in the Samoan population relate to adjustment difficulties and are, thus, social in origin. Mental health disorders are often secondary to environmental concerns (Markoff and Bond, 1980), and, therefore, analyses and information in this area are limited.

"Mental illness is vaguely defined and even less so acknowledged in the Samoan social framework" (Markoff and Bond, 1980, p. 195). Problems of anxiety, depression, and anger are manifested in behavioral illnesses that are believed to be spiritual in origin. Samoans call these illnesses ghost illnesses (*ma'i aitu*) and rely upon the treatment services of spirit priests or, if they are unavailable or unsuccessful, the services of Christian ministers. As a last resort, Samoans will turn to Western-trained practitioners for assistance. In American Samoa, the mental health clinic identified 336 cases of major psychiatric disorders in the population during 1988–1989, with the largest number of cases being major neuroses (Territory of American Samoa, Office of the Governor, 1990).

The range of social and psychological problems and issues confronting the Samoan population requires social service attention that draws upon cultural knowledge.

SOCIAL SERVICE INTERVENTION

Principles of Practice

The premise of this chapter is that social services for the Samoan population in the United States may be enhanced when variables in the cultural context are taken into consideration and incorporated into intervention planning and implementation. Knowledge and appreciation of variables such as historical background, cultural values, and behavioral norms are especially useful in guiding the worker toward more culturally sensitive practice. Given the retention of the mores of Samoan culture even in its transmission to American society, several principles of practice can be identified.

There should be a respect for the unique structure of the family system and an effort to design services that focus on the family rather than on the individual. Direct involvement or consultation of appropriate family members will help in assessing the scope of the problem and be especially critical in the successful implementation of treatment. For example, in a traditionally oriented Samoan family, if the chief of the extended family is not consulted, and intervention includes only the nuclear family (parents and children), then support from the extended family may be withheld.

Bilingual and bicultural workers are essential for the Samoan population and should be a part of the social service team. As noted earlier, the majority of Samoans are bilingual, with a substantial number speaking Samoan in their homes. A lack of understanding of the language will impede and may even be detrimental to service provision. For example, in the Samoan language, some words can have a dozen different meanings. "Stomach," "intestine," "breathing," or "getting to work" can all be interpreted from the Samoan word *manava* (Fiatoa and Palafox, 1980, p. 257). Conversely, there may be no Samoan words equivalent to Western terminology for concepts such as mental illness. It is important to understand the special nuances of the language.

Indigenous healing methods should be acknowledged, and, if necessary, appropriate actions to involve traditional practitioners should be taken. Many Samoans still believe in the power of spiritual healing and continue to seek the services of indigenous healers for illnesses that are usually behavioral (Territory of American Samoa, Office of the Governor, 1990). Physical methods used by these healers emphasize body massage and herbal preparations. When a client is involuntary and perceived as resistant, it may behoove the social worker to consult with persons familiar with traditional healing methods.

Conceptual Model of Intervention

A conceptual model of intervention for Samoans might include two components: education and treatment. Many of the problems and issues confronting Samoans in the United States hint more at social maladjustment than psychopathology. Problems such as child abuse, poverty, and unemployment, to a large extent, occur because the norms governing child-rearing, finances, and employment in Samoa and in the United States are different. Any psychopathology that is observed may often be secondary to environmental factors (Markoff and Bond, 1980). In these cases, a specialized form of education dealing with the problems and issues confronting Samoans would be most appropriate, Richard Markoff and John R. Bond (1980) suggest that this kind of education should focus on discussing and clarifying social and economic aspects of mainstream American culture to help Samoan clients in their adjustment to a different lifestyle. For example, in a social service program for Samoans in Hawaii, a radio program served as an educational adjunct to a more formal treatment program. The radio program occurred weekly for one hour in which the first half hour was devoted to a discussion about issues such as parenting skills and personal stress, and the second half hour provided for questions and comments from the audience.

In addition to education, treatment programs utilizing theories that are congruent with cultural variables are important. While there is a broad array of Western theoretical models and theories from which to select, behavioral theory, with its emphasis on observable behavior, clearly delineated procedures, and specific role responsibilities of the worker and the client, appears to be especially useful. In behavioral theory, the relationship of the worker and the client is contractual, with the worker and the client having specific roles and duties. The worker and the client collaboratively assess the problem, but it is the worker who takes the responsibility for recommending and implementing intervention strategies. Thus, the relationship may be perceived as active, directive, and hierarchical, with the worker assuming major responsibilities for the overall nature of intervention. The clear definition of roles and responsibilities in behavioral treatment is compatible with the Samoan emphasis on the hierarchy of roles within the family system and conformance to directive communication.

Satisfactory engagement of the worker-client relationship is essential to the establishment of clearly defined procedures of intervention. In behavioral theory, treatment goals are concrete and measurable, and the steps to achieve the goals are often specified in a contract developed between the worker and the client. Precise behavioral definitions of the problem and relevant environmental factors will enable the worker to make a comprehensive assessment and prescribe a suitable behavioral intervention plan. With Samoan populations, it is important to understand the cultural meanings of certain behaviors and to know what is normative and what is abnormal. Without such knowledge, the worker may be prone to bias, which will have detrimental effects on intervention. The benefit of such an intervention program is that it is focused and relatively quick. For Samoan clients who have a belief in the ritualized steps in activities and who need clearly defined goals and strategies, the behavioral process may be ideal.

Finally, the behavorial theory's emphasis on observable behavior is compatible with Samoan norms. Observable behavior should be clearly defined and subject to a form of measurement. In Samoan culture, the methods employed to deal with social control are direct and overt, and the Samoan lifestyle places greater emphasis on overt behavior than upon thought, feelings, and attitudes (Markoff and Bond, 1980). Thus, efforts to plan intervention according to behaviors seem more useful than insight-oriented or intrapsychic intervention plans.

Specific Skills for Intervention

Specific skills that are broadly characteristic of behavioral theory are applicable in work with Samoans. These skills can be described as part of the overall intervention process, which includes the following steps: worker-client engagement, problem assessment, intervention, and evaluation.

Worker-Client Engagement. A knowledge of the client's cultural history and the relevance of that cultural history to the client's present lifestyle is crucial to the development of the worker-client rapport. The engagement of the worker-client relationship is associated with factors such as trust and mutual respect. In order to achieve this, the worker needs to address the appropriate family member, usually a family spokesperson, and then identify and describe the specific role he or she is assuming in the context of the social service agency being represented. In some cases, a worker's command of the various levels of the Samoan language can reflect a degree of competence that may have a greater influence on the establishment of worker credibility than educational credentials. The worker may also choose to disclose personal information that may reveal that certain experiences are shared (e.g., place of birth or residence), thereby increasing credibility.

Problem Assessment. The problems or issues that are to be addressed need to be identified, described, and then translated into measurable components. Relevant goals for intervention are to be established. The ability to operationalize behavior in overt and concrete terms facilitate the description of preintervention behavior (baseline data) and postintervention behavior and aids in the evaluation of progress. For example, the Samoan child who is referred because of poor school performance may have the problem defined as different behaviors, including school absences, low test scores, and classroom rights. The goals for the behavioral intervention plan may include increasing school attendance and decreasing the number of low test scores and classroom fights. Intervention strategies will need to include the parents and possibly other siblings in school.

Intervention. The strategies for intervention will vary according to the problems assessed. The importance of the family has already been established, and a likely vehicle for intervention would be family treatment or groupwork. In a situation of child abuse, for example, there may be a combination of family counseling as well as group sessions that are educative in nature and focus on parenting skills. Samoan culture places such a strong emphasis on family approval and sanction that a group session in which other parents reinforce the learning of new skills is critical to intervention success. A specific behavioral skill called reframing, which is the use of a different set of words and behaviors to connote an intent, may also be useful in child abuse cases. The value in such a skill is that it validates the intent of a behavior and reframes the way in which the intent is offered. Samoan parents who believe that discipline is important to family functioning can continue to believe in the value of discipline but need to reframe the manner in which they discipline— for example, to use verbal communication rather than physical discipline.

Evaluation. An evaluation system that can be easily understood by both the worker and the client is important in the monitoring of progress in the intervention plan. On the one hand, it keeps intervention focused and may contribute to a sense of success and achievement in the reaching of goals. On the other hand, it may indicate that planned intervention is not helping the resolution of the problem, and alternative intervention plans may need to be explored. In the case of poor school performance noted earlier, evaluation may involve counting the number of times a child is able to attend classes during a one-month period. Evaluation may also be useful in assessing the success of outreach and contact with Samoan clients. With those Samoan clients who are involuntary, initial contact and first-time visits may be difficult. An evaluation system may include different monitoring levels in which the first level may be making telephone contact, a second level may be keeping an appointment, and a third level may be scheduling another visit.

CONCLUSION

With each new generation in the Samoan population residing in the United States, there will undoubtedly be progressive acculturation. Perhaps in time it will be more possible to view social and mental health issues from a Western perspective. In the interim, however, practitioners who serve that population must either come with or develop a deep appreciation for the culture and lifestyle of the Samoan people in order to better plan and implement effective intervention strategies.

It is important to acknowledge the enduring strength of "the Samoan way" and the manner in which communal and reciprocal values have served the Samoan people. It then becomes possible to appreciate how difficult it is for individuals and families who remove themselves from the security of that system by migrating to the United States.

At the same time, it is imperative that practitioners recognize the importance of assessing each individual and family in terms of the degree to which they adhere to traditional Samoan cultural norms and values. An understanding and appreciation of cultural norms and values, after all, offer practitioners a means by which to interpret behavior in a culturally congruent way.

REFERENCES

Alailima, F. (1982). The Samoans in Hawaii. *Social Process in Hawaii* 29: 105–115.
Alailima, V. J. (1972). Immigration, when and why they come. *Samoan Heritage Series*. Honolulu: University of Hawaii, College of Continuing Education and Community Service.
Betham, M. (1972). The family, the heart of Samoana. *Samoan Heritage Series*. Honolulu: University of Hawaii, College of Continuing Education and Community Service.
Bishop Estates/Kamehameha Schools (1983). *Native Hawaiian Educational Assessment Project*. Honolulu: Bishop Estates/Kamehameha Schools.
Brigham Young University, Language and Intercultural Research Center (1977). *People of Samoa*. Provo, Utah: Brigham Young University, Language and Intercultural Research Center.
Calkins, F. (1962). *My Samoan Chief*. Honolulu: University of Hawaii Press.
Fiatoa, L., and N. Palafox (1980). Samoans. In N. Palafox and A. Warren (eds.), *Cross-Cultural Caring: A Handbook for Health Care Professionals in Hawaii*. Honolulu: Transcultural Health Care Forum.
Franco, R. (1985). *Samoan Perceptions of Work: Moving Up and Moving Around*. Ann Arbor, Mich.: University Microfilms International, Dissertation Information Service.
——— (1978). Samoans in San Francisco, Western Samoa and the Catholic Church. In C. Macpherson, B. Shore, and R. Franco (eds.), *New Neighbors ...Islanders in Adaptation*. Santa Cruz: University of California, Santa Cruz, Center for South Pacific Studies.

Gratton, F.J.H. (1948). *An Introduction to Samoan Custom.* Papakura, New Zealand: R. McMillan Publisher.

Markoff, R., and J. R. Bond (1980). The Samoans. In J. F. McDermott, Jr., W. S. Tseng, and T. W. Maretzki (eds.), *People and Cultures of Hawaii: A Psychocultural Profile.* Honolulu: University Press of Hawaii.

Pirie, P. (1970). *Samoa: Two Approaches to Population and Resource Problems.* Honolulu: East-West Center Population Institute.

Rolff, K. (1978). The Samoan community in Oxnard, Southern California. In C. Macpherson, B. Shore, and R. Franco (eds.), *New Neighbors . . . Islanders in Adaptation.* Santa Cruz: University of California, Santa Cruz, Center for South Pacific Studies.

Satele, A. (1978). The role of the churches in northern California Samoan communities. In C. Macpherson, B. Shore, and R. Franco (eds.), *New Neighbors . . . Islanders in Adaptation.* Santa Cruz: University of California, Santa Cruz, Center for South Pacific Studies.

Shankman, P. (1978). The economic impact of outmigration on Pacific communities. In C. Macpherson, B. Shore, and R. Franco (eds.), *New Neighbors . . . Islanders in Adaptation.* Santa Cruz: University of California, Santa Cruz, Center for South Pacific Studies.

State of Hawaii, Department of Human Services (1988). *Child Abuse and Neglect in Hawaii.* Honolulu: State of Hawaii, Department of Human Services.

Territory of American Samoa, Office of the Governor (1990). *Mental Health Plan 1989–1991.* American Samoa: Office of the Governor.

Thompson, M. (1972). The Samoan in Hawaii today. *Samoan Heritage Series.* Honolulu: University of Hawaii, College of Continuing Education and Community Service.

Tuiasosopo, B. (1990, July). Interview with author.

U.S. Bureau of the Census (1988). *We, the Asian and Pacific Islander Americans.* Washington, D.C.: U.S. Government Printing Office.

CHAPTER 10

Chamorros

FAYE F. UNTALAN

INTRODUCTION

Called Guamanians by the U.S. Census, legislation, and the media, Chamorros are probably the least-known cultural and ethnic group of U.S. citizens. Guamanians are residents of Guam. Chamorro refers to the native or indigenous group of people in Guam and the Marianas Islands and to their culture.

This chapter is intended to provide a better understanding about Guamanians and Chamorros and their place and role in American society. It is further intended to highlight key variables of social service intervention and to examine the interface of culture and intervention. The perspective is based on the author's personal experiences and observations as a Chamorro who has studied social and cultural changes among the Chamorros in contemporary society.

HISTORICAL BACKGROUND

The island of Guam became a U.S. possession in 1898 after over 300 years of colonization by Spain. Until 1898 Guam and its sister islands of Rota, Tinian, and Saipan plus the other smaller uninhabited islands of the Marianas Islands were a single political entity. In 1898 when the Marianas Islands were severed as a political colony, Guam was ceded to the United States, and the other islands were given to Germany. Following the end of World War I, in 1918 the islands were transferred to Japan by treaty. Throughout these years of colonialization, the Chamorro race remained intact with cultural values and behavioral norms being maintained. Shifting foreign rule did not significantly alter their culture and traditions, their language, and their family ties in the Marianas.

The Americanization of the Marianas, however, caused intense Westernization and rapid social changes, which have eroded and continue to affect cultural traditions, family relationships, and the language. When the U.S. Congress established Guam as an unincorporated territory of the United States in 1950, the act created the term "Guamanian" to distinguish and identify the residents of Guam. The label Guamanian created a problem of definition and identity for the Chamarro people particularly with regard to language, customs, and traditions.

Chamorro is a racial, ethnic, and cultural term that describes the indigenous people of the Marianas Islands. The indigenous people of the Marianas identify themselves as Chamorros, speak a common language called Chamorro, and share common cultural traditions and customs. Chamorro, a native vernacular, is spoken throughout the Marianas Islands. There is no Guamanian language. Thus, the term Guamanian has serious implications when the U.S. Census counts people from Guam in the United States as Guamanians and the U.S. Territorial Census on Guam enumerates them as Chamorros.

The terms Guamanian and Chamorro are now used synonymously among the residents of Guam. When these definitions are applied to language and customs, it causes problems of identification and definition among the Chamorro people throughout the Marianas Islands. Shifting definitions, compounded by centuries of colonial rule, generate confusion in how people of Guam perceive themselves—as "Americans" or as "Guamanians" or as "Chamorros." These shifting definitions have affected their cultural identity, their attitudes and behaviors, and their needs for social services. The use of the label "Guamanian" to refer to the people of Guam is an American political action that has ignored the ethnic, racial, and cultural factors of these people. With regards to the indigenous Chamorros of Guam and the Northern Marianas, the change in definitions is a form of cultural and ethnic annihilation for those residing in the United States.

In-migration has also made a significant impact on the sociodemographic character of the Marianas Islands, Guam, and also Saipan. As the established center for the U.S. military and the administration of the U.S. Trust Territory of the Pacific, Guam and Saipan absorbed the early migration of other islanders throughout Micronesia who came for jobs and education. Later migration included Filipinos, Koreans, Taiwanese, and others from Southeast Asia, all of whom were seeking economic opportunities through jobs, better living conditions, business development, and economic expansion.

The Marianas Islands have in recent decades become a popular tourism site for the Japanese seeking recreation including golfing and, more

Table 10.1
Distribution of Guamanians in the United States by Region

UNITED STATES	GUAMANIANS
Total Population	30,695
Regional Distribution	
East	1,952
North	1,816
South	4,757
West	22,170
MAJOR CONCENTRATION BY STATES	
California	17,009
Washington	1,739
Hawaii	1,630
Texas	1,229
New York	1,017

Source: U.S. Bureau of the Census, 1988.

recently, gambling. These developments will change not only the ethnic and cultural character of the island people but also their social needs and problems.

SOCIODEMOGRAPHIC OVERVIEW

The 1980 Census was the first to count and identify persons in the United States originating from Guam as Guamanians. However, Chamorros from Guam have been migrating and settling in the United States as early as the 1920s (Untalan Munoz, 1979). The 1980 Census enumerated 30,695 Guamanians living in the United States (U.S. Bureau of the Census, 1988). Guamanians in this context can be inferred as Chamorros of Guam. Other nationalities who may live on Guam prior to this time have their own specific and more accurate race identifier (e.g., Filipinos and Caucasians).

Chamorros were found in all states. If the United States is divided into four regions (east, north, south, and west), the west had the largest concentration at 22,170 people, and California had the largest number at 17,009 Chamorros (Table 10.1). The 1980 Census taken on Guam

Table 10.2
Per Capita Income of Selected Groups in the United States and in Selected
States, 1979–1980

Selected Group	United States	California	Hawaii	Washington
Total (in dollars)	7,298	8,295	7,740	8,073
White	7,808	9,109	8,762	8,304
Black	4,545	5,710	5,437	5,867
American Indian, Eskimo, Aleut	4,577	6,030	6,244	5,006
Asian and Pacific Islander	7,037	7,243	7,351	6,233
Japanese	9,068	9,567	9,475	8,715
Chinese	7,476	7,946	9,422	7,202
Filipino	6,915	6,625	5,537	6,045
Korean	5,544	6,010	6,520	4,480
Asian Indian	8,667	8,159	10,165	7,245
Vietnamese	3,382	3,315	2,813	3,115
Hawaiian	5,691	7,169	5,328	5,845
Guamanian	5,533	5,747	4,249	6,288
Samoan	3,573	4,081	2,729	3,890

Source: U.S. Bureau of the Census, 1988.

revealed that there was a total of 105,979 persons with 47,825 Chamorros, 22,447 Filipinos, 26,901 whites, and 8,806 others. Thus, there are 47,825 Chamorro/Guamanians on Guam and 30,695 scattered throughout the 50 states. If undercount and other enumeration problems of the Census are discounted, these figures are significant in terms of Chamorro out-migration from Guam. While Chamorro migration is not the focus of this chapter, this demographic trend has serious implications for social and governmental policies for the islands. The distribution of Guamanians according to the 1980 Census is given in Table 10.1. Table 10.2 illustrates how Chamorros as a group fared economically in the United States compared with the general population. The per capita income of Guamanians in the United States was $5,533.

VALUES AND BEHAVIORAL NORMS

The social status of a Chamorro is determined by his or her family (Untalan Munoz, 1990). The family in Chamorro society is larger than the immediate or even intergenerational family. It is the constellation of family relationships by blood or by marriage, it has a group identity in a name (similar to a tribe or clan), and it has geographical dimensions such as a village or an area. Thus, to establish identity, a person may have to identify who his or her parents, grandparents, or significant relatives are, as well as the family group and the village from which he or she comes.

The family thus serves a very vital force in the life of a Chamorro. Considerable emphasis is placed on support, cooperation, and reciprocity among family members. Taking care of family is an integral part of an individual's personal success, and it reflects the success of the relationships within a given family. Kindness, compassion, friendliness, and generosity are strong values among Chamorros. Consequently, selfishness, lack of compassion, and individualism are viewed as negative behaviors and characteristics.

Traditional Chamorro family structure reveals that economic, social, and psychological functions are melded together in family relationships. Extended intergenerational families are common and typical among island peoples. The island-type of extended intergenerational family differs from the extended family where relatives reside in separate households and maintain only a social network of close communication with each other. In the island tradition of the intergenerational family, any combination of parents, grandparents, children, single aunts and uncles, and cousins may live in one household. They share resources and have clear roles and responsibilities to maintain family functions and relationships.

The sharing of resources, hospitality, and generosity are fundamental values common to many Pacific Island cultures. Such qualities are essential attributes in a small area, such as a self-contained island, where survival is dependent on an individual's relationship to other people and to nature.

The traditional island cultures were based on communal and mutual support, which resulted from a highly developed system of sharing and exchange, as well as from family organization regarding resource development and distribution. Struggle and competition for basic goods were largely unnecessary because goods were readily available and commonly shared. For example, food has been naturally abundant in the islands as evidenced by the plentiful breadfruit, taro, coconuts, bananas, and yams, which either have grown wild or have required very little tending. This natural abundance obviated the need for competition for basic foodstuffs, a fundamental component of survival. Furthermore, land and resources from the land were not viewed as properties of individuals.

Prior to World War II, the Chamorros had an economic lifestyle based on subsistence. Family members clustered around common family land

and shared the available food including agricultural crops and wildlife. As the primary social group on the island of Guam, the family has functioned as the basic nurturing and socializing force to maintain order and enforce social mores, values, and beliefs. Through the family, traditions have been continuously sustained and transferred from one generation to the next. In a society that has relied primarily on oral history, the elements of family cohesion and strong cultural ties were essential to the continuity of cultural heritage.

The traditional Chamorro family was sustained economically and psychologically from within as a result of the strong cohesive relationships among its members. Proximity of living has enabled family members to share in the care and rearing of children. Parents often lived near married children, or married children lived with parents and other unmarried siblings, aunts, and uncles in the same household. This system facilitated the sharing of child-rearing and promoted an enhanced process of socialization for the child.

Shared child-rearing is very useful in a family based on cultural milieu. Shared child-rearing provides the child with access to family members for affection, attention, and care. This access encourages interpersonal and social skills development in relating to a variety of individuals. These social skills and an environment of caring individuals are essential to a child's positive growth and development. Strong feelings of security and a positive ego can result. Furthermore, burdens or hardships resulting from the child's development, whether from illness or other problems, are also shared, thereby reducing stress and pressures on the natural parents or singular caretaker.

These cultural attributes are demonstrated in how the family functions and how social activities are conducted. *Chinchuli* is a practice of assistance and a social obligation given in cash or in kind. *Chinchuli* is given during such occasions as birth/christening, weddings, and funerals. The *chinchuli* practice establishes and maintains economic bonds among relatives and friends. The tradition is often extended to other occasions such as the family village fiestas or any other family celebration.

The village fiesta is a unique cultural activity among Chamorros. Influenced by Spaniards, the Marianas Islands was Catholic (at least under Spanish rule). The center of every village was the church; each had its own patron saint who was celebrated annually with religious and social festivities. During these annual events each village prepared a feast for all visitors who were welcomed to enter any home and participate in the fiesta. These fiestas are still a popular practice in most villages in the Marianas Islands of Guam, Saipan, Tinian, and Rota.

Christenings, weddings, funerals, and fiestas are important social functions that maintain family and social ties extending beyond mere social relationships. They include social and economic obligations as well. These forms of mutual assistance and social support are essential in maintaining the cultural values of generosity and kindness. Chamorros, as a group, look out for each other and do not hesitate to offer help regardless of relationships.

Ancestor worship is another cultural belief among Chamorros. Chamorros believe their ancestors, the *Taotaomona*, exist in various sacred places on the islands. They believe failure to show respect or to trespass uninvited or without permission into sacred places of the *Taotaomonas* may result in illness or tragedy. This belief serves to emphasize respect and nonviolation of others' properties. It also serves to explain illnesses and crises as forms of punishment due to a transgression or violation incurred by a family member or the victim. Ancestor worship is also a useful concept in a culture that advocates interdependence and social control.

PROFILE OF SOCIAL AND PSYCHOLOGICAL PROBLEMS AND ISSUES

The social and psychological problems experienced by and manifested among Chamorros today are imbedded in the turmoil and chaos resulting from rapid changes and value conflicts. High suicide rates among youth, alcoholism, drug abuse, family violence, and high crime rates are examples of problems confronting Chamorros today (Untalan Munoz, 1990).

Family dysfunction—a breakdown in traditional family relationships, mutual support, and cooperation—is manifested through alienation and failure to provide and maintain supportive relationships. As a result of this breakdown, social support is based more on social ties and relationships and less on familial reliance. Consequently, economic reciprocity, which has been a major aspect of Chamorro familial relationships, is declining. Family dysfunction for Chamorros today is highlighted by the universal trends in nuclear family composition, the residential distance among Chamorro family members, the severance of mutually owned and shared real estate property on Guam, and a breakdown in family social events and responsibility.

The sharing of children by a family, called *poksai*, is a cultural practice in decline. Similarly, the emphasis on respect and concern for the elderly is decreasing. Adults have forfeited their social obligation to the young to serve as models and parents, which before encouraged respect, care, and discipline among the young, as well as advocated the same regard for the elderly within family. As individuals began to share different values toward childcare and child-rearing, gaps and conflicts in these perspectives resulted in abandonment of the traditional roles and responsibilities formerly shared. Individualism and competition for survival surfaced as by-products of progress and change for the younger generations of Chamorros.

Rapid social changes coupled with increasing in-migration are causing major psychological stresses among the Chamorros. Powerlessness and lack of control over the changes occurring in the Marianas can be psychologically stressful and can lead to apathy and alienation (Untalan Munoz, 1990). The difficulties faced by people isolated by mountains or desert are not the same as those faced by islands sequestered by water. The Chamorros no longer have the models to prepare them to cope and adjust to the socioeconomic changes of the Marianas Islands nor the orientation to deal with a more aggressive and sophisticated immigrant population sanctioned by their mother country, the United States of America. The developing consciousness and awareness among the Chamorros are being manifested by hostility and anger, fueled by fear of being controlled and oppressed in their own homeland.

The situation for Chamorros in the United States is more difficult to assess because of the dispersement of this population and the limited data describing their circumstances. However, the profile of social and psychological problems of Chamorros in Guam may be used to extrapolate concerns of Chamorros in the United States. In general, the breakdown of cultural values and the deterioration of cultural identity may be even more exacerbated for Chamorros in the United States for several reasons. One reason is the difficulty in geographical accessibility of village and family support systems and the subsequent decline of values such as family reciprocity and sharing of roles. Another reason is the pervasive influence of Western values and behavioral norms on Chamorros in the United States and the struggle to maintain traditional cultural values when confronted with Western ideas.

SOCIAL SERVICE INTERVENTIONS

Principles of Practice

The cultural appropriateness of social services for Chamorros in Guam and in the United States can be guided by three major principles of practice.

1. A basic respect for the definition and identification of Chamorros as an indigenous group and a distinction of Chamorros from other ethnic groups should be exercised. To work from a cultural perspective with persons from Guam or other islands of the Northern Marianas, it is important to be able to differentiate between the native indigenous group—Chamorro—and other ethnic groups who have made these islands their residences but whose ethnic and cultural roots are elsewhere.

Without this understanding, the significance of the cultural perspective will be irrelevant in human service intervention.

2. Predicated on the strong cultural value of the family, practitioners need to conceptualize both assessment and intervention with Chamorros from a family context. In Guam and islands of the Northern Marianas as well as in the United States, cultural values of reciprocity and role interdependence are more critical for traditionally oriented Chamorros than values such as individual responsibility and independence (Untalan Munoz, 1990).

3. Similar to the emphasis on the cultural value of family, practitioners should design and deliver services that are compatible with the cultural value of social networks. An important cultural attribute among Chamorros is the development and maintenance of social relationships in which cultural traditions and activities are promoted. It is important that the practitioner understand and work with this emphasis on the collective.

Conceptual Model of Intervention

A conceptual model for working with Chamorros should be predicated on the previously discussed principles of practice. However, the reality is that social services have been designed and delivered according to a Western framework.

The incorporation of Guam as a U.S. territory in 1950 and the establishment of the Northern Marianas as a commonwealth in 1978 extended federal entitlement programs to the islands. These generally include aid to families with dependent children, child welfare, child protective services, public education support, aid to the elderly, Medicaid, public health services programs, and community mental health programs including drug and substance abuse programs.

These federal programs administered by the territories are consistent with federal guidelines for purposes and policies affecting service delivery design and modality. This form of conservative application is not without significant and serious consequences. While these islands are U.S. territories, the people, the culture, and, more important, the economic, social, and political infrastructures for social program planning, organization, and delivery fall far short of the conditions for which the federal programs were designed. Such programs were, in fact, formulated to deal with complex urban industrial cities in the United States. While similar problems may exist in the islands, the nature and dynamics are often quite different and thus require a different approach. For example, meals provided for the elderly in their homes are necessary when there are no family members and no one to cook and care for the elderly.

But in many cases, the elderly in the islands live with relatives. Often the food is an unnecessary assistance as well as unpalatable.

This form of assistance does not support the value of family unit and social responsibility. Such a practice promotes individual responsibility but undermines the role of the family as the primary caretaker of its members, young or old. The application of social welfare programs and social services intervention needs to be carefully examined and understood to determine the impact and consequences on the client, as well as the sociocultural dimensions and the meaning of the practice.

While there is a sizable population of Chamorros or Guamanians in the United States and clusters can be identified in specific geographical areas, there are no known formal programs or funded services, public or private, specific to Chamorro/Guamanians in any of the fifty states.

There are, however, many social clubs and organizations founded by Chamorro/Guamanian groups in the United States. Such social organizations can be found in almost every area where Chamorro/Guamanians reside. Interestingly, these types of organizations are not found on their home islands. Thus, these organizations can provide the social support and the opportunity to practice cultural traditions and activities from the islands, thereby promoting the indigenous and insular unity among those who choose to live away. Village feasts, weddings, christenings, and Liberation Day celebrations ameliorate the situation of isolation for Chamorros. Some of these social clubs and organizations were established as early as the 1950s. The Guamanian Association of Long Beach, the Sons and Daughters of Guam in San Diego, and the Chamorro Association of Southern California illustrate a few of the more than twenty organizations found in California alone. These organizations serve as a viable focus for social service delivery for Chamorro/Guamanians in the United States.

Chamorro/Guamanians are a tight-knit group. There is a strong tendency to look after each other and maintain social relationships. These are strong attributes of Chamorro/Guamanians. The utilization of these natural support groups can serve as an effective method in social service delivery. To illustrate this point, in a recent case a woman from Guam living in Hawaii was killed by her husband. The woman was not known to the Guamanian community in Hawaii. However, when the news revealed she was from Guam, the Guam military community and the Chamorro/Guamanians residing in Hawaii came together to help. Offers were made to take care of the baby, and a search party was organized by Guam's military personnel to look for the woman's missing body. The men organized the search on a voluntary basis during their free time.

Through these social networks, Chamorro/Guamanians away from their homeland provide social support, cultural reinforcement, and a strong sense of social identity to the members. Through these same networks, they are able to maintain cultural traditions, share resources, and enhance social ties.

Specific Skills

Certain considerations that highlight the skills component of practice should be emphasized. The practitioner needs to utilize skills that involve the family supports, maintain family cohesion, and strengthen relationships, which are important values among Chamorros. The family plays a significant role in social service intervention involving a Chamorro client. Because of strong and close ties, family members play a major role in the management of family members' problems and affairs. The extent and degree of family involvement are usually dependent on the relationships within that family context. Family involvement may include emotional support or actual assistance in kind and/or in cash. More important, the solution to personal and family problems is kept within the family support network, which is viewed as the appropriate place for such matters.

In addition, respect for personal and family privacy is necessary in a small socially oriented society, particularly where social controls can be severe. Thus, even away from their home islands, Chamorros are sensitive and concerned about how their behavior will affect family members. Confidential assurance must be communicated, and trust in that assurance is essential to effective involvement of Chamorros in social service intervention.

Chamorros are generally very resourceful. Given opportunities to participate in the solutions to their problems and needs, they can usually identify friends and relatives who can come to their aid. This method of client participation is useful in getting appropriate help as well as help that is more likely to be acceptable to the client. This is another way by which the vast and generous resource support networks found among Chamorros can be effectively utilized.

REFERENCES

Untalan Munoz, F. (1990). American policy: Its impact on Pacific Island families. *Pacific Ties, The Pacific Islander and Asian News Magazine at University of California, Los Angeles* 13 (3): 5, 7, 16, 23.

———. (1979). An exploratory study of island migration: Chamorros of Guam. Ph.D. dissertation, University of California, Los Angeles.

———. (1984). Family life patterns of Pacific Islanders: The insidious displacement of culture. In G. J. Powell (ed.), *The Psychological Development of Minority Group Children*. New York: Bruner-Mazel Publishers.

———— (1976). Pacific Islanders: A perplexed and neglected minority. *Social Casework* 57 (3): 179–184.

U.S. Bureau of the Census (1988). *We, the Asian and Pacific Islander Americans.* Washington, D.C.: U.S. Government Printing Office.

Workman, R. L., and J. E. Burton, Jr. (1982). A limited preliminary assessment of Guam's social service needs. A report prepared under Title XX grant for the Division of Social Services, Department of Public Health and Social Services, Guam, University of Guam.

III

Contemporary Problems and Issues

CHAPTER 11

Asian and Pacific Islander Elderly

JEANETTE C. TAKAMURA

INTRODUCTION

An ancient Chinese proverb bears a wish:

> May your happiness be as nice as the [Eastern] sea
> May your longevity be as high as the [Southern] mountain.

As Americans approach the twenty-first century, their longevity appears as "high as the mountain." Throughout the nation, more elders are living far beyond seven decades, with growing numbers becoming centenarians. So significant is the expansion of our elderly population that distinctions capturing their diversity are commonplace. Thus, older persons are often differentiated by age segments—as the "young old," "old," and "old old"—by needs—as "self-sufficient," "transitional," and "vulnerable" or "frail" elders (Executive Office on Aging, State of Hawaii, 1987, pp. 6–7)—and by psychographic characteristics—as "attainers," "adapters," "explorers," "martyrs," and "preservers" (Gollub and Javitz, 1989).

From from being dismissed as inconsequential, the burgeoning of the elderly population is now viewed as a Longevity Revolution with far-reaching implications for all sectors of society. Aging-related social, economic, and other opportunities and dilemmas are in visible competition for attention and dollars in the public and private domains.

One segment of America's population—the Asian and Pacific Islander Americans (APIAs)—provides us with an unusually rich opportunity to consider how best to prepare for and respond to the special needs and concerns of all elders and their families in the decades ahead. Among the most diverse of our nation's ethnocultural groups, the APIAs include people who enjoy the best longevity in the nation and in the world and comprise the fastest growing ethnic subpopulation in the United States (Gardner, Robey, and Smith, 1985). This chapter examines the phenomenon of aging in relation to APIAs and discusses service intervention strategies to be considered in work with these elders and their families.

DESCRIPTION OF THE ELDERLY ASIAN AND PACIFIC ISLANDER AMERICANS

America's elderly population is defined politically by federal laws such as the Social Security Act and the Older Americans Act. The Social Security Act's definition is more conservative, setting 65 years as the demarcation for old age. In contrast, the Older Americans Act utilizes 60 years as the standard.

Systematically gathered national data on minority older adults, their demographics, and their socioeconomic, health, and housing conditions are almost nonexistent, with the exception of data available through the U.S. Bureau of the Census and through such resource units as the National Center for Health Statistics (NCHS). According to the 1980 Census, elderly APIAs accounted for 6 percent of the total APIA population. In 1980, 79 percent of all elderly APIAs lived with their families (U.S. Bureau of the Census, 1988), a figure which may show a decline in the 1990 Census reports.

A great diversity characterizes APIA elders. That is, the socioeconomic status and other life conditions of the elderly APIAs differ by distinct ethnic groups, periods of immigration, and constraints imposed by the formal federal, state, and local policies and the informal social policies that dictate norms in such areas as race relations, immigration, housing, health, social welfare, labor and employment, education, business and economic development, and zoning. These factors in combination with genetic, lifestyle, and dietary considerations probably explain why Chinese and Japanese enjoy exemplary longevity while native Hawaiians have higher incidences of acute and chronic illnesses and functional impairments and shorter longevity rates.

The impact of formal and informal policies upon the full range of life opportunities and needs of APIAs is a subject unto itself and is nowhere more apparent than in their ethnic enclaves. Examples can be located, for instance, in America's many Chinatowns where the elderly descendants of immigrants who built America's transcontinental railroad are likely to interact with older immigrants from Hong Kong who are looking for investment opportunities. Here and in the "Little Manilas," "Little Seouls," "Little Japan Towns," and native Hawaiian communities, rural and urban redevelopment plans have threatened longtime residents with evictions and the disruption of familiar community patterns. In these instances, ethnic elders face some of the severest losses. These are losses of longstanding landmarks and buildings, of social networks and routines, and ultimately of aspects of their social and ethnic history, identity, and sense of security.

The diversity of APIA elders is also apparent in contrasting the extent to which APIA groups are comprised of the foreign-born. In one of the few studies to reconfigure and examine Census data, William T. Liu and Elena Yu (1985) found a wide range in the proportion of foreign-born APIA elders. Ranked at the high end were older Filipino and older Chinese, among whom 96 percent and 81 percent respectively were foreign-born. Elderly Japanese and Asian Indians tended by comparison to be American natives, with 43 percent and 28 percent foreign-born respectively (Liu and Yu, 1985). A wide variation also exists in the degree to which APIA elders may be Western, cosmopolitan, or traditional in their cultural orientations. While the Hmong are struggling to adapt to urban American life, some newly arrived Chinese, Japanese, and Asian Indians are comfortable with European as well as American ways.

As with most of America's ethnic minority elders, a greater percentage of elderly APIAs have incomes below the poverty level than do white elders. However, within-group variations in income levels are apparent. Liu and Yu's analyses establish elderly Asian Indians (17.4 percent) and Chinese (15.9 percent) as those who most often fall below the poverty level. Lower percentages (9.3 percent and 9.5 percent respectively) hold for elderly Japanese and Filipinos (Liu and Yu, 1985), who nonetheless are the poorest members of their own ethnocultural groups.

Comparatively high suicide rates have been noted among elderly Chinese and Japanese women and among Japanese men. Liu and Yu report, for example, that elderly Chinese women's suicide rates are three times higher between the ages of 65 and 74, seven times higher from 75 to 84, and ten times higher for those 85 and older than for elderly white women. Compared to elderly white men 85 years of age and older, Japanese men of the same cohort have suicide rates that are almost three times greater. These rates bring to mind the Japanese practice of *obasute*, which presents the self-imposed death of elders as an honorable alternative when village resources are inadequate to sustain everyone. Whatever the underlying causes, the suicide rates reveal the later years as far from idyllic for many APIAs.

The information that is available on APIA elders and their needs is sparse. An increased understanding of this population requires the commitment of adequate funding by Congress and data development initiatives focusing on minority elders.

DEFINITION AND SCOPE OF THE ISSUE

In 1900, the average life span in the United States was approximately 47 years. Americans 65 years of age and older accounted for 4.1 percent (or 3.1 million persons) of the U.S. population in 1900. As Americans approach the year 2000, they are enjoying an average of 73.88 years of life, with some APIAs claiming the best longevity in the nation. By the twenty-first century, there are expected to be 34.9 million older adults 65 years of age and older, comprising 13 percent of the U.S. population. Asserting that the next will be a "silver century," demographers also predict that the 65-and-over population will climb to 21.8 percent by 2030, when the last of the baby boom generation will have become elders.

A paper prepared by the Special Committee on Aging of the U.S. Senate reported that:

More people are . . . surviving into their 10th and 11th decades. The Bureau of the Census estimates that there were about 25,000 people 100 years or older in 1986 and that there will be over 100,000 by 2000. Because of the increase in the very old population, it is increasingly likely that the older persons will themselves have at least one surviving parent. (U.S. Senate, 1989)

Specialized knowledge and skills pertinent to aging-related physical and mental health and social and economic conditions are absolute requisites for work with older adults and their families.

Physical and Mental Health Conditions

Research studies conducted over the last decade on the biology and physiology of aging have debunked the most resilient myths of aging, which miscast older adults as predominantly decrepit, senile, withdrawn, and incapable. The general aging process is now known to be characterized by less than significant rates of physical and mental decline. Moreover, intelligence quotients have been observed to rise when mental activity and learning continue in the advanced years, despite any deceleration in computing time and other cognitive processes. In fact, dramatic changes in older adults mistakenly linked to aging are now attributed primarily to the ravages of chronic illnesses and to the contributory effects of heredity, preventive health behaviors, and socioeconomic variables.

Heart disease, cancer, and stroke are among the diseases that commonly present older adults with functional limitations, but Alzheimer disease and other dementias impose some of the most devastating and debilitating consequences. Although pseudodementias caused by drugs, depression, and cardiovascular and other diseases are treatable, Alzheimer disease cannot be diagnosed conclusively without an autopsy. Severe intellectual decline, progressing from the loss of memory and of the ability to compute to the loss of personality, speech, and control over bodily functions are characteristics of Alzheimer disease. Wandering and violent behaviors, extreme insomnia, the inability to recognize family and friends, and incontinence typically occur in persons with late stage Alzheimer disease. Research reports released in 1989 claim that the incidence of Alzheimer disease rises with advanced age far more dramatically than originally believed. Alzheimer disease is expected to remain a primary reason for long-term institutionalization during the 1990s unless a cure can be found via medical research.

Difficult and embarrassing for most elders and their families, urinary incontinence afflicts up to one out of five older adults residing in the community and nearly half of all elderly patients in nursing homes. Sometimes caused by neurological, psychological, environmental, and genitourinary conditions, incontinence responds to treatment in one out of three cases, when properly diagnosed.

Hearing and visual impairments are commonplace among older adults, with hearing impairments more prevalent among men and visual losses such as loss of depth perception, near- and farsightedness, the loss of ability to see certain colors, reduced visual scope, an inability to tolerate bright lights, and difficulties with transitions from dimly to well-lit environments noted more in women. Unless properly diagnosed, sensory losses suffered especially by the non-English-speaking APIA elder may be mistaken for noncompliance or incompetence, and depression, paranoia, and social isolation may be incorrectly treated.

Poor physical health and nutrition, the loss of friends and family members, and drug interaction effects are among the factors associated with depression in older adults. Older persons are not any less immune to mental health problems, but they are more likely to have chronic illnesses, to take several prescribed and over-the-counter drugs, and to experience multiple losses of significant others, familiar practices and routines, and longheld roles.

The foregoing discussion of age-related health and mental health conditions should substantiate the critical need for helping professionals with specialized training in geriatric practice. Professionals without such training are likely to commit gross errors in diagnosing and treating conditions associated with aging. Potential jeopardy and discrimination are heightened further when professionals also lack crosscultural training and fail to understand the stigma associated with some of the diseases prevalent in old age, how to serve the non-English-speaking and the culturally different, and the reliance of many elders upon folk remedies.

Social and Economic Conditions

There is a need to factor in the graying of the population as a major variable in social and economic planning efforts in American society. Elders are interested in maintaining part-time or flex-time work roles. However, there is strong evidence that employers are skeptical about the potential contributions of older workers. In this regard, an American Association for Retired Persons' commissioned study concluded that the commitment of American businesses' top management to older workers actually has been declining since 1985 (Yankelovich and Associates, 1989). Hence, the odds of minority elders in need of work securing decent employment are not heartening.

Older Americans include both persons with more discretionary income than any other age cohort and persons of greatly understated poverty. The high discretionary income levels of a sizable number of older adults have made them an attractive market segment. The service and retail industries are targeting "YEEPIES" ("youthful, energetic, elderly people involved in everything") and "SIPPIES" (senior independent pioneers"), aware of the fact that 75 percent of American's older adults are homeowners and that nearly three-fourths are unbridled by mortgages.

Consumer fraud and abuse specific to elders has followed on the heels of interest in the elderly market segment. Reports by Congress released in the mid- to late 1980s document the extent to which elderly consumers are being duped. Preying on health and other vulnerabilities, unscrupulous companies have made off with in excess of $10 million from older adults for quack drugs, useless devices, and Medicare supplemental insurance and long-term care insurance products with high premium rates and almost negligible benefit payout probabilities. For APIA elders, consumer protection issues revolve around the therapeutic value of folk medicines and curative aids, some deemed harmful.

As the nation grays, its elderly population grows disproportionately female. An abundance of evidence reveals that to be old and female is also to be impoverished. According to the Commonwealth Fund Commission on Elderly People Living Alone (1987), older minority women living alone on an annual income of $5,100 or less constitute the most vulnerable of all older adults. By the year 2020, it is expected that poverty among older Americans will be confined primarily to minority women living alone, giving special meaning to the term "feminization of poverty." The critical need to reexamine obstacles to female economic security, the male employment bias of Social Security, and the structure and characteristics of other sources of retirement income and then to construct necessary policy interventions may be expected to heighten significantly in the years ahead.

While the vast majority of older Americans enjoy good health, particularly those who are 85 years of age and older are more apt to experience functionally limiting chronic illnesses and to be among the nation's 5 percent of older adults receiving institutional long-term care. For most older persons, financial, emotional, and other long-term care burdens pose the most frightening and potentially devastating threat to the quality of their families' lives.

The level of concern among APIAs about long-term care is discernible in their establishment of special facilities and programs such as Kimochi and On Lok in San Francisco, Keiro in Los Angeles, and the Kuakini Medical Center's Hale Pulama Mau in Honolulu, all of which were designed to provide ethnically sensitive care to APIA elders who can no longer be cared for by family and friends in their own homes.

Two compelling trends with implications for long-term care are emerging in contemporary America. "Women-in-the-middle" who belong to the "sandwich generation" of caregivers of parents, spouses, and children are growing in number. Concomitantly, more women are joining the work force, causing experts to anticipate the labor force participation of women 45 to 60 years of age to reach 75 percent by the year 2000 (Crim, 1988). Without favorable labor and social policies in place, particularly APIA and other minority older women will be wedged between caregiving responsibilities, the need to work, and the lack of adequate work histories for earning decent pensions and benefits.

Policy issues with the greatest opportunity for transforming the future pertain to the basis for allocating fiscal and other scarce resources to different age segments. Already, detractors are saying that the older adults receive a disproportionate share of assistance from the government. Those who argue from this perspective fail to recognize that the Longevity Revolution requires a shift from paradigms that institutionalize retirement, underestimate longevity, cling to obsolete presumptions of large younger cohorts, and vilify old age. New paradigms must acknowledge the graying of America; promote the potential contributions of older adults in the workplace as volunteers, mentors, advocates, and moral arbiters; and otherwise reconceptualize and reconfigure the structures and processes of our society. Perhaps Andrew W. Achenbaum (1986) says it best when he writes, "we must rethink the meaning of 'age' in an aging society" (p. 28).

AGING AND CULTURAL TRADITIONS AND CONCERNS

Cultural values pertinent to aging and older adults are as diverse as the groups bound by the APIA rubric. One caveat thus must be underscored: Professionals must avoid stereotyping elderly APIAs and their concerns in the selection and implementation of helping processes.

Aging and Traditional Asian Cultural Concerns

Filial piety is a basic tenet in Confucian ethics, which capture values fundamental to Chinese society and have become the foundation for other Asian cultures. Confucianism stresses the importance of assuring happiness or quality of life in old age through the demonstration of respectful attitudes and proper behaviors. *Hsiao* or filial piety and *hsiao tao* or the way of filial piety and the bringing of happiness to elders are mentioned in several Chinese classics, including *The Analects, the Book of Rites,* and *The Book of Filial Piety.*

Old age is not regarded in negative terms in the traditional context. The word for "old"—*lao*—suggests respect, honor, and achievement. Hence, it appears in the phrases for "teacher" (*lao shih*), "old friend" (*lao yu*), government officials 70 years of age and older (*lao fu*), and political advisors during the Han and Tang dynasties (*san lao*). The aged were treasured, consulted for their wisdom-based longevity, and accorded vast authority over their households. Each year, younger persons honored elders through the *Hsiang Yin Chiu* ceremony with a banquet and special activities.

The significance of filial piety as a central concept is apparent in ancient Chinese history. Circa 2200 B.C., Emperor Yao purportedly bestowed the throne to Emperor Shun because of the latter's outstanding filial deeds. Written during the Tsin Dynasty to the Emperor by Li Mi to decline a court assignment in order to care for his ailing grandmother, the *Chen Ching Piao* is upheld as the ultimate statement of filial piety. Other legends in Chinese history tell of accomplishments and contributions in old age and of a special reverence for elders.

The traditional Japanese and Korean cultures have both been greatly shaped by Confucian ideals. Behaviors that reflected *oyakoko* or filial piety were expected of all children in traditional Japanese society. The young held *oya on* or obligations to parents and were expected to meet their *on* to their elders with feelings of deep gratitude by ministering to their needs, submitting to their demands, and otherwise caring for them. Not acting accordingly brought *haji* or great shame to the family name.

Filial piety and the social relationships prescribed by it are very much at the core of the traditional Korean culture. In keeping with Confucian dictates, traditional Korean social units ranging from the family to the national government characteristically have accorded supreme respect to older and higher ranked individuals.

Centuries of Indo-Malay, Spanish, and American influences have shaped the Filipino culture. Quite different from that of Far Eastern Asians, the traditional Filipino culture also gives primacy to the family and promotes the practice of *utang na loob* or a sense of obligation among younger members to their elders. Older members of the family are treated as wisdom figures and are addressed in honorific terms as *man-ang*, if an older woman, and *manong*, if an older man.

Aging and Traditional Pacific Islander Culture Concerns

Residing primarily in Hawaii and California, native Hawaiians comprise the largest Pacific Islander subgroup. Bound by the organizing concept of *'ohana* or family, native Hawaiians have traditionally accorded greater respect to their elders or *kūpuna* who serve as benevolent moral/ wisdom figures. *Kūpuna* are looked to for guidance, leadership, instruction, mediation, and facilitating harmonious interpersonal interactions.

The Samoans comprise the second largest of the Pacific Islander subgroups. Like all other APIA subgroups, the Samoans also value the family as the primary social unit and hold their elders in high regard. The *aiga* or extended family, led by a *matai* or chief, is the core unit of social organization in *fa'a Samoa*—the Samoan way. Older members are treated warmly and valued for their wisdom within the *aiga*, which also provides for their care.

In all APIA subgroups, elders have been accorded the highest degree of respect. They play important roles as wisdom figures, spokespersons, and decision makers. Because each traditional society was historically reliant upon a land-based, agricultural economy, families were stable social units, geographic mobility was rare, and interdependence, conformity, and adherence to traditions were essential for the orderly workings of the family, village, and larger community. The care of elderly members fell within the realm of responsibility of the family in all traditional Asian and Pacific Islander cultures.

Special Topics Related to Cultural Traditions and Concerns

Although Asian Americans tend to enjoy the best longevity in the United States and Pacific Islander Americans tend not to fare as well, the incidence of depression, Alzheimer disease, and other mental disorders that increase with age can bear special meanings for APIA elders and their families. Signs of mental disorders can be cause for tremendous alarm and shame, compelling families to bear caregiving burdens alone.

Two research studies completed in Hawaii in 1989 and 1990 suggest that APIA elder care attitudes may be difficult to ascertain. One study found that more than half of all Japanese American public employees were engaged in caregiving and that many of them reported that caregiving is a "source of personal satisfaction" and a way to "pay back" family obligations (Executive Office on Aging, State of Hawaii, 1990). Another reported that Japanese American adults do not feel "obligated" to care for their elders (KGMB Political Media Research, Inc., 1989).

Particularly among elderly APIAs who were immigrants, social and economic resources may be scant. The changing character of their ethnic enclaves, the mobility of other family members, their lack of mastery of the English language, the diminishing of social circles because of the death of relatives and peers, and woefully low fixed incomes and benefits are all factors that place them at risk. Many may be too old to attempt to return to the work force, and those who are not as old may lack the English language proficiency to seek anything but low-paying custodial, housekeeping, and other jobs.

Experts have long argued that access by elders to social welfare, health, and mental health programs for which they are eligible is constrained by such factors as a lack of awareness of these programs, distrust of the social service system, uncertainty as to how to navigate within it, and a preference for assistance from familiar others. However, it is important to recognize that the nonparticipation of APIAs is not entirely an anomaly. Joseph Veroff, Richard A. Kulka, and Elizabeth Douvan (1981) note that the vast majority of Americans tend to prefer informal help and resources. Specific to older Americans, some experts have found, moreover, that while less than 5 percent have used community mental health centers, one-third of the clientele eventually drop out.

While the preceding discussion asserts that elders and their families are best served by professionals with specialized gerontologic knowledge and skills, the following avers that social service interventions on behalf of minority elders must acknowledge and incorporate cultural differences and preferences.

SOCIAL SERVICE INTERVENTIONS WITH ASIAN AND PACIFIC ISLANDER AMERICAN ELDERS

Principles of Practice

Abraham Monk (1981) identifies a number of practice objectives that can be used as generic points of departure in constructing and selecting interventions for older clients. However, the following principles of practice are offered to facilitate work with elderly APIAs.

The importance of respect for older adults in general and for elderly APIAs specifically must be manifested in practice.

The decline of ageist attitudes has not kept pace with the rise of the Longevity Revolution. Even the best intentioned professionals frequently exhibit discomfort with their own aging and prefer younger clients. However, respect for older persons is not the only prerequisite in working with APIAs. A genuine appreciation of the cultural orientation of these individuals, devoid of stereotypes and misconceptions, is another fundamental requisite. This appreciation encompasses the diversity that characterizes the ethnic groups bound together by an all-encompassing rubric. Because America's treatment of its APIA citizens has been colored persistently by racism, helping professionals must be certain that they can offer APIAs nondiscriminatory assistance.

> *The clients' culturally based meanings of dilemmas and of help should be identified and utilized.*

Theoretical models and intervention strategies tend to perpetuate professional definitions of the meanings of human problems and legitimized solutions. Veroff, Kulka, and Douvan (1981) and others have documented incongruities between professional and lay views of human problems. For the elderly APIAs, culturally based explanations of dilemmas—such as a lack of *Yin-Yang* balance, the failure to understand appropriate roles and obligations or past transgressions that were unsatisfactorily addressed—fall outside of Western theoretical models. Moreover, legitimate APIA solutions may not be bound to verbal discussions or to the use of professionals.

> *Health, social, legal/civil rights, and client vs. professional issues should be distinguished from each other.*

Minority elderly clients are rarely versed in their legal and civil rights. They tend to be unfamiliar with social service and health institutions, the specific roles of different helping professionals, and Western therapeutic approaches. Many have been subject to racism and ageism and have concomitantly blamed and victimized. Professionals must honor their human and legal rights and be careful not to subjugate client interests in favor of those that ultimately serve the professions.

> *Ethnic consultants should be utilized to assure the primacy of the client and the provision of appropriate assistance.*

Professionals should assure the primacy of their APIA clients' needs by utilizing ethnic consultants to strive for accuracy in communications, crosscultural understanding, and culturally sensitive interventions. If necessary, the client's family should be recruited to assist as facilitators, particularly when clients do not speak English, subscribe to traditional or bicultural helping strategies, appear to be reserved, or are functionally limited by conditions such as dementias.

Theoretical/Conceptual Models of Intervention

To reiterate earlier observations, the diversity of the elderly population is nowhere more pronounced than among APIAs. If not for this reason alone, practice approaches must be eclectic, borrowing from the range of Western theoretical/conceptual models of intervention and, where possible and efficacious, from APIA alternatives. The selection, adaptation, and application of treatment techniques must be shaped by client assessment information that gauges the extent to which various Western approaches are or are not relevant.

The debate that has raged and the proposals that have been advanced since the 1970s reveal the unsettled state of crosscultural practice. James W. Green (1982) notes, for example, that there is "a general lack of genuinely cross-cultural conceptualization within social work, . . . and that theoretical deficiency is matched by a methodological one as well" (p. 28).

Lacking a definite theoretical model for crosscultural practice, professionals must develop a rich base of information through the client assessment process for use in selecting and adapting intervention models and strategies for application. Multidimensional assessments, which appear in Figure 11.1 can be utilized in the development of baseline data and care plans. For each client dimension, professionals should explore two questions: (1) What, if any, culturally based meanings does the client attach to elements within this dimension? (2) What, if any, culturally prescribed preventive and remedial actions does the client view to be legitimate? With the assistance of either family members or cultural consultants, professionals should also explore expectations held relative to helpers, helping behaviors, and outcomes to be achieved.

While professionals have available a multitude of practice theories and models from which to draw upon—including crisis intervention, problem solving, task centered, cognitive, gestalt, behavior modification, reminiscence, and reality orientation—they must consider when and how to draw upon them. Given the theoretical models of intervention deemed effective with certain problems and clientele and acknowledging each elderly APIA's own culturally defined requirements, professionals must seek and implement the answers to a final set of questions: What adaptations must be instituted in the application of specific strategies to accommodate cultural differences? What specific behavioral cues must be manifested in applying the adapted strategies?

SPECIFIC SKILLS FOR INTERVENTION

Because of the multidimensional nature of aging concerns, professionals must also have interdisciplinary teamwork skills. That is, they must be able to communicate effectively across disciplinary lines, represent their professional perspectives substantively, manage conflict, problem solve, facilitate multidisciplinary decisions, provide leadership, participate productively and with self-awareness, work toward trusting

Figure 11.1
Multidimensional Assessments to Use in Selecting Intervention Models

DATE	PROBLEM AREA SUMMARY AS OF (date) Circle all that apply	CULTURAL MEANINGS & SOLUTIONS	GOAL (desirable condition)	RANK	ANTICIPATORY PROBLEM (what the client is experiencing or will experience if not addressed)	CONTRIBUTING FACTORS (barriers, situational factors that impact upon the problem)	RESOURCES NEEDED (to move from undesirable condition to desirable condition)	QUANTITY OF HELP (frequency, duration, amount)	MONITORING INDICATORS (signs that indicate problem is being solved)
	Vision Hearing Mobility Health/ Medical								
	Mental Health								
	ADL IADL								
	Housing Architectural Barriers								
	Legal								
	Financial								
	Caregiver								
	Service Fragmentation								
	Behavioral								
	Cognitive Functioning								
	Other								

Source: Adapted from Takamura and Kimura, 1989, p. 66.

collaboration, and maintain accurate records (Takamura, Bermosk, and Stringfellow, 1978).

As the preceding discussion implies, flexible eclectic practice approaches are necessary to assist APIA elders and their families. Extant literature is in disagreement as to whether direct or nondirective counseling styles are effective with APIA clients (Atkinson, Maruyama, and Matsui, 1978; Mokuau, 1987). As a result, the appropriateness of one therapeutic approach over another may be determined by considering both the client's problem and the intersection of such variables as levels of educational attainment, generation, language(s) spoken, gender, and the richness of the ethnic community and of ethnocultural resources. As strong assessment data is utilized to determine appropriate theoretical perspectives and cultural orientations, professionals must be open also to the use of cultural consultants through whom they can provide understandable rationale for questions that are asked of clients, use descriptive or vernacular terms borrowed from clients' languages, and seek feedback on the pace, complexity, and depth of inquiry. Moreover, professionals must see that acknowledgment and use of elders' strengths and capabilities permeate throughout the entire helping process.

Theoretical orientation aside, several experts argue that rapport, credibility, and giving are important for the assurance of therapeutic success. Philip Tsui and Gail L. Schultz (1985) contend that rapport with Asian clients can be built if professionals inform clients about the purpose of questions, permit catharsis, respond to personal questions nondefensively, disclose personal information with proper emotional expressiveness, avoid creating shame and guilt, gather data slowly, and involve families in engaging clients—all actions which communicate connectedness, acceptance, sensitivity, and respect. Along slightly different lines, Stanley Sue and Nolan Zane (1987) purport that credibility or "the client's perception of the therapist as an effective and trustworthy helper" and a "gift" or "a meaningful gain early in therapy" are critical components that determine effectiveness (pp. 39–40). Of course, some of the foregoing are intangible concepts with meanings and behavioral cues that, from the client's perspective, can differ from person to person. And, at least one—"gifts" such as "anxiety reduction, depression, relief, cognitive clarity, normalization, reassurance, hope and faith, skills acquisition, a coping perspective, and goal setting"—should be pursued for any client, regardless of ethnocultural background (Sue and Zane, 1987, p. 42). Finally, Stanley Sue and J. K. Morishima (1982) also remind professionals that the universalization or normalization of problems, when appropriate, can relieve elders and their families from unnecessary shame or feelings of moral degradation.

The ability to utilize life review or reminiscent therapy is also important in work with older persons who may need to reach into the past to complete "unfinished business" or to be reassured of the significance of innate strengths and previous accomplishments. To encourage access to long forgotten, intimate memories, professionals can use program materials that are ethnically specific. For an elderly Japanese woman, for example, professionals can bring *mochi* (rice flour) cakes that are typically eaten on *Hana Matsuri* (Girl's Day) to trigger discussions of times past.

Reality orientation techniques can also be utilized by geriatric professionals to assist older persons to remain oriented in time and place. With elders who have retained a strong ethnocultural identity, reality orientation interventions can mean using calendars with ethnic holidays and vernacular descriptors.

Professionals who choose to work with APIA elders must have training in gerontologic/geriatric and crosscultural practice. Because definitive, comprehensive, crosscultural theoretical and methodological approaches do not yet exist for the counseling professions, professionals must be able to use multidimensional assessments to capture accurately clients' problems, strengths and resources, needs and limitations, expectations, and cultural orientations and to select and modify therapeutic interventions.

Case Example

Intervention can mean many things including information, education, referral, the securing of supportive services, social activities, modified pharmacotherapy, and psychotherapy. When family members are involved in elder care, intervention may also include respite and counseling for caregivers.

The following example demonstrates how professionals can work with elderly APIAs and their families.

Ed and Hisae Ito, a Nisei (second-generation Japanese) couple, were referred to a neighborhood health center by police who responded to a distressed missing persons call from their daughter Anne and found Ed wandering, disheveled, disoriented, bruised on his forehead, and exhausted in a park across town. He had a fever of 104 degrees and was clearly in weak physical condition. A former cashier at a small grocery store, Hisae seemed to rely on Anne, a college student studying to be a teacher. Beside herself with fear and worry, Hisae revealed that Ed has a chronic heart condition and tends to tire easily. Bilingual, she seemed overwhelmed with Ed's frailty.

Active listening was used as Hisae and Anne ventilated their fears. They were told that a series of questions would be asked of them in order to identify the cause of his wandering and fever and the best course of action to help him and them. They were asked for Ed's doctor's name; the names and amounts of his medications—prescription, over-the-counter, and folk; their understanding of his health condition; a description of his usual behaviors and affect; and their account of the events leading up to his wandering and disappearance. This information was given to Ed's doctor, who approved a multidimensional assessment. The meanings of Ed's conditions and treatments were explored with the two Ito women. Anne revealed that Hisae was afraid that Ed had lost his mind and that they were both wondering how to explain what happened to outsiders and how to care for him.

Although Alzheimer disease was a possibility, the assessment revealed that Ed had significant hearing loss, a severe case of the flu, and that he had mixed at least eight prescription and nonprescription medications for his heart condition and the flu, triggering the disorientation. With information from the geriatrician, the nurses taught Hisae and Anne how to monitor his drug intake and about the dangers of multiple medications. They were told that drug interaction effects are common, can be prevented, and are not shameful. By asking them to restate the information, the tone and clarity of communications particularly to Hisae were checked. Some role playing and rehearsals were demonstrated with Anne and observed by Hisae to help them explain what happened to outsiders. They were assured that Ed was not *kichigai* (crazy). The Itos were given a regimen to help better manage Ed's heart condition and pointers on dealing with hearing loss, including instructions on how to use reality orientation. They were also engaged in problem solving toward less stressful caregiving. A call was placed to their Area Agency on Aging and a respite companion was secured for once-a-week visits, on a sliding scale basis, to keep Ed company and relieve them. Through the Area Agency, Hisae and Anne also learned about a free stress management/caregiver training course in which they enrolled.

CONCLUSION

Due to the growth of both elderly and minority populations in America in the decades ahead, helping professionals will need to prepare themselves for effective practice with these populations. The diversity that is characteristic in older cohorts of APIAs makes them a challenging group to serve. Lacking comprehensive, definitive theoretical and methodological points of departure, professionals need to acquire sound knowledge and skill bases pertinent to gerontologic/geriatric and cross-cultural practice to construct sensitive interventions informed by solid assessment data. Thus prepared, the "silver century" will be a fulfilling one.

NOTES

Chinese American and Japanese American women have average longevity rates in excess of 80 years.

Native Hawaiian elders are more likely to be functionally impaired than are other elders, according to *The Native Hawaiian Elderly Needs Assessment Report (Age 55 and Over)* by Alu Like. Native Hawaiian elders experience heart conditions at a rate that is 1.8 times greater than for non-Hawaiians. Other conditions that occur at higher frequencies among native Hawaiians are diabetes, hypertension, obesity, and cancer (Alu Like, 1989, p. ii).

Research announcements in the early months of 1990 suggested optimistically that a cure for Alzheimer disease may be in the offing. The use of fetal tissue implants, chemical interventions, and other experimental treatments was reported to be showing positive results.

REFERENCES

Achenbaum, A. W. (1986, Winter). America as an aging society: Myths and images. *Daedalus* 115: 13–30.

Alu Like (1989). *The Native Hawaiian Elderly Needs Assessment Report (Age 55 and Over)*. Honolulu.

Atkinson, D., M. Maruyama, and S. Matsui (1978). Effects of counselor race and counseling approach on Asian Americans' perceptions of counselor credibility and utility. *Journal of Counseling Psychology* 25 (1): 76–83.

Commonwealth Fund Commission on Elderly People Living Alone (1987). *Old, Alone and Poor*. Baltimore.

Crim, S. (1988). *Employees and Eldercare*. Washington, D.C.: Bureau of National Affairs.

Executive Office on Aging, State of Hawaii (1990). *Caring for the Elderly Family Members: The Impact on Employed Caregivers. A Report on a Survey of State Government Employees Who Are Caregivers to Older Adults*. Honolulu.

———. (1987). *Comprehensive Master Plan for the Elderly: Update 1987*. Honolulu.

Gardner, R. W., B. Robey, and P. G. Smith (1985). Asian Americans: Growth, change, and diversity. *Population Bulletin* 40 (4): 3–43.

Gollub, J., and H. Javitz (1989). Six ways to age. *American Demographics* 11 (6): 28–35.

Green, J. W. (1982). *Cultural Awareness in the Human Services*. Englewood Cliffs, N.J.: Prentice-Hall.

KGMB Political/Media Research, Inc. (1989, September 8–19). Family Life in Hawaii: A Survey for KGMB-TV. Washington, D.C.

Liu, W. T., and E. Yu (1985). Asian/Pacific American elderly: Mortality differentials, health status, and use of health services. *Journal of Applied Gerontology* 4 (1): 35–64.

Mokuau, N. (1987). Social workers' perceptions of counseling effectiveness for Asian American clients. *Social Work* 32 (4): 331–335.

Monk, A. (1981). Social work with the aged: Principles of practice. *Social Work* 26 (1): 61–68.

Morris, R., and S. A. Bass (1982). Successful aging. Address delivered to American Psychological Association, Washington, D.C.

Sue, S., and J. K. Morishima (1982). *The Mental Health of Asian American.* San Francisco: Jossey-Bass.

Sue, S. and N. Zane (1987). The role of culture and cultural techniques in psychotherapy: A critique and reformulation. *American Psychologist* 42 (1): 37–45.

Takamura, J., L. Bermosk, and L. Stringfellow (1978). *Health Team Development Program.* Honolulu: John A. Burns School of Medicine, University of Hawaii.

Takamura, J., and P. Kimura (1989). *Preparing Professionals for Geriatric Practice in Social Welfare Settings.* Honolulu: School of Social Work.

Tsui, P., and G. L. Schultz (1985). Failure of rapport: Why psychotherapeutic engagement fails in the treatment of Asian clients. *American Orthopsychiatric Association* 55 (4): 561–569.

U.S. Bureau of the Census (1988). *We, the Asian and Pacific Islander Americans.* Washington, D.C.: U.S. Government Printing Office.

U.S. Senate (1989). Aging America: Trends and Projections. An information paper by the Senate Special Committee on Aging, 101st Congress, 2d Session. Washington, D.C.: U.S. Government Printing Office.

Veroff, J., R. A. Kulka, and E. Douvan (1981). *Mental Health in America: Patterns of Help-seeking from 1957 to 1976.* New York: Basic Books.

Yankelovich, D., and Associates (1989). *Business and Older Workers Current Perceptions and New Directions for the 90s.* Washington, D.C.: American Association for Retired Persons.

CHAPTER 12

Family Violence Among Pacific Islanders

SHARLENE MAEDA FURUTO

INTRODUCTION

Family violence is a serious problem that has existed throughout history and may be increasing or at least becoming more visible. It refers to abuse, neglect, or exploitation through physical, sexual, and emotional acts by family members on family members. Social service workers recognize the multiplicity of variables needing to be examined in the assessment and treatment of family violence in the 1990s. One significant variable to consider when working with people is ethnic and cultural background and the impact of that culture on people's lives. W. Devore and E. G. Schlesinger (1987) espouse the view that social work practice must be attuned to values related to ethnic group membership and position in the social stratification system. In Hawaii, where approximately 77 percent of the population are people of color, primarily of Asian and Pacific Islander descent (U.S. Bureau of the Census, 1988), social workers should better understand ethnicity for more effective intervention.

The premises of this chapter are threefold: (1) Family violence is increasingly more visible in the United States; (2) culture is fundamental in the development of attitude and behavior related to family violence; and (3) culturally sensitive social work practice can be used successfully to intervene in family violence. While family violence may be directed at children, partners, parents, and the elderly, this chapter focuses on family violence as it relates to children and women. Specifically, this chapter examines family violence in Hawaii among two Pacific Islander groups, Samoans and native Hawaiians, in which there is a disproportionate number of cases of abuse. Information addressing the problem as well as on social service intervention for the perpetrators of family violence is provided.

DEFINITION AND SCOPE OF THE PROBLEM

Family Violence with Children

The number of abused and neglected children in the state of Hawaii has been steadily increasing. The State of Hawaii Department of Human Services records indicate a 149 percent increase in the number of confirmed reports of child abuse and neglect in Hawaii from 1980 through 1988. Confirmed reports increased from 1,057 in 1980 (State of Hawaii, Department of Human Services, 1988a) to 2,309 in 1988 (State of Hawaii, Department of Human Services, 1990b). Since 1980, approximately 52 percent of all child abuse and neglect reports were confirmed by social workers.

While victims of child abuse are heterogeneous in terms of social class, age, and gender, a few trends characterizing the population do emerge. In 1987, 34 percent of child abuse and neglect victims were between 6 and 12 years of age, 55 percent were girls, and 20 percent were referred by schools. Of the 17 percent of the children who possessed special characteristics, a little over half were diagnosed to have learning disabilities, emotional disturbances, or birth complications. While 83 percent of the abused and neglected children did not require medical treatment, 15 percent did require treatment, 2 percent required extended treatment, and .12 percent were permanently disabled. Since 1980, at least twenty-three children were known to have died from their injuries (State of Hawaii, Department of Human Services, 1990b).

Physical abuse continues to be the most common type of abuse and neglect. In 1988 there were 1,313 confirmed cases of physical abuse (State of Hawaii, Department of Human Services, 1990b). Threatened abuse and neglect increased 2,088 percent from 43 confirmed cases in 1980 to 897 confirmed cases in 1987. A possible reason for this substantial increase is the broadened definition of abuse and neglect that is reflected in legislation that took effect in 1985 and includes any child who is "subject to any reasonable foreseeable, substantial risk of being harmed" (Chapter 350, 1987).

Family Violence with Women

It is difficult to estimate the scope of the problem of battered women in Hawaii. There are no state laws requiring an agency to compile such data. Generally, statistics are quoted in terms of number of arrests made for spouse abuse; number of homicide victims killed by their former husbands or boyfriends, number of restraining orders issued, and number of battered women served in emergency shelters (Oahu Spouse Abuse Task Force, 1986).

Arrests serve as one indicator of the scope of the problem. In 1986 there were less than 300 arrests made for spouse abuse; however, a family violence statute (HRS 709–96, Abuse and Family and Household Members statute) that offers clearer guidelines and stronger enforcement was invoked in 1987 bringing about an increase in arrest cases. In that year there was an increase of arrests for household member abuse, with 923 cases being reported (State of Hawaii, Honolulu Police Department, 1990b). Arrests also increased in 1987 due to a policy change in the Honolulu Police Department requiring police officers to arrest offenders if there were visible injuries or if the women complained of pain. Each arrest necessitates a court hearing, with a guilty plea having a consequence of a jail sentence and/or social service intervention. The number of arrests for family violence is high, but it may not accurately reflect the scope of the problem because many situations of family violence do not end in arrests. In 1989 there were approximately 3,000 arrest and nonarrest cases of family and household member abuse against adults, with the vast majority of them being against women.

Battered women often become homicide victims. From 1980 through 1989, a total of fifty-one women were homicide victims; all deaths were committed by the women's spouses, boyfriends, or exhusbands (State of Hawaii, Honolulu Police Department, 1990b). Furthermore, the use of drugs by male murderers seems to be taking a more prominent role in cases (State of Hawaii, Honolulu Police Department, 1990a).

Women who have been battered can request that a restraining order be processed against the perpetrator with hopes that he will not approach and hurt her. In Honolulu, restraining orders requested by battered women increased from 164 in 1980 to 1,720 in 1987 (Alert, 1988).

Hundreds of battered women flee their homes annually and seek refuge unknown to their perpetrators. There are six emergency civilian shelters throughout the state and one military-operated shelter. These shelters provide service to the more than 1 million persons residing in Hawaii. Shelters for battered women received over 4,700 crisis calls for assistance and provided shelter for 1,716 women and children during 1987–1988. The capacities of the shelters are insufficient. In 1987, shelters were forced to turn away 390 families (Alert, 1988). Thus, there is a strong need for additional shelters.

POPULATION DESCRIPTION

Perpetrators of Child Abuse in the Samoan Population

Of all the abused and neglected children in Hawaii in 1988, 6 percent were Samoan (State of Hawaii, Department of Human Services, 1990) despite the fact that approximately 0.4 percent of the statewide population was Samoan (State of Hawaii, Department of Human Services, 1988b). Statistics indicate that in 1980 and again in 1988, girls had a greater likelihood of being abused than boys and that the greatest number of abused Samoan children lived in one urban community heavily populated by Samoans (State of Hawaii, Department of Human Services, 1990). In 1980 the most common age for an abused child was 5 years; however, in 1988, the most common ages were 7 and 15 (State of Hawaii, Department of Human Services, 1990).

Samoan adults are overrepresented as perpetrators of physical abuse and neglect, with an average of 6 percent of all perpetrators in the 1980s being of Samoan descent (see Table 12.1). A profile of the perpetrator reveals him to be the father's child, between the ages of 18 and 40, with some high school education or a high school diploma. There is a critical need to examine the influence of culture on child-rearing practices and discipline and to address the prevention of child abuse and neglect among Samoans.

Perpetrators of Spouse Abuse in the Native Hawaiian Population

Accurate statistics ascertaining the ethnic background of perpetrators of spouse abuse are not comprehensively or consistently collected. Informal and anecdotal reports from human service providers, however, indicate that native Hawaiian men, in proportion to the total population size, are overrepresented as perpetrators.

An overall description of the batterer in Hawaii is that he was abused as a child and is between 23 and 45 years of age (Fuqua, 1986). He is unable to negotiate relationships of equality and feels threatened by a mate who moves toward independence by going to school, finding her own friends, or getting a job. He denies or minimizes his violence, often does not believe the mate is hurt or feels threatened, and many times is sexually abusive as well.

RELATIONSHIP OF THE PROBLEM TO CULTURAL TRADITIONS AND CONCERNS

Culture plays an extremely significant role in determining one's attitudes and behaviors. L. E. Davis (1984) claims that despite the many factors that affect individuals, none has as clearly or as consistently demonstrated its potency as has skin color. Color remains one of the most accurate predictors of populations being at risk and of the quality of life experiences for an individual.

Others emphasize the need to be cautious with research findings re-

Table 12.1
Ethnicity of Child Abuse and Neglect Perpetrators in Hawaii, 1980–1988 (percent)

ETHNICITY & Percent of Total Population in 1986*	1980	1981	1982	1983	1984	1985	1986	1987	1988
Other	NA	6.8	6.8	5.7	3.6	3.0	3.6	2.9	4.2	3.1
SE Asians	NA	.5	.4	.9	1.1	1.5	.3	.6	.8	.8
Black	2.3	3.0	4.2	2.6	5.7	5.0	6.1	5.1	4.9	5.2
Chinese	4.8	2.0	.8	1.0	1.4	1.9	2.2	.9	1.3	1.2
Filipino	11.3	9.2	10.8	11.7	9.3	9.4	8.8	10.0	9.5	10.6
Hawaiian	20.7	20.0	21.5	17.6	17.0	21.5	21.7	18.3	22.1	23.8
Japanese	23.0	4.5	5.0	4.1	4.4	2.6	4.0	3.7	3.8	3.0
Korean	1.3	2.1	1.0	1.0	2.1	1.9	.9	.8	1.3	1.0
Mixed	11.3	5.7	5.7	8.2	15.2	12.4	15.0	16.4	14.5	14.9
Puerto Rican	0.4	2.0	1.4	1.4	1.5	1.1	1.0	1.5	1.6	2.1
Samoan	0.4**	7.9	8.2	6.4	6.1	6.0	5.9	6.1	5.9	6.0
Unknown	1.2	3.9	3.4	8.6	2.8	3.3	4.9	5.8	4.5	4.9
White	23.4	32.4	30.7	30.8	29.8	30.4	25.6	27.8	25.6	23.4
Total	100.1%	100%	99.9%	100%	100%	100%	100%	99.9%	100%	100%

NA = not available.

* Excludes persons in institutions or military barracks, on Niihau, or in Kalawao. Based on a sample survey of 17,107 persons.

** There is a disagreement as to how many Samoans resided in Hawaii, from a low of 3,830 (State of Hawaii, Department of Human Services, 1988b) to a high of 14,349 (U.S. Bureau of the Census, 1988).

Sources: State of Hawaii, Department of Human Services, 1988a; 1988b; 1989; 1990.

lated to race. These researchers attribute the higher violence rates of people of color due not to ethnicity but instead to stress, frustration (Straus, Gelles, and Steinmetz, 1980), and attitudes about the use of physical punishment and the degree of social support for parents (National Center on Child Abuse and Neglect, 1984).

Nevertheless, one's response to stress and frustration, one's attitude about the use of physical punishment, and the degree of social support from parents are derived from one's culture, which is normally linked to one's ethnicity. Hence, the basic premise that culture is fundamental in the development of attitudes and behavior remains true.

It is important, then, to understand the cultural traditions of an ethnic group and the impact culture makes on problem identification and resolution if social service providers are to better manage social problems such as child and spouse abuse. Cultural information on Samoans and native Hawaiians will enhance an understanding of these groups and be useful in the development of culturally sensitive social services.

Cultural Traditions and Concerns in Samoan Culture

Traditionally, Samoans are born into a highly structured society that commands obedience at every level. The unit of social organization is the extended family (*aiga potopoto*), wherein a child has many relatives who provide multiple parenting. A very young child enjoys the "golden age of childhood" (Ritchie and Ritchie, 1981) when punishment is not inflicted. Harsh punishment may begin about the age of three (Markoff and Bond, 1980) and oftentimes is administered by any of many extended family members, including older siblings.

Natural parents do not necessarily play a dominant role in child-rearing during the years the child is in school; instead that role belongs to peer and sibling groups of the family and village. Parental sternness has been considered a sign of love (Dubanoski and Snyder, 1980). Women in villages rely on the women's committee (*komiti*) for counsel and support on parental roles and responsibilities (Freeman, 1983).

Each extended family is influenced tremendously by chiefs and ministers. The chief (*matai*) performs judicial, executive, and ceremonial functions. In addition, the chiefs have the right to punish individuals for infractions of cultural law. The minister (*faife'au*) is also highly regarded in traditional Samoan culture because of the locus of power placed with the church (Antilla, 1980). Both the chiefs and ministers play key roles in decisions affecting families troubled by social problems. Children learn from a very young age to obey and to hold the highest respect for both the chief and the minister.

The traditional Samoan lifestyle (*fa'a Samoa*) has undergone change as Samoans have migrated from American and Western Samoa to Hawaii and other west coast states since the 1950s. Samoans in Hawaii experience the loss of the extended family, erosion of the close guidance of chief and minister, and increased conflict or disruption of other basic cultural traditions.

The severity and tolerance threshold of Samoan parents differs from that of the American majority and from the accepted standard of American professionals such as social workers (Markoff and Bond, 1980). Among the reasons for the high incidence of abuse and neglect of Samoan children are: (a) The authoritative cultural base allows for physical discipline which other cultures would view as abuse; (b) parents feel physical discipline is expected and effective and hence have little incentive to adopt milder styles of discipline that are more acceptable to the host country; (c) multiple parenting is not available to relieve the adult from child-rearing or to keep the abuser from disciplining the child too harshly; (d) like other ethnic minorities, Samoans have become identified as a group prone to social problems; (e) Samoan parents frequently do not conceal the effects of the abuse and readily admit to the incident; and (f) parents adhere to the biblical teaching that to spare the rod is to spoil the child (Freeman, 1983). These reasons, indicative of *fa'a Samoa* and the marginal conditions under which many Samoans exist, create the preconditions for children to be abused and neglected.

Cultural Traditions and Concerns in Native Hawaiian Culture

Most anthropologists agree that following an emigration several thousand years ago from the Malay Archipelago to the Pacific (McDermott, Tseng, and Maretzki, 1980), a culture unique and isolated evolved in Hawaii. This societal structure was stratified, and there were clearly dictated daily activities and roles. Adults and children understood their roles and responsibilities.

The introduction of Western culture to Hawaii came in 1778 with the arrival of Captain James Cook. A cultural loss hypothesis suggests that such an introduction of Western influences brought about a demise of native Hawaiian cultural traditions. B.B.C. Young (1980) reflects that such a change has contributed to economic, educational, social, and political events that have negatively impacted the lifestyles of native Hawaiians. The loss of culture is manifested in the inordinate needs of native Hawaiians in education, housing, land, health, employment, and economics. In addition, psychological concerns such as depression, personal inadequacy, and powerlessness are associated with the sense of cultural loss (Bishop Estates/Kamehameha Schools, 1983).

Even with the demise of many cultural traditions, there are several values that are evident in the 1990s. Native Hawaiians continue to value the family (*'ohana*) where youngsters are taught their duties, behavior is outlined, needs are maintained, and respect is accorded to the elders. Native Hawaiian children, particularly boys, are expected to be mischievous and to stand up for themselves, even to the point of fighting, and not turn to adults for sympathy or help with peer problems. Furthermore, boys become sensitive to dominance relationships and are loathe to accept a position inferior to another child.

Another value of native Hawaiians is their preference to work as a group rather than individually. Native Hawaiian children perform better when rewards are to be used for the benefit of the group rather than for the individual. Relationships should also be free of conflict (Young, 1980). While conflicts may occur, it is unacceptable to resolve conflict openly and through confrontation. Rather, disagreements are almost always suppressed, denied, or avoided. A belief many native Hawaiians regard to be important is the maintenance of harmony (*lōkahi*), particularly as it exists among the individual environment, and the supernatural or spiritual.

SOCIAL SERVICE INTERVENTION

There is a grave need for social services in Hawaii to prevent family violence and treat victims and perpetrators; however, the theoretical and conceptual information on family violence among Samoans and native Hawaiians is limited. There are a few ethnic models developed for working with persons of color that may have applicability for work with Samoans and native Hawaiians (Devore and Schlesinger, 1987; Gallegos, 1982); however, research documenting the applicability of these models is unavailable. The following information highlights some of the major principles of practice and key skills that may be useful with native Hawaiians and Samoans by describing programs that service these populations in Hawaii.

Principles of Practice

There are many guidelines that may be offered for social service intervention with Samoans and native Hawaiians, but there are two principles of practice that are imperative in establishing an efficient and appropriate worker-client relationship and facilitating intervention success.

First, there should be an understanding and incorporation of basic cultural traditions and values in social service intervention. In the area of family violence, the cultural value of groups and, in particular, the family is very appropriate. Underlying this principle is the belief that for many Samoans and native Hawaiians, the family is more important than the individual and that social service intervention, either through process or content, should focus on the needs of this group.

Second, it is useful to have bilingual and bicultural social service providers working with Samoan and native Hawaiian clients. Many Samoans, while bilingual, speak their native language at home and with other Samoans; thus, it is helpful if providers are able to understand the special nuances of the Samoan language. Providers who are knowledgeable about the cultures are better able to develop worker-client relationships and assess and treat problems that may be due to culture conflict.

These two principles are at the foundation of the program described in the following sections, which address education and prevention of child abuse among Samoans and treatment of perpetrators of spouse abuse among native Hawaiian clients.

Education and Prevention Programs for Child Abuse Among Samoans

Much can be done to prevent abuse and neglect among Samoans in Hawaii by helping Samoan adults and youth go through the adaptation process to the host country. Since Samoans are traditionally a group-oriented people, workers should consider specialized culturally sensitive group sessions for the chiefs, pastors, parents, and youth in homes, schools, Samoan organizations, and especially in churches.

The adaptation process consists of two parts: (1) Samoans acculturate individually and collectively to the host country's norms, values, attitudes, and expectations; and (2) Samoans learn, understand, use, and manage organizational structures and processes of the host country (e.g., educational, marketing, employment, transportation, social, and family systems). For example, there needs to be instruction regarding the American family, including family structure, roles, and responsibilities of members, lifecycle events with an emphasis on childhood and adolescence, and realistic expectations, styles of communication, dimensions of child/adolescent-rearing, various forms of discipline, anger management, social resources, and so on. Such information would help Samoans become more aware of the American family, better assist them in integrating and adapting, and share with them another perspective for living in Hawaii or in other states. The task is difficult and subtle, and in most cases the educational effort needs to be an integral part of a supportive and directive counseling program.

Discussions during group sessions should also include indigenous Samoan resources and concepts that strengthen the family, such as family loyalty, ethnic pride, use of a chief or pastor or other respected person to mediate disputes, hierarchical deference, social harmony, ceremonial obligations, and religious beliefs and the church.

The church and the pastor in Hawaii have taken on new roles and responsibilities when compared to their traditional roles in the Samoan village, to the extent that serious consideration should be given to actively including the church and the pastor in adaptation/prevention programs. S. C. Antilla (1980) notes that the church is now the main contributor for the maintenance of cultural traditions, and the church is becoming more influential than chiefs. The church minister, once obligated only to preach and be supported by the church members, is increasingly becoming more of a working person in Hawaii. Most ministers are gainfully employed and actively participate in volunteer or paid social services. Many pastors voluntarily provide counseling in schools, interpret for the courts, serve on boards or organizations, or help at immigration services.

It is recommended that group sessions have two facilitators, one possibly a Samoan social worker and the other a pastor. Group formation and preparation could follow the same general guidelines used when working with members of the dominant society, although particular attention should be paid to: (a) selecting the facilitators and members since many Samoans are reluctant to discuss family problems with other Samoans who may know their family members; (b) using scenarios and having parents describe or role play what they would do in a given crisis; (c) teaching and using a problem-solving approach with the parents, defining the problem from their cultural perspective; and (d) keeping the group intimate to encourage participation.

Skills social workers use, such as empathy, active listening, and self-disclosure, are compatible with Samoan clients for the most part. Social workers should recognize the following distinctions, however: (a) In a worker-client relationship, Samoans will likely be passive, low-verbal communicators who look toward the floor as an indication of respect for the worker's authority, and many Samoans will expect the worker to state what the client should do; (b) even with probing, it is sometimes difficult for the worker to have the client express feelings, behaviors, and experiences concretely or specifically; and (c) confrontation, if used, should be done gently at first (e.g., "Why don't you try talking with your son?" rather than, "Hurting your son as you did is against the law. You should talk with him first.")

Samoans concur that the only method they know and therefore use to discipline a disobedient child or teenager is physical punishment. Physical punishment is a parental responsibility and is administered with the intention of teaching the child to obey family rules. Human service workers need to provide Samoans with the opportunity to learn alternative styles of child discipline and thus help to prevent abusive incidents.

Treatment Programs for Battered Women Among Native Hawaiians

In Hawaii there are a few group programs that address the problem of battered women by focusing on the native Hawaiian male perpetrators. In analyzing these group-oriented programs, the following dimensions contribute to the cultural sensitivity of these programs: (1) one or both cofacilitators are native Hawaiians and may be former battered women perpetrators; (2) cofacilitators are knowledgeable of the native Hawaiian culture and confidently share this knowledge in an organized, methodical manner; (3) cofacilitators have a high regard for native Hawaiians and the native Hawaiian culture, traditions, practices, and values; and (4) the group curriculum uses native Hawaiian terminology, examples of native Hawaiian families, and visuals of native Hawaiian individuals.

One program for male batterers has a high number of perpetrators who are of mixed ethnic background, including those of part native Hawaiian ancestry. The traditional curriculum on power-control-anger management issues is supplemented with curriculum on native Hawaiian culture. The cultural content relevant to native Hawaiians in the 1990s includes both traditional and contemporary beliefs and concepts such as the family (*'ohana*), ancestral spirits (*'aumākua*), enlightenment (*umeke*), empowerment (*ho'omana*), and harmony (*lōkahi*).

More specifically, perpetrators learn how the value of harmony was traditionally present in native Hawaiian daily life, how the once harmonious traditional family lifestyle was impacted negatively by the rapid introduction of the Western system, and how select concepts and skills are needed today to cope satisfactorily amidst stress factors. Group leaders describe the traditional native Hawaiian family (*'ohana*) as one that supported one another, worked together, and loved each other; sought and heeded the goodness and wisdom of their ancestors (*'aumākua*); removed denial and defense mechanisms to allow for enlightenment (*umeke*) and behavioral changes; and worked toward empowerment and self-control (*ho'omana*) in order to maintain the family harmony (*lōkahi*).

The overall curriculum focuses around power, control issues, and anger management. Discussion topics include anger, body signals, self-talk, and alternatives for dealing with anger. Included in the curriculum is instruction regarding behavior control, psychological anger, sex role beliefs, assertiveness, communication, problem resolution, and appropriate expression of feelings. Perpetrators learn concepts and skills they need to bring back the traditional harmonious family lifestyle into their own homes. This program, together with individual and family counseling, have helped a number of families better cope with family violence in their stressful lives.

CONCLUSION

A growing problem in Hawaii is family violence. Each year approximately 4,000 reports of child abuse and neglect are made to the Child Protective Services unit of the Department of Human Services, and about 50 percent of these reports are confirmed. From 1980 to 1987, 21 deaths and 28 permanent disabilities were recorded due to child abuse and neglect. The extent of the battered women problem is more difficult to estimate, but in 1988, police made approximately 4 arrests per day due to domestic violence. In 1989, police responded to about 1,000 domestic cases a month. Shelters for battered women and their children are insufficient, and many women are being turned away.

While the statistics are grim and the services insufficient, there are some indicators of progress. Enactment of new laws and changes in agency policies in the 1980s have helped in defining abuse and neglect and have clarified roles and powers of social workers, police, and courts. In addition, there are a few innovative education and treatment programs that demonstrate how culture and social services can be integrated in work with Samoan and native Hawaiian clients. It is these types of incremental changes that will promote the hope that there will be an end to family violence.

REFERENCES

Alert (1988, September). *Woman Abuse: A Crisis in Hawaii.* Honolulu: Hawaii State Committee on Family Violence.

Antilla, S. C. (1980). The role of the church/minister in the Samoan community in Hawaii: As compared with a Samoan village. Unpublished manuscript.

Bishop Estates/Kamehameha Schools (1983). *Native Hawaiian Educational Assessment Project.* Honolulu: Bishop Estates/Kamehameha Schools.

Chapter 350 (1987). Hawaii Revised Statutes, vol. 6. Honolulu: State of Hawaii.

Davis, L. E. (ed.) (1984). *Ethnicity in Social Group Work Practice.* New York: Haworth Press.

Devore, W., and E. G. Schlesinger (1987). *Ethnic-Sensitive Social Work Practice.* Columbus, Ohio: Merrill Publishing Company.

Dubanoski, R. A., and K. Snyder (1980). Patterns of child abuse and neglect in Japanese and Samoan Americans. *Child Abuse and Neglect* 4: 217–255.

Freeman, D. (1983). *Margaret Mead and Samoa: The Making and Unmaking of an Anthropological Myth.* Boston: Harvard University Press.

Fuqua, C. S. (1986). The dark side of aloha. *Honolulu* 21 (4): 79–80, 82–83, 108.

Gallegos, J. S. (1982). The ethnic competence model for social work education. In B. White (ed.), *Color in a White Society*. Silver Spring, Md.: National Association of Social Workers, Inc.

Markoff, R. A., and J. R. Bond (1980). The Samoans. In J. F. McDermott, Jr., W. S. Tseng, and T. W. Maretzki (eds.), *People and Cultures of Hawaii: A Psychocultural Profile*. Honolulu: University Press of Hawaii.

McDermott, J. F., Jr., W. S. Tseng, and T. W. Maretzki (eds.) (1980). *People and Cultures of Hawaii: A Psychocultural Profile*. Honolulu: University Press of Hawaii.

National Center on Child Abuse and Neglect (1984). *Perspectives on Child Maltreatment in the Mid–80s*. Department of Health and Human Services Publication No. OHDS 84–30338. Washington, D.C.: U.S. Government Printing Office.

Oahu Spouse Abuse Task Force (1986). *Breaking the Cycle of Violence: A Report on Spouse Abuse on Oahu and Recommendations for Change*. Honolulu: Child and Family Service.

Ritchie, J., and J. Ritchie (1981). Child rearing and child abuse: The Polynesian context. In J. Korbin (ed.), *Child Abuse and Neglect: Cross Cultural Perspectives*. Berkeley, Calif.: University of California.

State of Hawaii, Department of Human Services (1989). *Child Abuse and Neglect Registry*. Honolulu: Program Development, Family and Adult Services Division and Planning Office.

——— (1990). *Child Abuse and Neglect Registry*. Honolulu: Program Development, Family and Adult Services Division and Planning Office.

——— (1988a). *A Statistical Report on Child Abuse and Neglect in Hawaii 1980–1987*. Honolulu: Program Development, Family and Adult Services Division and Planning Office.

——— (1988b). *A Statistical Report on Child Abuse and Neglect in Hawaii 1988*. Honolulu: Program Development, Family and Adult Services Division and Planning Office.

State of Hawaii, Honolulu Police Department (1990a). *Homicide Summaries for 1980–1990*. Honolulu: Criminal Investigation Division.

——— (1990b). *Tallies of Persons Arrested for Abuse of Family and Household Members*. Honolulu: Research and Development Division.

Straus, M. A., R. J. Gelles, and S. K. Steinmetz (1980). *Behind Closed Doors*. New York: Anchor.

U.S. Bureau of the Census (1988). *We, the Asian and Pacific Islander Americans*. Washington, D.C.: U.S. Government Printing Office.

Young, B. B. C. (1980). The Hawaiians. In J. F. McDermott, Jr., W. S. Tseng, and T. W. Maretzki (eds.), *People and Cultures of Hawaii: A Psychocultural Profile*. Honolulu: University Press of Hawaii.

CHAPTER 13

Social Literacy for Asian and Pacific Islander Youth

MICHAEL J. MANOS

INTRODUCTION

Social relationships are the heart and soul of human development. The value of community and the privilege of contribution are predicated on the face-to-face transactions of human relationships. From relationships, people sense their own uniqueness and, with others, accomplish what they could not do alone.

Relationship building is truly important yet difficult when cultures with different underlying values come together. Such is the case in the United States where immigration from Asia and the Pacific regions is surging (Gould, 1988). We are experiencing an exploding diversity of multicultural relationships in which people must recognize the social signals from other cultures as well as their own. As cultural intermingling continues, today's youth in particular have a special set of issues as they attempt to build crosscultural relationships with peers and adults.

The ability to recognize and use the social signals of culture to build relationships is called social literacy. Social literacy is the ability to distinguish and use behavior appropriate to social situations. Social literacy is not a gift bestowed upon some and denied others, nor is it behavior acquired by happenstance. It occurs by design. People *learn* to behave well with each other.

In many ways, social literacy is like language literacy. People use the symbols of language to guide behavior—a novice chief reads a cookbook to prepare a meal; a traveler consults road maps to arrive at a particular place. Just as people learn to recognize and use the symbols of language in order to cook and travel, so people learn to recognize and use the symbols of cultural behavior in order to work with and relate to others to accomplish goals and share experiences. Social literacy allows people to use the symbols of human behavior to promote relationship. As language literacy requires fluency with semantic skills, so social literacy requires fluency with social skills.

It is the purpose of this chapter to discuss the fundamentals of social literacy with Asian and Pacific Islander American (APIA) youth. The following sections provide: (1) a description of the Asian and Pacific Islander youth population; (2) the particular problem these youth face in American culture; (3) the relationship of social literacy to cultural tradition; and (4) examples of social service intervention based on a longitudinal research project in Hawaii.

DESCRIPTION OF ASIAN AND PACIFIC ISLANDER AMERICAN YOUTH

The grouping of Asian and Pacific Islanders by the 1980 U.S. Census includes a variety of subcultures with an array of heterogeneous characteristics. Asian Americans include Japanese, Chinese, Filipino, Korean, East Indians, Vietnamese, Thai, Laotian, and others of Southeast Asia. Pacific Islanders include native Hawaiians, Chamorros, Samoans, Fijians, Tahitians, and other groups of the Micronesia, Melanesia, and Polynesia areas of the Pacific. Asian and Pacific Islander youth comprise about 16 percent of the youth population of the United States. Population concentrations are highest in the states of California, Hawaii, New York, Illinois, Texas, New Jersey, and Washington, in rank order. Of all APIA, 58 percent live in the west and 90 percent have settled in big cities or their surrounding suburban areas. Population concentrations are highest in just five cities—45 percent of the total APIA youth population live in Los Angeles, San Francisco, New York, Chicago, and Honolulu. (These and subsequent data are compiled from U.S. Bureau of the Census, 1988.)

APIA youth come from younger families and families that are generally larger than the national norms. The median age—that is, the age at which half the population is older and half younger—is 28.4 years versus the national median age of 30. Of Asians, the Vietnamese are youngest with a median age of 21.5 years; of Pacific Islanders, Samoan families are youngest at 19.2 years. The average family size for APIAs is 3.8 members, higher than the national average of 3.3 members. Vietnamese and Samoan families are largest with an average of 5.2 members; Japanese and Asian Indian families have the lowest average (3.6 and 3.5 respectively). One reason APIA families are larger is that children younger than 18 years old tend to live with their parents; 85 percent live with their parents compared with the national average of 77 percent.

The number of two-parent households (84 percent) is about the same as the national average (83 percent).

The trend in education for APIAs is mixed; 42 percent of Asian men and 26 percent of Asian women are college graduates. This is twice as high as the national average of 20 percent men and 13 percent women. (The Vietnamese are exceptions to this overall trend; only 18 percent of the men and 8 percent of the women complete college.) Pacific Islanders, on the other hand, are about half the national average, as only 10 percent of men and 6.3 percent of women complete college. High school graduates among Pacific Islander populations are more comparable to national averages of 67 percent for men and 66 percent for women. About 69 percent of Hawaiian, Samoan, and Guamanian men and 63 percent of these women graduate from high school.

In summary, APIA youth come from younger, larger, two-parent families. These families are concentrated in the western United States in urban areas or their surroundings. For Asian youth, education beyond high school is a priority. Pacific Islanders, however, tend not to have as open an access to education.

DEFINITION AND SCOPE OF THE ISSUE

The acculturation of APIA youth into mainstream American society is not on a smooth course as evidenced in arrest rates for legal and status offenses. Often cited as evidence of alienation and social illiteracy, these offenses are on the upswing. Whereas the arrest rates for white and black youth have declined or remained the same throughout the 1980s, arrests for APIA youth have steadily risen holding constant the increase in the APIA population. In 1988, APIA youth contributed about 1.1 percent of the violent crimes and 1.7 percent of property crimes in the U.S. juvenile population (U.S. Department of Justice, Federal Bureau of Investigation, 1989). In 1980, APIA youth contributed only 0.6 percent of the total number of violent crimes and 1.0 percent of property crimes. Status offenses (e.g., truancy or curfew violations that are offenses for juveniles but not for adults) show a steeper upward trend. APIA youth account for about 2.4 percent of the total curfew and loitering violations in the country and about 1.7 percent of the runaways (U.S. Department of Justice, Federal Bureau of Investigation, 1989). These figures are not particularly significant at first glance, but they represent a 380 percent increase in curfew/loitering violations and an 89 percent increase in runaways since 1980, again, holding constant population increases (percentages of the total in 1980 were 0.5 percent and 0.9 percent respectively). Statistics from particular localities support this national trend. In Hawaii, for example, Hawaiian and part-Hawaiian youth comprise about 12.3 percent of the total youth population. The incidence of Hawaiian youth in detention and correctional facilities, however, is 36.5 percent, nearly three times their corresponding percentage in the general population (Honolulu Police Department, 1980–1987).

What significance do these statistics have for social work intervention? School dropouts, substance abuse, teen pregnancy, and other legal and status offenses are strongly influenced by youths' ability to use the skills of relationship (Asher, 1983; O'Donnell and Tharp, 1982). The development of social literacy appears to be a problem of growing proportions for APIA youth as they live in the realities of discrimination associated with minority status. APIA youth are the country's fastest growing minority (Gould, 1988) and thus are especially susceptible to the difficulties of growing up within the confines of a dominant culture; they must learn to successfully participate in two worlds—their own and that of their adopted society. As a result, the stressors of cultural conflict, minority group status, and social change may act to impede the learning of social skills (Sue and Morishima, 1982) critical to social literacy. When social skills are not learned, youth tend not to build supportive relationships outside their natal cultures and do not successfully adapt to the dominant community (Mortland and Egan, 1987).

RELATIONSHIP OF SOCIAL LITERACY TO CULTURAL TRADITIONS

For youth in the United States, the challenges of relationship are magnified by the clash of culture and color. We live in a society that is becoming increasingly complex and pluralistic, where members of diverse ethnic and cultural backgrounds greet each other in the common interactions of everyday life. Ethnic identities are challenged as people of different backgrounds intermingle. Behaviors that carry a particular meaning for one group may be unrecognizable or misread by another. A refined sense of social acumen is required because youth must not only rely on their own history and culture to determine how to behave; they must learn and be tolerant of the behaviors of other cultures as well. In a classroom in Honolulu, for example, a black youth who had recently moved to Hawaii from the midwest was trying to attract the attention of a Filipino girl sitting several seats away. He quietly blew air through his teeth to make a soft hissing noise thinking that by doing so she would turn to notice him. The teenage girl rebuffed his overtures outright. To her, hissing was not a signal of friendly interest; it was the way men call prostitutes.

The clash of culture is particularly apparent in established institutions such as schools. J. D'Amato (1988) describes the cultural practice of "acting" among low income Hawaiian children at the beginning of the school year:

> Hawaiian children learn to use the idea and forms of "acting" both to combat and to come to terms with adult authority. Playful mischievousness is used to entertain adults and to win applause for spirit; defiance—though never approved—is used to earn a certain measure of respect (D'Amato, 1986). Hawaiian children preserve the meanings of "acting" in their behavior at school. "Acting" in classrooms begins and sometimes ends with mischievously playful challenges to teacher authority. In the right circumstances, however, playful challenges may escalate to sharp and bitter resistance. (p. 530)

The problems of APIA youth in adapting to the dominant culture and, in turn, the dominant culture accepting and including APIAs can be explored from three perspectives. (See Tharp, 1988, for this discussion related to education.) The first involves the notion of *cultural deficit*. Members of minority cultures are described as deficient in the social skills needed to survive in the dominant culture. From this perspective, minority youth would be taught the social skills of the dominant culture with only casual regard for the compatibility of those skills with the natal culture. Culture deficit advocates tend to ignore minority strengths altogether while propounding the virtues of the dominant culture.

The second point of view has largely replaced the ethnocentric context of cultural deficit. The *cultural difference* theory emphasizes the strengths of culture. From this framework, social skills of both cultures are taught. Children and youth learn to use skills of the dominant culture in those situations where such skills will produce desired outcomes while maintaining ethnic identity and practices. Cultural difference proponents allow for respectful coexistence of cultures. As tolerant of culture as this theory appears to be, there is the danger that it leads to stereotyping. Emphasizing only ethnic differences opens the opportunity for people to create cultural caricatures. Thus, in Hawaii, for example, Caucasians are talkative, Hawaiians are lazy, Chinese are thrifty, and so on.

Cultural compatibility proponents suggest that social literacy requires no "correct" set of skills to be learned. The skills of the dominant culture are not best practices (i.e., social deficit), and the characteristics of the natal culture are not merely to be tolerated (i.e., social difference). Cultural compatibility suggests that relationship skills exist in all cultures and that regardless of the social skills taught or learned, youth will translate them into what is appropriate for a particular social situation. The basic ingredients for social literacy already exist with youth and do not need to be added to or added on—they need to be translated to fit particular situations. Thus, for example, when a Hawaiian girl is taught to respond to the teasing of a peer, though the skill steps she learns may be from a program characteristic of Caucasian culture, she will grasp the intent of the skill, use the skill steps that fit the style of communicating with which *she* is accustomed, and engineer a successful outcome from the interaction. Cultural compatibility includes natal distinctions and uses the learning of a child's lifetime to promote social literacy. Thus the worldviews of culture are not sacrificed; rather, they are included. It is this approach that best supports social work intervention for social literacy.

APIA youth are socially literate in the context of their own cultures, but often they are not fluent in the social skills of mainstream American culture. The importance of translating the social skills of the natal culture to fit a variety of social situations cannot be overemphasized. In a study by G. Higa, M. J. Manos, and A. Yempuku (1987), for example, disadvantaged APIA youth who had little prior contact with the behavioral expectations of American schools and businesses tended not to use social skills that empowered them in novel situations; mainstream youth did use such skills. In this study, youth who had learned to translate their natal culture behavior into effective social skills showed a social fluency that altered their relationships dramatically. Those APIA youth who are versed in the behavioral expectations of mainstream American society have not necessarily *adopted* the dominant ways as their own but have successfully *translated* the skills of their own histories into skills that work in the dominant culture. In other words, such youth have continued to use behavior congruent with their own worldviews and have done so outside of their natal environments. They are, in effect, socially literate in both their natal cultures and the dominant culture.

Social Literacy and Asian and Pacific Islander Worldviews

Two traditional APIA worldviews have relevance to a culturally compatible model for social literacy training. First, Asian and Pacific Islander cultures emphasize the collective rather than the individual. This is especially so with family, where the individual family member is subordinate to the welfare of the family as a whole. The family unit is traditionally a formal patriarchal structure with a vertical flow of power and authority (Kitano, 1974; Sue, 1973). Directly related to the family structure of authority is the emphasis on kinship, interdependence, and loyalty. Familial interdependence and loyalty demand role conformance and respect for parents, other elders, superiors, and ancestors. Levels of reciprocal obligations exist between parent and child. The child obeys and is dutiful to the parents and elders, and, in exchange, parents are responsible for educating and supporting the child (Kitano, 1974). Strong emphasis is placed on "knowing one's place in the arrangement of things," as well as on the suppression of individualistic behaviors that might interfere with the smooth functioning of the family.

Second, APIA cultures emphasize cooperation over conflict. People from these cultures are socialized to exercise self-control and emotional restraint. S. Nakao and C. Lum (1977) suggest that self-control is manifested when people do not openly challenge the viewpoints of others. Rather than directly confront someone on an issue or problem, APIAs tend to withhold comment, partially agree, or find areas within which cooperation can continue. This is done in order to encourage cooperation and to avoid unpleasant, nonconstructive confrontation.

An example of the relevance of social literacy training to cultural worldviews is in native Hawaiian culture. Native Hawaiian families are structured around sibling caretaking (Gallimore, Boggs, and Jordan, 1974). The family is interdependent, members share work, and children are to be obedient to parental authority. Childcare is shared by siblings as well as parents and is regarded as training for adolescents. A strong sense of affiliation is developed. In Hawaiian families, opportunity for the expression of social skills abounds given the atmosphere of affiliation and togetherness. Though direct confrontation and negotiation with parents are not allowed, interactions with siblings and with peers are encouraged given the degree of shared child caretaking. Hawaiian children tend not to use the skill of negotiation with parents, for example, but it is invaluable as a means of dealing with friends, brothers, and sisters.

SOCIAL SERVICE INTERVENTION: A PROGRAM FOR SOCIAL LITERACY FOR APIA YOUTH

Principles of Practice

There are several basic principles that provide guidelines for social literacy with APIA youth.

Cultural worldviews and traditions should be incorporated into social skills training, but the skills themselves do not need to originate from specific APIA populations. Skills pertaining to worldviews that emphasize the collective (e.g., family) and that promote cooperation and conflict resolution may be more relevant to particular APIA intervention, but such skills need not be normed on APIA youth.

The role of the social worker is to present basic skill steps and to encourage culturally appropriate modification. Given the diversity of APIA populations and the dearth of culturally sensitive programs in social literacy training, the worker needs to present generic skill steps and to coach youth in translating the steps into those unique to the youth's culture.

The role of the youth is to adapt the generic skills steps to his or her cultural context. Youth participating in social literacy programs will learn skills and, with guided practice, translate them into culturally compatible behaviors. To be socially fluent, youth must discriminate the appropriate time to exercise the translated skills.

Conceptual Model of Intervention

The success that people have in interpersonal relations is a function of two critical components: (1) a supportive social network (with whom people do things), and (2) a large and varied behavioral repertoire (what people do) (O'Donnell and Tharp, 1990). Social networks are comprised of all the people with whom one associates. Within social networks, people form friendships, start families, complete projects, solve problems, and do all the things that people do together. Social networks both generate and perpetuate cultural behavior. The behavioral repertoires of people within networks are called social skills. Social skills are complex interpersonal behaviors that enable one to generate satisfactory outcomes in interpersonal relations. They are actions that, when performed in social situations, lead to a positive exchange between people or, if nothing positive occurs, at least help avoid negative outcomes (Bellack and Hersen, 1979).

Though repertoires and networks are reciprocal in that networks influence behavior and behavior in turn influences networks, a person who is socially skilled has at his or her disposal the means by which to make new associations. Social skills thus become the building blocks for relationships. Research shows that good social interactional skills are important for youth in that they affect peer relations (Marshall and McCandless, 1957; Hartup, Glazer, and Charlesworth, 1967), adult interpersonal adjustment and assertiveness (Bellack and Hersen, 1979), social maladjustment (O'Donnell and Tharp, 1982), and delinquency (Spence and Marzilier, 1981). Children who lack social skills generally experience social isolation, rejection, and diminished happiness (Michelson, Sugai, Wood, and Kazdin, 1983). Social competence in childhood is strongly related to later social, academic, and psychological functioning.

Children learn social skills in much the same way they learn to do many other things—they imitate others using skills, and, in turn, they are reinforced for their imitating. Studies show that young children imitate older children (Abramovitch, Carter, and Lando, 1979), preschool children reinforce and encourage each others' behavior (Lamb and Roopnarine, 1979), and peers influence each other to manage aggression (Hartup, 1979).

Most social skills programs have evolved from work with relatively homogeneous, generally white populations with little consideration given to the compatibility of such behaviors to minority cultures. These programs generally are based on a cultural deficit model where the social skills taught are normed on behavior characteristic of the dominant culture. Social behavior of the dominant culture, however, may not work for APIA youth and may even come to shape dysfunctional behavior for them. In some Asian Pacific Island cultures, for example, behavior such as averting eye contact or remaining silent in the presence of another can signify respect and honor. In the dominant culture such behavior may appear to be social withdrawal. Behavior perceived by members of the dominant culture to be withdrawal may arouse members of the dominant culture to intrude on the minority members' personal thoughts and feelings. This in turn may press the minority member to further self-effacing and apologetic behavior. Repeated intrusion of this kind may eventually turn what was respectful behavior into outright escape from intrusion. What was respect now becomes withdrawal.

Cultural compatibility, the conceptual strategy discussed earlier, is useful for the design and implementation of a social literacy project for APIA youth. This is so because social behavior among APIA populations is so diverse and because teachers and counselors may not have the time or the organizational capacity to teach different versions of skills (e.g., a Japanese, Hawaiian, Chinese, Filipino, Samoan, Thai, and so on version of negotiating). Teachers teach basic skills and trust students to know what to do with them. It is important to encourage students to use them in a way that is consistent with cultural histories. Prior to introducing each skill, teachers may give a variation of the following instructions:

The skill you are about to learn is *A* way of interacting with someone. It is not *THE* way. *YOU* know what to do. Use these steps as guidelines; try them; practice them; see what works. Though we will learn them exactly as they are, you decide how you will use them. The skills are like money in the bank—they are available for you to use for whatever purposes you choose.

Specific Skills for Intervention: The Youth Development Project

The Youth Development Project was an ongoing investigation of social literacy with APIA youth (Manos, 1990). It was a school-based program designed to accomplish two tasks: (1) to teach basic social skills, and (2) to give students the opportunity to exercise skills with their classmates. Fourth- through eighth-grade children were taught eighteen to twenty-six social skills. These included such skills as greeting others, giving compliments, responding to teasing, giving and accepting negative feedback, persuading others, active listening, and joining a group. In order for students to use the skills they were taught, teachers organized students into cooperative learning teams. Children were heterogeneously grouped to allow for varying ethnicities and ability levels (Manos, 1985). The contrived learning groups were actually specially constructed social networks that permitted students to use social skills to solve group academic and recreational tasks.

The children who participated in the project were primarily Hawaii-born. They included native Hawaiian, Japanese, Filipino, and Caucasian youth. Other groups such as Chinese, Thai, and Vietnamese children were also represented though in smaller numbers (Manos, 1988).

Because students were learning skills that originated within the dominant culture rather than within their own natal culture, skill training at first took on an air of stiffness and at times seemed unnatural. Later, however, as students gained fluency in "translating," training flowed easily. With the appropriate coaching of a teacher who kept the students' ethnic identity foremost, social skills become an avenue through which ethnic identity was expressed. For the Japanese child, for example, the social skills could be used to express *on* or the deep sense of obligation to one's parents (Johnson, 1977; Kitano, 1969). Skills also related to *oyakoko* or filial piety, especially of a child to his or her parent (Kitano, 1969).

Social skills training for multicultural participation, from the perspective of cultural compatibility, requires a set of basic skills taught by a trainer who has implicit trust in the cultural history of his or her students. The teacher of social skills merely drops the mantle of authority and empowers students to adapt and to translate skills to fit life as it occurs.

There are two basic components to teaching social skills: assessment and training. Assessment entails identifying the situations and interactions that repeatedly occur. Assessment is organized around such questions as: What is the child doing? What happened? With whom does the situation occur? Who usually seems to be present when it does? Where does it occur and when? Clear patterns present themselves. For instance, some youth will have excellent peer relationships but will have little positive contact with adult authority figures. Other youth will have persistent altercations with one or two friends over a problem like gossiping.

The training approach always begins with assessment. Without assessment, training becomes a hit-or-miss proposition. When the situations and interactions are clearly specified, the trainer can focus on them. For the child who does not complete assignments, training may focus on the skills of requesting help and following instructions. For the youth who has difficulty with her parents, negotiation and problem solving skills may be appropriate. For the child who is continually teased, the skill of giving negative feedback may be useful.

Training procedures for APIA youth differ little from traditional methods. Procedures follow a discuss-model-practice-feedback sequence with loopbacks to model and practice. When a skill is introduced, the trainer first discusses it with participants. This discussion reviews reasons why the skill is useful, the situations in which youth may find the skill useful, and a summary of the skill steps to be learned. The teacher then models the skill. He or she sets up a role-play situation by outlining a setting and a cue that introduces the action. To introduce the skill of giving positive feedback, for example, the setting could be two students passing in the hall between classes; the cue is the greeting one gives to the other.

When the skill has been discussed and modeled, it is the students' turn to practice through role play. As in the modeling scenario described above, a setting and cue are selected and the skill steps are enacted. After participants have had an opportunity to role play, enactments are discussed, and each member is given feedback as to his or her performance. It is in this discussion that the youth's cultural adaptations of skills are encouraged and developed by the teacher. An important element of discussion is discrimination training. Discrimination training is assisting the child to discern when it is appropriate to use a certain skill. Exploring the many possible situations that might have occurred in the previous few days in which a specific social skill could have been used is an effective method to do this. It allows children the opportunity to explore their relationships and to determine the behaviors that support those relationships.

Case Examples

Following are verbatim accounts of three situations in which children were videotaped as they role played in the classroom. The first situation involves three 12-year-old boys. The first boy (#1), a part-Hawaiian, is approached by two others, a part-Hawaiian (#2) and a Japanese (#3), who want him to go shoplifting. The skill that is demonstrated is "saying no." The specific steps as they were taught are outlined below (Schumaker, Hazel, and Pederson, 1988). Children in all examples speak in their local dialect.

1. Face the person.
2. Make eye contact.
3. Use a serious voice tone.
4. Keep a serious facial expression.
5. Have a straight body posture.
6. Say something nice to the person.
7. Say "No."
8. Give a reason for not doing the activity.

9. Suggest something else to do.
10. Say "No" again and leave if the person will not listen to you. If the person does listen to you, go do the other activity.

The skill as it was role played follows:

1: Hi.

2 & 3: Hi. What do you want to do today?

1: I going to the dollar ramp.

2: For what? Skateboard?

1: Yeh.

2: Oh, the last time you did that you broke your leg.

1: So?

2: Why not come Safeway with us? We going stealing. Mo' bettah.

3: Got all kind stuff. Got candy, "Transformers," all kind stuff.

1: That ain't the right thing to do.

2 & 3: It is! Good fun. Yeh!

1: What if you was the manager and two kids came steal from you?

2: They wouldn't anyway 'cause they would be scared . . . but us not scared.

3: Come wid us!

2: Chicken.

1: I not chicken. I not stupid like you.

3: Then how come you don't come wid us?

2: Yeh. You chicken that's why. Look. You even growing feathers.

1: Because that ain't the right thing to do.

3: Come wid us!

2: Chicken. You scared.

1: Because that ain't the right thing. You guys can do what you guys like. I like going. (He walks away.)

In this instance, boy #1 stands up to his friends while he essentially uses only three of the skill steps—saying no, giving a reason, and leaving. He refuses to acknowledge his friends' taunts and avoids further conflict by leaving.

In the second example two 11-year-old girls approach each other. The first (#1), a part Hawaiian, is asked by the second, a Korean (#2), to shoplift. Again, the skill demonstrated is "saying no."

1: Hi, Chuko.

2: Hi, Tiffany. Hey, c'mon wid us, go shoplift.

1: Nah.

2: Why not?

1: Because people have to pay money for that kind of stuff.

2: So?

1: So you like get caught and go to jail?

2: We not going to get caught!

1: Yeh, they got cameras and stuff all over the place.

2: So?

1: You like go do something else instead?

2: Like what?

1: We go cruisin'.

2: (Pause) Okay.

In this instance, girl #2 does not taunt her friend and thus girl #1 has the opportunity to suggest something else for them to do together.

The final example is that of a part-Hawaiian boy teasing a Japanese girl. Both are 12-year-olds. The skill the girl uses is "responding to teasing." The teacher taught her to use the following skill steps (Schumaker et al., 1988):

1. Face the person.
2. Make eye contact.
3. Use a serious voice tone.
4. Have a serious facial expression.
5. Keep a straight body posture.
6. Ask the person to stop. Say "Stop" without anger.
7. Tell the person that you don't like it.
8. If the person will listen, explain or give a reason.
9. Say "Thanks" if the person stops. Then change the subject.
10. Excuse yourself and leave if the person continues to tease you.

The girl modified and used the skill effectively in the following way:

B: What books you reading?

G: *The Flowers* and *Behind the Attic Wall.*

B: Oh, those junk books! Look at this, brah. Modern Air Combat Book! F-14 Tomcat and all! Junk, you! You no can even read this kine good books. Junk books you read!

G: Can you please stop teasing me?

B: No!

G: Excuse me, but I have to go.

B: Go then!

In her interaction with the boy, the girl does not tolerate the presence of conflict. After making her request, she leaves.

CONCLUSION

This chapter explores the fundamentals of social literacy for APIA youth. Social skills training for social literacy follows a cultural compatibility model that deemphasizes ethnic-specific training (such as creating a Chinese, Japanese, Filipino, or so forth version of negotiating) and encourages the translation of skills into those compatible with youths' natal culture. The ultimate goal of social skills training is to empower youth to manage social interactions with people of diverse cultures. It is to provide youth with the freedom to build relationships and participate with others regardless of cultural background. It is *not* a goal of social skills training to supplant an individual's ethnic identity and to have Hawaiian, Samoan, Japanese, Korean, Chinese, and Filipino youth speak and act like members of the dominant culture. Social literacy for multicultural participation gives greater expression to an already rich ethnic identity. Though alone it will not solve the complex problems of a pluralistic society, social literacy training enhances the quality of relationships within cultural diversity.

This discussion focuses on social literacy for youth, but all those who live and work in culturally diverse communities are charged with the responsibility of learning the behavioral symbols of the others' culture. Cultural compatibility is not a vestment of minority status; it is an opportunity for people to relate to people.

REFERENCES

Abramovitch, R., C. Carter, and B. Lando (1979). Sibling interaction in the home. *Child Development* 50: 997–1003.

Asher, S. R. (1983). Social competence and peer status: Recent advances and future directions. *Child Development* 54: 1427–1434.

Bellack, A. S., and M. Hersen (1979). *Behavior Modification: An Introductory Textbook.* New York: Oxford University Press.

Coleman, J. S. (1987). Families and schools. *Educational Researcher* 16 (6): 32–38.

D'Amato, J. (1988). "Acting": Hawaiian children's resistance to teachers. *The Elementary School Journal* 88 (5): 529–544.

——— (1986). "We cool, tha's why": A study of personhood and place in a class of Hawaiian second graders. Ph.D. dissertation, University of Hawaii.

Gallimore, R., J. W. Boggs, and C. Jordan (1974). *Culture, Behavior and Education: A Study of Hawaiian-Americans*. Beverly Hills, Calif.: Sage Publications.

Gould, K. H. (1988, March-April). Asian and Pacific Islanders: Myth and reality. *Social Work* 33 (2): 142–147.

Hartup, W. W. (1979). Peer relations and the growth of social competence. In M. W. Kent and J. E. Rolf (eds.), *Primary Prevention of Psychopathology. Social Competence in Children*, vol. 3. Hanover, N.H.: University Press of New England.

Hartup, W. W., J. A. Glazer, and R. Charlesworth (1967). Peer reinforcement and sociometric status. *Child Development* 38: 1017–1024.

Higa, G., M. J. Manos, and A. Yempuku (1987). Social skills assessment of disadvantaged and mainstream youth. *Pacific Educational Research Journal* 3 (1): 19–31.

Honolulu Police Department (1980–1988). *Annual Statistical Report*. Honolulu: City and County of Honolulu.

Johnson, C. L. (1977). Interdependence, reciprocity and indebtedness: An analysis of Japanese American kinship relations. *Journal of Marriage and the Family* 39: 351–364.

Kitano, H. L. (1969). *Japanese Americans: The Evolution of a Subculture*. Englewood Cliffs, N.J.: Prentice-Hall.

——— (1974). *Race Relations*. Englewood Cliffs, N.J.: Prentice-Hall.

Lamb, M. E., and J. L. Roopnarine (1979). Peer influences on sex-role development in preschoolers. *Child Development* 50: 1219–1222.

Manos, M. J. (1985, July). Youth Development Project: Preventive intervention in delinquency—Revised project description (Report No. 317), Center for Youth Research, University of Hawaii.

——— (1988, October). Youth Development Project: Preventive intervention in delinquency—Three year evaluation report, 1984–1987 (Report No. 338), Center for Youth Research, University of Hawaii.

——— (1990, December). Youth Development Project: Program summary (Report No. 355), Center for Youth Research, University of Hawaii.

Marshall, B. R., and H. R. McCandless (1957). Sex differences in social acceptance and participation of preschool children. *Child Development* 28: 421–425.

Michelson, L., D. P. Sugai, R. P. Wood, and A. E. Kazdin (1983). *Social Skills Assessment and Training with Children: An Empirically Based Handbook*. New York: Plenum Press.

Mortland, C. A., and M. G. Egan (1987, May-June). Vietnamese youth in American foster care. *Social Work* 32: 240–245.

Nakao, S., and C. Lum (1977). Yellow is not white and white is not right. Masters thesis, School of Social Welfare, University of California, Los Angeles.

O'Donnell, C. R., and R. G. Tharp (1982). Community intervention and the use of multi-disciplinary knowledge. In A. S. Bellack, M. Hersen, and A. E. Kazdin (eds.), *International Handbook of Behavior Modification and Therapy*. New York: Plenum Press.

——— (1990). Community intervention guided by theoretical development. In A. S. Bellack, M. Hersen, and A. E. Kazdin (eds.), *International Handbook of Behavior Modification and Therapy*, 2d ed. New York: Plenum Press.

Schumaker, J. B., J. S. Hazel, and C. S. Pederson (1988). *Social Skills for Daily Living*. Circle Pines, Minn.: American Guidance Service, Inc.

Spence, S., and J. S. Marzilier (1981). Social skills training with adolescent male offenders—II: Short-term, long-term and generalized effects. *Behaviour Research and Therapy* 19: 349–368.

Sue, D. W. (1973). Ethnic identity: The impact of two cultures on the psychological development of Asians in America. In S. Sue and N. Wagner (eds.), *Asian-Americans: Psychological Perspectives*. Palo Alto, Calif.: Science and Behavior Books.

Sue, S., and J. K. Morishima (1982). *The Mental Health of Asian Americans*. San Francisco: Jossey-Bass.

Tharp, R. G. (1988). Psychocultural variables and constants: Effects on teaching and learning. Report prepared for the Center for Studies of Multicultural Higher Education, University of Hawaii and Native Hawaiian Vocational Education Program, Alu Like.

U.S. Bureau of the Census (1988). *We, the Asian and Pacific Islander Americans*. Washington, D.C.: U.S. Government Printing Office.

U.S. Department of Justice, Federal Bureau of Investigation (1980–1989). *Uniform Crime Reports for the United States*. Washington, D.C.: U.S. Government Printing Office.

Chapter 14

Future Directions in Social Services: Asian and Pacific Islander Perspectives

Daniel S. Sanders

INTRODUCTION

Trying to predict the future direction of social services for Asian and Pacific Islander Americans (APIAs), despite its value in planning and delivering social services for APIAs, is fraught with difficulties. There are assumptions to be made and inferences to be drawn on the basis of current realities, regarding likely societal trends, changes in the workplace, demographic changes, and the beliefs, hopes, and aspirations of a complex immigrant subculture that are open to questions.

First, there are hazards in predicting the future, including the future directions of social services. There is considerable arbitrariness in the effort to identify and to predict future developments, be they societal changes, changes in family patterns, or social policies and services impacting the family. Second, at least in some instances the effort to predict future trends has tended to be a fad. Such tendencies are unfortunate and stand in the way of efforts to anticipate and to meet future needs. Third, in discussing APIAs' perspectives, the views of several somewhat disparate groups have to be noted and, insofar as possible, commonalities in values, orientation, and thinking identified (Green, 1982). Fourth, even within a particular ethnic group under the umbrella term "Asian and Pacific Islanders" there are variations among individuals and groups depending on their time of arrival as immigrants, level of education, nature of occupation, and their generational status.

Despite these difficulties, efforts need to be made to identify future trends in social services, at least on the basis of current realities and emerging new developments. This is vital if social services are to respond positively to the challenge of being more proactive than reactive in meeting human needs. Increasingly in the future, social workers and other human service professionals will be faced with the task of dealing with complex social and psychological problems such as family violence, substance abuse, delinquency, and poverty that call for a more community-based, preventive, and developmental approach in the delivery of social services. This chapter examines those factors that are an integral part of future predictions and plannings of social services for APIAs. It describes a futuristic orientation and specific implications for social work and social services with APIAs.

ASIAN AND PACIFIC ISLANDER AMERICANS

The umbrella term "Asian and Pacific Islander Americans" refers to members of somewhat disparate nationality groups whose heritage can be traced to the Asian continent and to the Pacific Islands (Green, 1982). It is clear that the term "Asian and Pacific Islander Americans" represents a very complex subculture in American society. Any attempt to generalize or draw inferences regarding their perspectives would have to take note of the many differences that are evident among these ethnic groups. Hideki A. Ishisaka and Calvin Y. Takagi (1982) point out that in analyzing differences among Asian American groups it is helpful to identify family lifestyles, taking into account such factors as language, socialization, religious beliefs, cultural values, family roles, and child-rearing practices. They also refer to likely variations between the older immigrant families, the newer immigrant families, and the descendants of the first-generation (American-born) immigrants. This is not to deny certain commonalities such as respect for authority, commitment to education, strong family ties, and cooperative efforts.

The need to explore further these and other commonalities, despite the differences such as varying beliefs, values, history of immigration, and economic status, is essential to identifying APIA perspectives regarding future directions in social services.

FUTURISTIC CONSIDERATIONS

A futuristic orientation is essential if social work and social services are to respond to the challenge of developing an effective and culturally sensitive system. Despite the difficulty in predicting the future, efforts should be made, at least on the basis of present realities, to identify future developments. Perhaps a reliable way of predicting the future is to understand critically the present.

It is evident that social work and the provision of social services in dealing with human problems are often on a reactive and crisis basis. Historically, social services emerged in Western societies as an organized response to the social problems that came in the wake of industrialization. The traditional role of social services based on a remedial model has been to minimize or to contain the negative impact of industrialization on individuals and families. However, a futuristic orientation in planning and delivery of social services involving an anticipatory stance will help considerably in breaking loose from the traditional model (Sanders, 1988).

Following the industrial revolution, in most industrial societies in the West, social welfare and social services had a marginal role. This is not to deny the positive developments in the emergence of the concept of a welfare state such as efforts toward universal services and the viewing of social services increasingly as a social right. Despite these and other positive elements, economic development was the dominant theme, and social welfare and social services tended to be necessary appendages. While there were notable exceptions in particular countries and in specific time periods, it is evident that limited attention was given to issues of social justice, human rights, disintegration of community life, and the impact of industrial technology on people.

Social forecasters and critics such as Alvin Toffler (1974) and John Naisbitt (1984) refer to the breakdown of the postindustrial society and the emergence of new realities that social work practitioners, social policy analysts, and decision makers need to take note of in the planning and delivery of social services. The anticipatory stance in dealing with individuals and societal problems becomes crucial in the context of the societal changes and the complex problems in the postindustrial society. Toffler (1974) refers to the breakdown of the postindustrial society (the second wave) and the emergence of the third wave, where earlier problems are further aggravated, giving rise to more complex problems.

In societies experiencing the industrial revolution (Toffler's second wave) and its aftermath, there was almost exclusive emphasis on economic development, mechanization of work, concentration of workers in factories, and mass production and consumption As mentioned earlier, insufficient attention was given to social development, equitable distribution of resources, and the quality of life of all people. The emergence of the third-wave economy, Toffler maintains, signifies a radical change in the postindustrial society. As evidence of this change, he points to the present crisis in the world industrial society. Mass production and mass distribution are viewed less and less as advanced methods of economic activity. There are indications (as Toffler puts it) that the economy is "demassifying." In the complex changes that Toffler identifies as part of the third-wave economy, he predicts that people will produce goods and services not so much for profit as for their own use (Toffler, 1974).

Both Toffler (1974) and Naisbitt (1984) in referring to the breakup of the industrial society, point to the anachronistic nature of current socioeconomic organizations and institutions. They discuss new ways of thinking and organizing the economy, the work life, family life, and leisure that have implications for social work and the planning and delivery of social services in the future. Toffler, in identifying some of the likely trends in the future, goes so far as to specify a third-wave economy sector referred to as "prosuming"—that is, production for consumption largely by consumers. In the third-wave economy, the changes produced include deemphasis of mass production, emergence of non-profit networks, greater emphasis on employee participation in decision making, and the development of electronic co-ops and familial teams (Toffler, 1974).

Naisbitt (1984) similarly foresees trends such as the growing interaction between "high tech" and "high touch" and the potential for redis-covery of the capacity to be creative and effective from the bottom up. He also refers to a shift away from heavy reliance on institutional help to greater self-reliance, a change from dependence on hierarchical systems to informal networks, and, not the least of the changes, a growing realization that humankind is part of a global village.

Impact of Changes on APIAs

These current realities and emerging developments impact all segments of society. However, special attention needs to be given to the negative impact of prospective societal changes on populations such as ethnic minorities, the elderly, new immigrants, and victims of economic deprivation, especially the ethnic poor and the homeless. At a minimum, this calls for cultural sensitivity and understanding of ethnic lifestyles in social work practice with various minority groups, including APIAs.

APIAs, as one of the fastest growing minority groups, are likely to experience more changes and intergenerational problems impacting parents, children, and the elderly in the future. It is evident from present sociodemographic trends in the United States that there are increasing numbers of elderly persons, infants, and young children at risk who require adequate care. The emerging data also suggests that the population of children under 18 years old is changing rapidly to the point where minority children will constitute the majority child population early in the twenty-first century. While this prediction is mainly in relation to Hispanic children, it reflects, at least to some extent, the situation regarding APIAs. The change, social analysts point out, will most likely be due to immigration and differential child-bearing among varying populations (Sarri, Vinter, and Steketee, 1988).

FUTURE DIRECTIONS IN SOCIAL SERVICES FOR APIAs

Several factors will be operative in varying degrees in shaping future directions in social service for APIAs. The emerging social and technological changes will necessitate ongoing critical assessment of the role of public welfare, the relationship between public and private social service agencies, and the phenomenon of private practice. There will be experimentation with new forms of participation between professionals and clients and between producers and consumers on the basis of mutually shared purposes and authority. Clearly, the barriers between professionals and clients, the paternalism of professionals, and the powerlessness of the users of services will have to be changed.

The following are some of the specific developments in future social services that are likely or desirable. First, if social services are to respond creatively to the emerging changes, they need to develop a more holistic, broad-based framework for the delivery of services. This is in keeping with the APIAs' tradition of a holistic perspective to viewing the community, culture, and ecological context. This holistic perspective embodies all events related to life, relationships, and services. There is less of the dichotomy of body and mind, psyche and soma (Green, 1982). A holistic perspective will influence the design of future services. APIAs, increasingly in the future, will require a broad range of integrated services, somewhat akin to the multiservice centers that are prevalent among Pacific-Asian communities today. This multiservice model with the potential of increasing community usage of services by ethnic minorities will be in contrast to the present highly specialized, fragmented services (Green, 1982). An essential aspect of the multiservice model of service delivery is the importance of providing culturally appropriate help with bicultural and bilingual expertise. The provision of culturally sensitive social services, taking into account the knowledge and skills background of workers, will increasingly be a feature of social services.

Second, in the future, there is likely to be emphasis on a change from remedial to a more preventive and developmental perspective in social services (Sanders, 1988; 1982). The developmental perspective in social work and social services, among other things, embodies a fundamental philosophical stance in work with people in a helping role that is positive, open to social change, and committed to maximizing the inherent strengths and capacities of individuals, families, and communities. In relation to APIAs, for example, this will involve positive, creative use of their networks or spiritual traditions in supporting the individual. It is evident that APIAs' worldviews are, at least to some extent, influenced by their religious systems of thought and their traditional heritage. For example, traditional values guiding Chinese family life have been drawn from the Confucian philosophy and system of thought. There is emphasis in the Confucian system of thought on harmony and the development of right relationships in the family, community, and the larger society. Similarly, Buddhism and Hinduism, with their emphasis on respect for life, compassion, and selfishness, exercise influence in the lives of many APIAs. As part of the developmental approach in the provision of social services, social workers could play a creative role in making use of positive elements in ethnic and cultural diversity with potential for growth and harmony.

Third, there will increasingly be a crosscultural, pluralistic perspective in work with people and in the delivery of social services. A vital component of this is the provision of social services more sensitive to cultural traditions and beliefs. APIAs function at least in two environments: their own cultural environment and that of mainstream society. Service providers need to be aware of and sensitive to the immigration history, traditions, and events that have shaped the lives of APIAs. This is especially important in designing services for special groups such as the elderly. A crosscultural/international perspective is also important in dealing with complex social problems such as refugee problems, AIDS, and family violence that transcend national and cultural boundaries, with the increasing trend of global interdependence.

Fourth, there will be greater emphasis on the total family and family support systems in formulation of social policy, in treatment of clients, and in social service delivery in the future. In work with APIAs, for example, the policy analyst and the practitioner alike need to take note of the strong family ties, sense of mutual obligations, and family and friendship networks. The Western value of individualism that undergirds social work approaches is somewhat alien to the indigenous value system of some of the societies in the Asian-Pacific region. Related to this is the concern for and loyalty to others, which is an integral part of the lifestyles of APIAs. Individualism is deemphasized. There is considerable emphasis on the family in relation to the individual influencing individual interactions within the family and outside the family. Both therapeutic approaches and social services will increasingly be based on the understanding of the family as an "interdependent whole."

Emphasis will be on making available both treatment services and resources to strengthen family ties among members. Related to this will be the increasing emphasis on the evaluation of social policies and services to determine their impact on the well-being of families. Also, there will be increasing efforts to foster positive family policies designed to undergird and strengthen family functioning.

Fifth, there will be emphasis on ethical considerations and issues of equity in the planning and delivery of social services. Issues of equal accessibility of services and appropriate services in terms of cultural background will be increasingly emphasized. In the case of APIAs, for example, the lack of culturally appropriate services from the outside is a key factor in reinforcing the arrangement of obtaining help from within their communities. The reluctance to obtain help from mainstream agencies, analysts point out, has been at least partly due to the fact that these ethnic groups have been largely ignored by the mainstream social services (Green, 1982).

There will be ethical considerations in service delivery and in concerns related to the negative impact of social policies and services on vulnerable groups such as women, children, the elderly, and ethnic minorities. Human service professionals and administrators of social services will be increasingly faced with value dilemmas in the future in dealing with policies and services related to childcare, surrogate motherhood, and institutional care of the frail elderly, to mention only a few. These issues will highlight further the need to critique social services, to define social problems, and to design social services to respond in culturally appropriate ways, free from bias and ethnic stereotyping.

Sixth, social services in the future are likely to be less bureaucratic, involving more clients and consumers in the planning and delivery of services. This will be in keeping with the predictions related to industry of deemphasis on mass production and the search for nonbureaucratic structures more responsive to consumer needs.

The predictions referred to earlier regarding production for consumption largely by the consumer and the attendant changes of greater emphasis on employee involvement and participation in decision making, the emergence of nonprofit networks, and the development of cooperative efforts and familial teams, to the extent that they are likely to happen in the future, will have a significant impact on the social service delivery system. These likely changes will have a positive effect on the future use of social services by ethnic minority groups, including APIAs.

Already there is some evidence of production and service delivery, in both economic and social spheres, being more responsive to the interests and needs of consumers and clients. In the social sphere the response to the high-tech health care delivery system involving increasing costs and impersonal atmosphere in hospitals and clinics has results, for example, in the growth of the hospice movement, the development of health co-ops, the fostering of childcare networks and the reappearance of midwives (Naisbitt, 1984; Sanders, 1988). This is also evident in the development of the "people's medical society," which is committed to the view that the people who should alter the practice of Medicare are the people it is practiced on—the consumers (Inlander, Levin, and Weiner, 1988).

CONCLUSION

It is clear that the emerging societal changes necessitating greater responsiveness to consumers, involvement of consumers in shaping policies, and the development of less bureaucratic structures are likely to have considerable influence on the planning and delivery of future social services.

The predominant concept of clients as impersonal cases in a technological and industrial service culture will continue to be under attack. Increasingly, in this context, the service bureaucracy will be viewed from the position of the user rather than the practitioner or the administrator of social services. This likely change in the perception of the service user as a consumer rather than a client will necessitate a critical look at the nature of the relationship and the transaction between "seeker" and "helper," opening up new possibilities (Perlman, 1975).

The future developments regarding the welfare state concept, the likely shifts in philosophy, the ongoing role of the federal government, and the likely public-private partnership in service delivery are all critical factors that are likely to influence social services (Khinduka, 1987).

In keeping with the trends of an increasingly pluralistic society, there will be a push, particularly by ethnic minorities including APIAs, for social services to be more responsive to the culture, belief systems, and religious traditions of the clients and consumers. In developing the necessary pluralistic perspective, there is likely to be a greater understanding and appreciation of ethnic and cultural diversity, the need for alternate approaches, and a conscious effort to break loose from limiting and distorting cultural biases in future social services. Increasingly, there will also be commitment to both developing services and resources in efforts to help people.

A key consideration in the context of these changes is whether the definition of social problems and the planning and delivery of social services (including social work practice) will be operative within a framework of social change or social control. It is vital that the future planning and delivery of social services to all people, including APIAs, stems from a philosophy of people-oriented development, involving positive institutional and policy change, the provision of tangible supports, and the empowerment of people—especially those that are most vulnerable in society.

Here, social movements—especially client and consumer movements—will have an increasingly vital role in the future in providing positive supports and enhancing the clients'/consumers' sense of confidence and capacity to collaboratively effect change. For ultimately, despite past experiences and likely ongoing difficulties, the goal is one of empowering the consumers and clients to exercise greater control in shaping policies and services that impact their lives.

REFERENCES

Gould, K. H. (1988, March-April). Asian and Pacific Islanders: Myth and reality. *Social Work* 33 (2): 142–147.

Green, J. W. (ed.) (1982). *Cultural Awareness in the Human Services*. Englewood Cliffs, N.J.: Prentice-Hall.

Inlander, C. B., L. S. Levin, and E. Weiner (eds.) (1988). *Medicine on Trial*. New York: John Wiley and Sons.

Ishisaka, H. A., and C. Y. Takagi (1982). Social work with Asian and Pacific-Americans. In J. W. Green (ed.), *Cultural Awareness in the Human Services*. Englewood Cliffs, N.J.: Prentice-Hall.

Khinduka, S. K. (1987). Social work and human services. In *NASW Encyclopedia of Social Work*, vol. 2. New York: National Association of Social Workers.

Naisbitt, J. (1984). *Megatrends*. New York: Warner Books.

Perlman, R. (1975). *Consumers and Social Services*. New York: John Wiley and Sons.

Sanders, D. S. (ed.) (1982). *The Developmental Perspective in Social Work*. Honolulu: University of Hawaii, School of Social Work.

——— (1988). Futuristic considerations in social work. In D. S. Sanders and J. Fischer (eds.), *Visions for the Future: Social Work and Pacific-Asian Perspectives*. Honolulu: University of Hawaii, School of Social Work.

Sarri, R. C., R. Vinter, and M. Steketee (1988). *The Future of Social Work and Social Work Education: Final Report of the Interdisciplinary Seminar*. Ann Arbor: University of Michigan School of Social Work.

Toffler, A. (1974). *The Third Wave*. New York: Bantam Books.

Index

Acculturation: among Asian and Pacific Islanders, 3, 5, 14, 30; among Filipinos, 108; among Hawaiians (*kānaka maoli*), 140–41, 146; among Japanese, 62, 69, 74; among Samoans, 211; conflict in Chinese culture, 88; difficulties among youth, 219; stress among Vietnamese, 121–23

Achenbaum, Andrew, 191

Asian and Pacific Islanders: definition, 234; history, 29; mental health problems, 4–5; models for service delivery, 12; racism, 6; sociodemographic information, 3–4, 29, 236; stereotypes, 5; stressors, 5–6; underutilization of services, 6–12

Barnes, V., 141

Barringer, Herbert, 135

Bilingualism: for Asian and Pacific Islanders, 8, 11, 15, 24, 50, 237; for Filipinos, 112; for Japanese, 71; for Samoans, 158, 164, 166, 211; for Vietnamese, 126

Bolman, W., 50

Bond, John, 165

Bourne, Peter, 87–88

Bowles, Dorcas, 23

Brown, Timothy, 5

Buddhism, 38–40, 42, 63, 72, 124, 238

Bui, Diana, 120

Bulato, J. C., 109

Calkins, Fay, 161

Chamorros: ancestor worship, 177; definition, 172; family, 174–77, 179, 181; family dysfunction, 177–78; historical background, 171–73; skills of the worker, 181; social clubs and organizations, 180; social service intervention, 178–81; sociodemographic information, 173–74; values and behavioral norms, 174–77

Cheung, F.M.C., 41–42

Child abuse: in Hawaiian (*kānaka maoli*) families, 141, 206; in Samoan families, 31, 161–62, 167, 205–6

Chinese Americans: acculturation, 88; family unit, 84–85; historical background, 79–82; intergenerational conflict, 87–88; racism, 86–87; role of the worker, 89–92; skills of the worker, 93; social and psychological problems, 86–88; social service

intervention, 88–93; sociodemographic information, 82–84; values and behavioral norms, 84–86
Chinese psychologies, 40–42
Church, Timothy, 107
Communication, 8, 28, 74–75, 90–92, 108, 165, 195, 212
Confucianism, 41–42, 84, 124, 192, 237–38
Coping: of Asian and Pacific Islanders, 10; of Chinese, 85–86, 89; of Vietnamese, 120
Council on Social Work Education, 23
Cultural awareness approach, 25–26
Cultural compatibility, 221–22, 225
Cultural-competent model, 25
Cultural deficit, 221
Cultural difference, 221

D'Amato, John, 220
Davis, Larry, 24, 25, 206
Devore, Wynetta, 23, 25, 26, 27, 31, 203
DeVoss, G., 43
Douvan, Elizabeth, 194, 195
Draguns, Juris G., 28, 49
Dual perspective, 25

Elderly, Asian and Pacific Islander: cultural values related to aging, 191–93; definition, 186; multidimensional assessments, 196–97; Older Americans Act, 186; physical and mental health conditions, 188–89; skills of the worker, 196–99; social and economic conditions, 190–91; Social Security Act, 186; social service intervention, 194–200; sociodemographic information, 186–87
Enriquez, Virgilio, 105, 106
Ethnic-competent practice, 21, 22, 25, 32
Ethnic-competent worker, 22, 32–33
Ethnic enclaves: Chamorros, 180–81; Chinese, 81–82; Vietnamese, 120–21, 123, 127
Ethnic-sensitive practice approach, 25, 27–28, 32

Family: Asian and Pacific Islander, 222, 238; Chamorro, 174–77, 179, 181; Chinese, 84–85, 87–88; Filipino, 99, 104, 106, 109; Hawaiian (*kānaka maoli*), 138–40; Japanese, 42–43, 67–69, 71–72; Samoan, 158–61, 164, 208–9; Vietnamese, 123–25, 127–28
Family violence: against children, 31, 141, 161–62, 204, 209; against women, 204–5; cultural concerns related to, 206–10; definition, 203; education and treatment programs, for Samoans, 165–66; Hawaiian perpetrators of spouse abuse, 206; Samoan perpetrators of child abuse, 205–6; skills of the worker, 212, 213; social service intervention, 210–14; treatment programs for Hawaiians, 213–14
Filial piety, 41, 42, 84, 192, 226
Filipinos: family, 99, 104, 106, 109; historical background, 98–99; post–1065 immigration problems, 102–4; religion, 106: skills of the worker, 111–12; social and psychological problems, 102–4; social service intervention, 107–12; sociodemographic information, 99–102; values and behavioral norms, 104–7
Folk healing: in Asian cultures, 9; in Chinese culture, 41–42, 89; in cultural awareness approach, 26; with culturally different clients, 50; in Hawaiian (*kānaka maoli*), 9, 32, 45, 147; in Japanese culture, 32, 72–73; in Samoan culture, 163, 164–65; in Southeast Asian culture, 9
Forbes, Ken, 141
Franco, Robert, 156, 163

Gallegos, J., 22, 25, 32
Glidden, C., 70
Gratton, F.J.H., 160
Green, James, 22, 25, 26, 196

About the Editor and Contributors

NOREEN MOKUAU is an Associate Professor and chair of the baccalaureate social work program at the University of Hawaii at Manoa, School of Social Work. She has engaged in research and published in areas associated with health and mental health concerns of multicultural populations, with an emphasis on Asian and Pacific Islander groups. Her recent works have focused on native Hawaiian health, spiritualism as a component of practice, and family-centered indigenous healing.

JENNIFER ABE is completing her doctoral training in clinical psychology at the University of California, Los Angeles. She graduated from Wheaton College with a B.A. in psychology in 1985 and has been actively involved in the ongoing research activities of the National Research Center on Asian American Mental Health at UCLA. Some of her projects have included examining psychological maladjustment among Asian American college students and looking at predictors of post traumatic stress disorder (PTSD) among Southeast Asian refugees. Currently, Abe is finishing her dissertation entitled, "Are Asians 'Situationally-Oriented'?: Exploring the Situational Responses of Asian and White American College Students."

AMEFIL AGBAYANI is Director of Minority Student Programs at the University of Hawaii at Manoa. She received her B.A. in political science from the University of the Philippines and her M.A. and Ph.D in political science from the University of Hawaii at Manoa. Her teaching and research interests are in the areas of education and politics, minority students, multicultural and bilingual education, immigration, and Filipinos in Hawaii. She is the chair of the Hawaii Civil Rights Commission and vice president of the National Association of Asian and Pacific American Education.

KEKUNI BLAISDELL has been Professor of Medicine at the University of Hawaii at Manoa, John A. Burns School of Medicine, since the school's establishment in 1965. He was also acting interim director of the university's Center for Hawaiian Studies from 1987 to 1989. He wrote the health section for the 1983 U.S. Congress Native Hawaiians Study Commission Report and was a member of the consortium that produced the E Ola Mau *Native Hawaiian Health Needs Study Report* of 1985. These activities led to the founding of E Ola Mau (Live On). This Hawaii-wide indigenous Hawaiian health workers organization participated in the final wording and passage of the U.S. Congress Native Hawaiian Health Care Act of 1988 and is currently facilitating the development of community health programs by *kānaka maoli* for *kānaka maoli* under this federal legislation.

NATHAN CHANG received his Masters of Social Work degree from the University of Hawaii at Manoa in 1975. From 1981 to 1989, he served as the director of a bilingual counseling program for Samoan residents of the State of Hawaii. He is a founding member of the Samoan Service Providers Association, a nonprofit social service agency based in Honolulu. He has also served as a consultant to that organization and is a member of its board of directors. Currently, he is a specialist at the University of Hawaii at Manoa, School of Social Work, doing minority student recruitment and retention.

STEPHEN FUGITA is Associate Professor of Psychology and Ethnic Studies at Santa Clara University. His areas of expertise include the Japanese American community and minority mental health. He and coauthor David O'Brien have two books being published this year: *Japanese American Ethnicity: The Persistence of Community* and *The Japanese American Experience*.

SHARLENE MAEDA FURUTO is a Professor and Social Work Program Coordinator at the Brigham Young University–Hawaii, where she has been since 1975. She has done cross cultural research with Samoans and Southeast Asians, and her book *Social Work Practice With Asian Americans* is expected to be released in early 1992. From 1988 to 1990 she served as the National Association for Social Workers Hawaii Chapter president, and she was recently honored as the Outstanding Social Worker of Hawaii.

KAREN HUANG a native of Taiwan, graduated Phi Beta Kappa with high honors and then earned her Ph.D. in clinical psychology at the University of California, Berkeley. She completed her clinical training at the Harvard Medical Center–affiliated Children's Hospital and Massachusetts General Hospital in Boston. Currently Dr. Huang is a Psychology Department affiliate and staff psychologist at Stanford University specializing in young adult/late adolescent Asian/Pacific Islanders development. Dr. Huang also has a part-time private practice and provides management consulting aimed at increasing pluralism in corporate America.

KAREN L. ITO is a cultural anthropologist specializing in medical and psychological anthropology. She has conducted research and published articles on Asian and Pacific Islander Americans in the area of cultural interpretations of illness and cultural constructions of self. She is currently a postdoctoral fellow at the National Research Center on Asian American Mental Health at UCLA completing a monograph on native Hawaiian interpretations of self and affective social relationships.

MICHAEL J. MANOS completed doctoral studies in education and clinical psychology at the University of Arizona. He gained solid experience in multicultural education by designing educational programs with Native Americans in Arizona and with Asian and Pacific Islander immigrants in Hawaii. He later concentrated on juvenile delinquency and delinquency prevention in Hawaii. His current research investigates the role of social networks and social competence in contributing to youth development in multicultural populations. At the University of Hawaii at Manoa, Dr. Manos is an Assistant Researcher of the Center for Youth Research, Social Science Research Institute, and Assistant Professor at the College of Education.

JON K. MATSUOKA received his doctorate from the University of Michigan in 1984 and is currently an Associate Professor of Social Work at the University of Hawaii at Manoa. He has conducted research and published scholarly works in the area of mental health and Pacific-Asian peoples. He has investigated the themes of social change, stress, and mental health as they relate to a variety of populations, including native Hawaiians, Pacific-Asian Vietnam veterans, and Vietnamese refugees. He is coeditor of a recently published book, *Peace and Development*.

JONATHAN Y. OKAMURA is Program Coordinator of the Center for Studies of Multicultural Higher Education at the University of Hawaii at Manoa. A social anthropologist by training, he has done field research on Filipino immigrants in Honolulu and on Hanunuo Mangyans, an upland cultural minority in the Philippines where he has also taught. His research interests and scholarly works are in the areas of ethnicity, ethnic relations, and minority higher education.

PAUL PEDERSEN is a Professor of Education in Counselor Education at Syracuse University. He is the author, coauthor, or editor of seventeen books, thirty-five book chapters, fifty-seven articles, and nineteen other monographs primarily on multicultural counseling and communication. He was director of the National Institute of Mental Health–funded DISC (Developing Interculturally Skilled Counselors) four-year project at the University of Hawaii at Manoa and the East-West Center. He taught at universities in Malaysia for two years and in Indonesia for three years while conducting research on youth and student attitudes. He was a counselor at the International Student Office for eight years while on the faculty of Psychoeducational Studies at the University of Minnesota.

DANIEL S. SANDERS was Dean and Professor of Social Work at the University of Hawaii at Manoa from 1971 to 1986 and at the School of Social Work at the University of Illinois at Urbana-Champaign from 1986 to 1989. At both institutions he directed programs of international social welfare, and he was the founder and first president of the Inter-University Consortium for International Social Development from 1980 to 1989. He presented over thirty papers at national and international conferences, authored eleven books and monographs and numerous journal publications and book chapters on a variety of social welfare topics such as peace and development, ethical issues, social work values, and the role of immigrants. His contributions to the profession of social welfare were at the forefront of his life until his death while attending the National Association of Social Workers Conference in San Francisco in 1989.

DEBBIE SHIMIZU received a Masters in Social Work degree from the University of Hawaii at Manoa, School of Social Work. She is currently a program specialist for the undergraduate program in the School of Social Work and the program coordinator for the Public Service Program; a cooperative progam between the University of Hawaii at Manoa, School of Social Work, and various departments of the state government. She is also a board member of the National Association of Social Workers–Hawaii Chapter and chairs the Continuing Education Committee. Shimizu was the production manager for a videotape on culturally sensitive practice and has presented lectures on Social Work in the United States to students visiting from Japan.

STANLEY SUE is Professor of Psychology at UCLA and Director of the National Research Center on Asian American Mental Health. Prior to the faculty appointment at UCLA, where he was also Associate Dean of the Graduate Division, he served for ten years on the psychology faculty at the University of Washington and from 1980 to 1981 was Director of Clinical-Community Psychology Training at the National Asian American Psychology Training Center in San Francisco, an APA-approved internship program. His research has been devoted to the study of the adjustment of, and delivery of mental health services to, culturally diverse groups.

JEANETTE C. TAKAMURA is currently Director of the Executive Office on Aging, Office of the Governor, State of Hawaii. Prior to this she was Assistant Professor and Gerontology Projects Coordinator of the School of Social Work, University of Hawaii at Manoa, and Instructor and Health Team Development Program Director at the School of Medicine and the School of Social Work, also at the University of Hawaii at Manoa. In addition to serving as an officer on the Board of the National Association of State Units on Aging, Dr. Takamura is a member of several other national boards and committees; has provided consultation in the public and private sectors on gerontology issues, organizational development, and interdisciplinary team work; and maintains a professional interest in long-term care, employment, the use of technology, and women's issues as they relate to population aging.

DAVID T. TAKEUCHI is a sociologist and the Associate Director of the National Research Center on Asian American Mental Health at UCLA. His research interests revolve around educational and mental health issues in minority communities. He has published articles on educational achievement in Hawaii, predictors of psychological distress among native Hawaiians, social structural factors related to psychiatric problems among African Americans, and access to educational and mental health programs among different racial and ethnic groups. Recently, he has begun analyses of minority children mental health issues.

LAURA UBA teaches anthropology classes on Asian Americans and psychology classes at California State University, Northridge. Most of her research has been in the area of Asian American mental health. More recently, her research has focused on Asian American sexual behavior, the supply of Asian American health care providers, and the relationship between trauma experienced and financial and physical well-being among Southeast Asians.

FAYE F. UNTALAN is an Assistant Professor in the School of Public Health at the University of Hawaii at Manoa and is Principal investigator of a grant focusing on interdisciplinary training in the area of child abuse and neglect in Hawaii. She is currently editing a book, *Interdisciplinary Perspectives on Child Abuse and Neglect*, and has published several articles, book chapters, and technical reports on Pacific Islander health, mental health, and social-service-related issues. She is known for her work on the immigration and adjustment of Chamorros in the United States.